T0262511

HOW GOD GROWS

a GIRL of

WISDOM and GRACE

Published by Barbour Publishing, Inc., 1810 Barbour Drive, Uhrichsville, Ohio 44683, www.barbourbooks.com

Our mission is to inspire the world with the life-changing message of the Bible.

Member of the
Evangelical Christian
Publishers Association

Printed in China.

002198 1024 HA

INTRODUCTION

Hi! I'm JoAnne Simmons, and my daughters are Jodi and Lilly. I got a lot of help from them as I wrote this because they're close in age to you, and God's currently growing them to be girls of wisdom and grace. Actually, you know what? Even though I'm a grown-up, He's still growing me to be one too. Anyone who knows Jesus never stops growing in wisdom and grace, and that's awesome!

I'm praying for you as you read this. I may not know you specifically by name, and I may never actually meet you. (That would be super fun if we did meet, though! We should have ice cream too!) But I'm positive that God, who does know you by name and counts every hair on your beautiful head, knows if and when you will read this book. He has put you in my mind and on my heart and given me an opportunity to write words to encourage you in your love for Him and your relationship with Him. Will you join me in these devotions to learn more about how God wants to grow you in His wisdom and grace and what the Bible says about how we should live?

I pray you find each devotional in this book to be a bit like an icy-cold Popsicle on the hottest, heaviest summer day—cool and refreshing and dripping with sweetness, a supernatural kind of sweetness that comes from the awesome joy of knowing the one true God made you, sees you, loves you, and wants to help you, by His grace—with everything!

A DOWNPOUR OF GRACE

Where sin increased, grace increased all the more.
ROMANS 5:20 NIV

Have you ever acted really mean or selfishly toward someone and didn't even say you're sorry, yet the person went right on loving you and taking care of you and giving you good things? Then you know what grace is. Grace is best defined by experiencing it. Good parents, especially, know how to love with grace like that because they learn it from their heavenly Father.

The ultimate, most amazing grace is the kind that God offers. He gives it to anyone who believes that He is the one true God and that He sent His Son, Jesus, to die on the cross to shed His blood to cover our every sin. Not only that, but He rose back to life to be our Savior who gives us eternal life. That's the incredible message of the gospel! It's because of Jesus' death (that took the place of our sin) and His resurrection (that triumphed over the death that sin causes) that God can offer everyone grace.

God doesn't just offer grace like a little sprinkle, either. No, when we come to Him, He pours it on us like the heaviest rainfall. Have you ever played in the rain? Like you dance with delight in a really good downpour, God wants you to dance in the grace He showers on you. He wants you to know grace and grow in it every day, experiencing His love and forgiveness and His power to help you in all things.

Dear God, even when I don't deserve it, You love and care for me so much anyway. That's grace, and I'm so thankful for it. Amen.

Day 2

THE BEGINNING OF WISDOM

The works of His hands are faithful and right.
All His Laws are true. They stand strong forever and ever.
They are done by what is true and right. . . . The fear of the
Lord is the beginning of wisdom. All who obey His Laws
have good understanding. His praise lasts forever.
PSALM 111:7–8, 10

So what is wisdom, exactly? . . . Is it just being smart and reading lots of books? Is it what you get once you've lived so long that you're old and wrinkly? Well, you can gain *knowledge* by reading lots of books and living a long time, for sure; but *wisdom* comes from the one true God, who teaches us how to apply the knowledge we gain over the years. Wisdom basically means being able to figure out right from wrong and having good sense or good judgment. That might not sound popular and cool, but God's wisdom really is awesome! Having it and using it makes for the best kind of life. And the Bible tells us that the fear of God—meaning having faith in and respect for God—is the beginning of wisdom. So, do you want to have wisdom, and do you have faith in and respect for God? Then keep on reading!

Dear God, I've never thought much about having wisdom.
Could You please help me grow in this area and teach
me what You want me to know? Thank You! Amen.

LET IT GO!

*Then Peter came to him and asked, "Lord, how
often should I forgive someone who sins against
me? Seven times?" "No, not seven times,"
Jesus replied, "but seventy times seven!"*
MATTHEW 18:21–22 NLT

If you haven't heard Elsa's "Let It Go" song at least a zillion times in the last few years, then you must have been living under a troll's rock. I might be exaggerating. . .but only a little. ☺ Whether you're terribly tired of the song or happily humming it right now, a great way to apply its three little key words is when you're needing to forgive someone.

Since Jesus offers us so much grace, we are called to give grace and forgiveness easily and abundantly to others. When Peter asked Jesus in the Bible how often he should forgive someone and suggested seven times, Jesus said multiply that times seventy! He didn't mean it in the literal way—that once you get to 490 times of forgiveness you're done and you can hold on to any grudges you want forevermore. He meant it in a way that whatever you're thinking is the right amount to forgive, go FAR above and beyond that and keep on forgiving again and again.

---

*Gracious God, You are so good to forgive me again and again. . .and
again. Help me remember that when I need to forgive others. Amen.*

Day 4

JESUS IS THE ONLY WAY

*Jesus told him, "I am the way, the truth, and the life.
No one can come to the Father except through me."*
JOHN 14:6 NLT

To have true faith in and respect for God (which then leads to gaining wisdom) means that you will want to have a relationship with Jesus Christ as your Savior. Jesus is God in human form who came to earth as a baby to grow up and live and love and show all people the way to have a relationship with God in heaven forever. Then Jesus died on the cross to save people from the bad things they do, their sin. Three days later He rose again to prove that He could conquer death and offer eternal life to all who believe in Him alone as their Savior from sin. If you have never prayed to ask Jesus to be your Savior, then pray something like this:

Dear Jesus, I believe in You as God and Savior! You died on the cross to save me from my sins, and You didn't stay dead. You rose again! And because that's true, I trust that You will give me eternal life too. Please help me to live my life following Your ways and growing in Your love and wisdom. Amen.

Day 5

SOFTEN YOUR HEART

*"If you forgive those who sin against you, your heavenly
Father will forgive you. But if you refuse to forgive
others, your Father will not forgive your sins."*
MATTHEW 6:14–15 NLT

God is so serious about giving grace and expecting us to do likewise that He says in His Word that He will not forgive people who refuse to forgive others. Real forgiveness is not just *saying* you forgive someone, either. It's *acting* like it too. Ephesians 4:31–32 (NIV) says, "Get rid of all bitterness, rage and anger, brawling and slander, along with every form of malice. Be kind and compassionate to one another, forgiving each other, just as in Christ God forgave you."

Bitterness and anger are often what we hold on to when we haven't truly forgiven someone, and this scripture urges us to get rid of it *all*! Instead of letting our hearts harden up with bitterness and anger, when we truly forgive, our hearts soften with compassion and grace—and gratitude that God forgives us so much. Our heavenly Father has such a soft heart toward us, and we are called to soften our hearts toward others too.

---

*Dear Father, it can be SO hard, but please help me to fully and
truly forgive, letting go of all anger and keeping my heart soft
and tender toward those who have done me wrong. Amen.*

Day 6

ASK GOD FOR IT

If you do not have wisdom, ask God for it. He is always ready to give it to you and will never say you are wrong for asking. You must have faith as you ask Him. You must not doubt. Anyone who doubts is like a wave which is pushed around by the sea.

JAMES 1:5–6

Once you have accepted Jesus as your Savior and have begun a new life of faith in the one true God, then you can begin to ask God for His wisdom. God loves you and is interested in every single thing about you. In everything you do and think and say throughout your days—in your home with your family, at school with classmates and teachers, in your activities with friends, and even when you're just hanging out by yourself—God wants to help you. He wants you to ask for and apply His wisdom as you make choices and learn and grow. Don't ever doubt it. God doesn't want you to be like a wave that's pushed around by the sea. No, if you constantly use His wisdom in your life, you will be strong and stable, ready and able to do the good things God planned for you when He created you.

Dear God, please give me lots and lots and lots of wisdom for everything in my life. Help me to trust You and use that wisdom exactly the way You want me to. Amen.

Day 7

MAKE IT LOOK EASY

*Jesus said, "Come to me, all of you who are weary and carry
heavy burdens, and I will give you rest. Take my yoke upon
you. Let me teach you, because I am humble and gentle
at heart, and you will find rest for your souls. For my yoke
is easy to bear, and the burden I give you is light."*
MATTHEW 11:28–30 NLT

Grace also means how you handle things or carry yourself. You've
probably heard a good ballerina described as having grace. She
dances smoothly and beautifully and makes her hard work look easy.
Have you ever seen *The Nutcracker* at Christmastime? There are so
many graceful dancers and beautiful scenes, and such lovely music!

The grace that God gives is like the word *graceful* describing a
ballerina, because God's grace *does* help you handle things smoothly
and carry yourself well. Being a Christian and having God's grace
does not guarantee that everything that happens in your life will be
easy and nice, but He will help you handle hard things in smooth and
beautiful ways. Also, He will take on the work of each difficult thing
and help you make it look easy because you're depending on Him.

---

*Dear Jesus, life can be so hard sometimes, but You give me grace
to handle it well. You make things easy for me when I depend
completely on You for love and strength. Thank You! Amen.*

Day 8

YOUR HELPER, THE HOLY SPIRIT

*"The Helper is the Holy Spirit. The Father will send
Him in My place. He will teach you everything and
help you remember everything I have told you."*
JOHN 14:26

Jesus promised His followers that after He died and rose again and went to heaven, He would not leave them alone. He would send the very best Helper—God's Holy Spirit who comes to live in each person who asks Jesus to be their Savior. So if you have asked Jesus to be your Savior, then you have the Holy Spirit in you too. When you ask God for wisdom, you can remember that He is right there inside you, ready to give wisdom to you right away and help you know what to do and think and say in any kind of situation.

*Dear God, thank You for Your Holy Spirit living in me. Help me to
learn and grow in all the things You want me to know. Amen.*

Day 9

GRACE FOR THE MESSES

God loves you and has chosen you as his own special people. So be gentle, kind, humble, meek, and patient. Put up with each other, and forgive anyone who does you wrong, just as Christ has forgiven you.
Colossians 3:12–13 cev

When Jodi, Lilly, and I were first brainstorming ideas for this very book, we had a funny situation in need of grace. We went to a coffee shop for some treats while we worked together. (Sharing treats always makes work a little more fun, right?) But not long after we sat down, a major spill caused hot cocoa to spread over the table and all down Lilly's pants. She was soaked and had to walk to the restroom looking a major mess in front of a room full of people and then ride forty minutes home feeling quite sticky! We needed grace to handle that situation. Our instant reactions were shock, annoyance, anger, frustration. . .you get the idea. But we all chose to let those first reactions go and instead decided to laugh and make the best of the situation. We focused on the blessings that the hot chocolate wasn't too hot, no one was hurt, and nothing was ruined. We wiped the table, easy-peasy, and the pants washed clean in the laundry! Another blessing was that the baristas gave us fresh hot cocoa!

Let the grace that God constantly gives you fill every single moment of your life so that you can handle anything and everything—no matter if it's a major messy situation or just a minor spill—with a supernatural kind of calm, cool collectedness.

Dear God, help me give grace to others too, no matter what kind of mess we're in. Amen.

Day 10

TREASURE TROVE, PART 1

*All the Holy Writings are God-given and are made alive
by Him. Man is helped when he is taught God's Word.
It shows what is wrong. It changes the way of a man's life.
It shows him how to be right with God. It gives the man who
belongs to God everything he needs to work well for Him.*
2 TIMOTHY 3:16–17

God can communicate with us in any way He chooses. He shows us He is real by His amazing creation all around us. He proves Himself faithful to us when we talk to Him and He answers our prayers. He shows us His love in infinite ways and through the many people who take care of us and encourage us and bless us. And He speaks to us in written words, especially through the Bible. When we choose to believe it as God's main way of teaching and guiding us, and then read it, follow it, and put it into action in our lives, it is an absolute treasure trove of the wisdom we need.

---

*Dear God, please help me to love Your Word and all
the wisdom You give to me in it. Help me want to read
it every day and learn more about You and how You
want to guide me in the best kind of life. Amen.*

Day 11

TREASURE TROVE, PART 2

*God's Word is living and powerful. It is sharper than a sword
that cuts both ways. It cuts straight into where the soul and
spirit meet and it divides them. It cuts into the joints and bones.
It tells what the heart is thinking about and what it wants to
do. No one can hide from God. His eyes see everything we do.
We must give an answer to God for what we have done.*
HEBREWS 4:12–13

God's Word, which is full of wisdom for us, is not just some ancient
book that should gather dust on a shelf. It is alive and powerful as we
read it, and God uses it to speak to us. More scriptures that show us
how powerful and important God's Word should be to us are these:

- ✿ "Everything that was written in the Holy Writings long
  ago was written to teach us. By not giving up, God's
  Word gives us strength and hope" (Romans 15:4).

- ✿ "How sweet is Your Word to my taste! It is sweeter than
  honey to my mouth! I get understanding from Your Law
  and so I hate every false way. Your Word is a lamp to my
  feet and a light to my path" (Psalm 119:103–105).

*Dear God, please speak directly to me through Your Word every
day. Guide me and help me to listen and obey well. Amen.*

TREASURE TROVE, PART 3

The grass dries up. The flower loses its color.
But the Word of our God stands forever.
ISAIAH 40:8

Since the Bible is our main source of wisdom given to us by God, we should make reading it a regular part of our daily lives. We shouldn't just flip through it here and there. We shouldn't just carry it to church and not touch it the rest of the week. If you spend time in it regularly, you will learn more and more about God and His people and how He wants His Word to guide you in your life today. The Bible has sixty-six books in all, and they are separated into the Old and New Testaments. Throughout this devotional, we'll talk a little about each of the books to help you understand the purpose of each one and grow in your knowledge of the Bible so that you might want to learn more from it to grow in wisdom and faith and relationship with God for your whole life!

Dear God, please help me to love Your Word and
spend time reading and studying it regularly. I want to
grow in wisdom and grow closer to You! Amen.

Day 13

BOLD CONFIDENCE

*So let us come boldly to the throne of our gracious
God. There we will receive his mercy, and we will
find grace to help us when we need it most.*
HEBREWS 4:16 NLT

If I ever had the chance to visit the Oval Office to meet the president or Buckingham Palace to meet the king of England, I'd probably trip over my own clumsy feet, forget what I wanted to say, and nervously laugh too much. What would you do?

What about with God in heaven on His throne? Being almighty Creator God of the whole universe is kind of a big deal. The biggest deal ever, actually! Too many people don't respect Him anymore or even believe in Him at all. That's awful, but it doesn't mean He isn't still the one true God and isn't on His throne, sovereign over all His creation. He's there and always will be, and He'll always be the biggest deal, the one worthy of the most respect and honor and praise. What's so incredible about God's grace is that because of it, you can go to God, not timidly, not with shaking legs and a quivering voice, but boldly to receive even more grace to help you with whatever you need.

---

*Dear God, I am so thankful for Your amazing grace
that lets me come boldly to You with anything I need.
Please keep growing my confidence in You! Amen.*

Day 14

WISDOM FROM THE BOOK OF GENESIS

In the beginning God made from nothing the heavens and the earth.
GENESIS 1:1

The word *genesis* means "beginnings." That's fitting for the title of the very first book of the Bible! In this book, written by Moses, we learn about the beginning of our earth and how God created it. We learn about the very first people, Adam and Eve. We also learn how sin began when Adam and Eve chose to disobey God. We learn about Noah and the ark. (That's our favorite story in Genesis! We love animals!) And we learn about the beginning of God's special family of people, the Israelites, through whom He would send His Son, Jesus Christ, to offer salvation to all people. You can learn much from the book of Genesis if you take time to study it.

Dear God, thank You for the book of Genesis. Help me as I read it and keep coming back to it in the future. Teach me what You want me to learn from it to apply to my life and to share with others. Amen.

Day 15

GETTING TO KNOW GOD

Grow in the grace and knowledge of our Lord and Savior Jesus Christ.
2 PETER 3:18 NLT

Do you know *all* about who God is? No one here on earth knows everything about Him, but a Christian's goal is to keep knowing Him better. He's the best giver of grace, and the more you know about Him, the better you are!

It seems confusing sometimes, but it's important to understand about God that He exists in something called the Trinity, which means three in one. He's God the Father, God the Son, and God the Holy Spirit. He's not three different gods but all the same single God; He just exists in three forms, kind of like there are three forms of water—liquid, frozen, and steam. Their forms don't change the fact that they are all water. That example still doesn't explain the Trinity fully, but it's a start to try to wrap our human minds around the Trinity of God.

When your brain is spinning about God, remember that you don't have to figure it all out! That's the beauty and wonder of faith! Keep trusting that God's Word is true and that His Holy Spirit helps you, little by little, to understand more about Him as you read your Bible and go to church and worship Him!

God, You are awesome and sometimes confusing too. But I trust You! Please grow me in grace and faith, and help me keep learning more about who You are. Amen.

WHAT LOVE IS

We have come to know and believe the love God has for us. God is love. If you live in love, you live by the help of God and God lives in you.

1 JOHN 4:16

What are your first thoughts when you think of love? When we think of it, we think of love for each other in our family, love for our friends, and love for our two silly dogs, Jasper and Daisy. We care about each other and want to help each other, no matter what, even if we get mad at each other sometimes. We bring joy and laughter to each other as we spend time together. The reason we know anything at all about love is because God is love and He showed us His love through His Son, Jesus, who loves us so much that He died to save us. People have a lot of mixed-up ideas about what love is, and so we constantly need to ask God to give us *His* wisdom about love and how best to share love with others.

Dear God, You are love and You show love better than anyone else. Please give me Your perfect wisdom about knowing real love and sharing real love in the best and healthiest ways—Your ways—my whole life. Thank You! Amen.

Day 17

WHAT'S IN A NAME?

In the beginning God created the heavens and the earth.
GENESIS 1:1 NLT

God's many names in the Bible tell us more about who He is and how He loves us. The first Hebrew name of God in Genesis 1:1 is *Elohim*, and it's a name that describes God's power and might and the fact that He is the Creator.

When you're facing something really hard in your life, maybe dealing with a difficult friend or a really stressful situation, stop and think about who exactly you have on your side. *Elohim! Powerful, mighty, and Creator God!* Call out to Him at any and every moment and believe that the almighty God of all the universe sees you, your problems, and your fears and wants to help you. Keep calling to Him, have faith in Him, and wait for Him to help you in His perfect timing! Romans 8:31 (NLT) says, "If God is for us, who can ever be against us?" And Psalm 118:5–7 (NLT) says, "In my distress I prayed to the LORD, and the LORD answered me and set me free. The LORD is for me, so I will have no fear. What can mere people do to me? Yes, the LORD is for me; he will help me."

Elohim, You are powerful and mighty, and You are on my side! I praise You and ask You to help me with the problem I'm facing. Amen.

OBEY AND HONOR

Invest in truth and wisdom, discipline and good sense, and don't part with them. Make your father truly happy by living right and showing sound judgment. Make your parents proud, especially your mother.
PROVERBS 23:23–25 CEV

Maybe sometimes you get a little tired of being reminded by your parents that you need to obey. But it's not just parents who tell their kids to obey. *God* is the one who put that rule in place first. It's one of the Ten Commandments. Exodus 20:12 says, "Honor your father and your mother, so your life may be long in the land the Lord your God gives you." And Ephesians 6:1–3 says, "Children, as Christians, obey your parents. This is the right thing to do. Respect your father and mother. This is the first Law given that had a promise. The promise is this: If you respect your father and mother, you will live a long time and your life will be full of many good things."

It might not always feel fun, but obeying and honoring your parents is the right and wise thing to do. Don't forget that we parents must obey too—we should always be obeying God our heavenly Father.

Dear God, please help me not to disobey my parents.
Help me to have a good attitude and remember that
You have called me to honor and obey my parents and
most importantly to honor and obey You! Amen.

Day 19

THE ONE AND ONLY

But Moses protested, "If I go to the people of Israel and tell them, 'The God of your ancestors has sent me to you,' they will ask me, 'What is his name?' Then what should I tell them?" God replied to Moses, "I AM WHO I AM. Say this to the people of Israel: I AM has sent me to you." God also said to Moses, "Say this to the people of Israel: Yahweh, the God of your ancestors—the God of Abraham, the God of Isaac, and the God of Jacob—has sent me to you."
EXODUS 3:13–15 NLT

Yahweh or *Jehovah* is another of the names of God in the Hebrew language. This means "I AM WHO I AM." With this name, God shows that He is the one and only God. There is no one and nothing higher or worthy of all honor and praise!

Is your calendar pretty jam-packed with stuff you have to do? It's hard not to let all the activities and responsibilities and people in your life get in the way of your relationship with God. But it's so important to keep Him first in your life and spend time with Him each day, praying and reading His Word. He is your Jehovah and there is no one else in all of time who is as great as He is, and He wants you to spend one-on-one time with Him every chance you get! How cool is that?

Jehovah, You are truly the greatest, and it's so awesome that You want to spend time with me. Amen.

WISDOM FROM THE BOOK OF EXODUS

God saw the people of Israel and He cared about them.
EXODUS 2:25

The word *exodus* means "departure," and the main purpose of the book of Exodus, written by Moses, is to share how God rescued His people, the Israelites, out of slavery in Egypt. You've probably heard some of the stories in Exodus of the plagues on Egypt and how God parted the Red Sea (amazing!) for His people to safely walk through when the Egyptians were chasing them down. Exodus is when we first learn of the Ten Commandments too. Do you know all of them? If not, look them up in Exodus 20:3–17. And don't stop there. You can learn much from the book of Exodus if you take time to study it.

Dear God, thank You for the book of Exodus. Help me as I read it and keep coming back to it in the future. Teach me what You want me to learn from it to apply to my life and to share with others. Amen.

Day 21

GOD THE FATHER

You received God's Spirit when he adopted you as his own children. Now we call him, "Abba, Father."
ROMANS 8:15 NLT

I hope you have a wonderful father in your life, and I'm so sorry if you don't. Either way, you always have your heavenly Father, whom the Bible encourages you to call Abba, which translates like "Daddy."

That means you don't have to think of God like some unapproachable dictator dad in the sky, but you can go to Him with anything. He wants to hug you close and keep you safe, comfort you when you cry, listen when you want to vent, and love you through all of your life. He is so awesome that He's almighty, all-powerful, all-knowing Creator God, worthy of all praise and honor and respect, yet He longs for you to know Him like a cozy and cuddly daddy who wraps you in big bear hugs. Picture your heavenly Father that way. Respect and honor and obey Him, and also bask in the snuggly, warm love He offers you every moment of every day. He never leaves you or lets you down (Hebrews 13:5).

Abba, You're my heavenly Daddy, and I'm so thankful that You're with me and love me so much. Amen.

Day 22

WISDOM FOR SIBLINGS

*Pray and give thanks for those who make trouble for you.
Yes, pray for them instead of talking against them. Be happy
with those who are happy. Be sad with those who are sad.
Live in peace with each other. Do not act or think with
pride. Be happy to be with poor people. Keep yourself from
thinking you are so wise. When someone does something
bad to you, do not pay him back with something bad.*
ROMANS 12:14–17

"It was the best of times; it was the worst of times" is the famous opening line from a famous old book called *A Tale of Two Cities* by Charles Dickens. It makes us think of times with siblings because they sure can have the best of times and worst of times together, right? Jodi and Lilly know all about that. And so do I, from growing up with three siblings. Sometimes brothers and sisters need to ask for a double, or even triple, dose of God's wisdom in the worst of times. This scripture in Romans 12 can help in a huge way. If siblings read it and apply it, they will greatly improve their relationships and have far more "best of times" than "worst of times."

---

*Dear God, please help me to have mostly good times with
my siblings. Please help us to follow the wisdom in Your
Word to have great relationships together. Amen.*

Day 23

GOD PROVIDES

"Go into your house with your sons and shut the door behind you. Pour olive oil from your flask into the jars, setting each one aside when it is filled."
2 KINGS 4:4 NLT

What a cool miracle God worked through Elisha to provide for a woman whose husband had died and who was about to lose her sons to slavery to pay debts her husband had owed. From one flask of oil, she was able to miraculously fill many, many jars and then sell the oil, earning enough money to pay the debts plus enough for her and her sons to live on.

Just like He provided for this widow, God will always provide what you need too. One of His names is Jehovah-Jireh (Genesis 22:14), which means "the God who provides." Anytime you might be worried for yourself and your family about having money to pay bills or buy food, think about this story and ask God to help you like He did the widow. According to His perfect will and timing, He will make sure you have exactly what you need at exactly the right moment. Trust in His goodness and grace. Trust that He is your constant provider.

Jehovah-Jireh, You have always provided for me, and I know You always will. Help me to keep trusting You for everything I need. Amen.

Day 24

LOVE AND FORGIVE

Peter came to Jesus and said, "Lord, how many times may my brother sin against me and I forgive him, up to seven times?" Jesus said to him, "I tell you, not seven times but seventy times seven!"
MATTHEW 18:21–22

Sometimes the people you love the most are the ones who can drive you crazy the most, right? We get it. We spend more time with the people we love most, and that means there is more opportunity to annoy each other and fight. But there's also more opportunity to love and forgive each other too. And the Bible says that because God loves and forgives us so much, we should do the same and forgive others bunches too—seventy times seven as much! That's a math problem that means however much you first think you might need to forgive, you need to go way above and beyond that amount. . .because God goes way above and beyond at loving and forgiving you. We need His wisdom to know how to love well and forgive well too.

Dear God, please help me to do my best at forgiving others in above-and-beyond kinds of ways like You forgive me. Amen.

Day 25

GOD IS PEACE

*And Gideon built an altar to the Lord there and named it
Yahweh-Shalom (which means "the Lord is peace").*
JUDGES 6:24 NLT

The world sure is full of too much fighting, turmoil, and trouble. If you pay attention to the news, you feel like it's everywhere, all the time. That can be so stressful if you let it constantly fill your mind. So don't! Instead, focus on the fact that a name of God in the Bible is Yahweh-Shalom or Jehovah-Shalom. It means "the Lord is peace." He is your constant peace, and He is the only hope for peace for the world.

You cannot possibly control the events of this world or even all the events right around you or in your own home and activities. But you can "do your best to live at peace with everyone" as Romans 12:18 (CEV) urges you. You can't do that on your own, of course. It's far too easy to get into a squabble with someone, especially brothers or sisters, right? ☺ You can only do your best at living in peace with everyone by asking God to help you and believing in Him and depending on Him for true peace. And when you mess up, you can ask God to forgive you, ask for forgiveness from the person you were in conflict with, and then start fresh again, trusting that God's grace covers your mistakes.

---

*Jehovah-Shalom, please steady me always
with Your unfailing peace. Amen.*

Day 26

WISDOM FROM THE BOOK OF LEVITICUS

*The Lord said to Moses, "Say to all the people of Israel,
'Be holy, for I the Lord your God am holy.'"*
LEVITICUS 19:1–2

The book of Leviticus gives detailed instructions about how God wanted the Israelites to live and to worship Him. Our one true God alone is holy and worthy of all devotion and praise! We hope you love to sing to Him like we do! The instructions in Leviticus also included sacrifices that the Israelites should make to God, but one day all those sacrifices would be replaced by God's Son, Jesus Christ, making the ultimate sacrifice by giving His life on the cross to pay for the sin of all people forever. You can learn much from the book of Leviticus if you take time to study it.

---

*Dear God, thank You for the book of Leviticus. Help me
as I read it and keep coming back to it in the future.
Teach me what You want me to learn from it to apply
to my life and to share with others. Amen.*

Day 27

OUR HEALING GOD

"I am the LORD, who heals you."
EXODUS 15:26 NIV

I'm guessing you know someone who is currently struggling or has struggled with cancer or another disease. Maybe they've overcome the disease, or maybe it overcame them. My heart aches for the loss of our loved ones in this world. In that aching, it's so comforting to know that our God is called Jehovah-Rophi, which means "our God heals." I cry out to God sometimes, "Why, since You can heal here on earth, don't You always do it, and so many people die way too young, and we have to miss them?" When I just can't understand, I trust in the many promises of God, especially that "for those who love God all things work together for good" (Romans 8:28 ESV) and that "the LORD is near to the brokenhearted" (Psalm 34:18 ESV).

Just because God doesn't always answer yes to our prayers to heal someone on earth does not mean He is not the Great healer. He is. It's just that sometimes healing for a person can only come when they've died here on earth and gone on to heaven, where God provides perfect new bodies that will never, ever get sick. With Jesus as our Savior, we have such a perfectly healthy life waiting for us for eternity, and we trust that our healer God is good and knows exactly what He's doing.

Jehovah-Rophi, I trust that You care and You heal in Your perfect timing. Please hold me so closely and comfort me when a loved one has gone to heaven to be healed. Amen.

Day 28

BE HONEST ABOUT EVERYTHING

The Lord hates lying lips, but those who speak the truth are His joy.
PROVERBS 12:22

Since God hates lying lips, then so should we! And that means we should be honest about everything—big things and little things. If we are, then we become trustworthy people. Bosses and leaders and teachers notice consistent honesty, and good ones usually want to reward us and give new opportunities because of it. Luke 16:10–12 says, "He that is faithful with little things is faithful with big things also. He that is not honest with little things is not honest with big things. If you have not been faithful with riches of this world, who will trust you with true riches? If you have not been faithful in that which belongs to another person, who will give you things to have as your own?"

Dear God, please help me never to lie, even about little things.
I want to be wise and honest and trustworthy in all things. Amen.

Day 29

UNCHANGING

"I am the LORD, and I do not change."
MALACHI 3:6 NLT

Let's talk ice cream! When I was younger, I couldn't imagine why on earth just plain vanilla was the most popular flavor of ice cream in America. That's still true according to my quick Google search for statistics. I'm *still* not sure how anyone picks ordinary vanilla when they could have soooo many different flavors involving yummy chocolate. Not to mention the fun colorful flavors like Blue Moon and Superman! I could never just pick the same kind of ice cream all the time, especially vanilla, which is good, of course (but so much better with a bunch of hot fudge and sprinkles!). I want variety!

Variety and change in ice cream are great, but I don't like too much variety and change in life. I want some things to remain the same, and yet there's never any guarantee of that. Life can change in an instant in all sorts of ways. That's why it's so important to know that there is one true constant in all of life—God! He is immutable, which means unchanging. Aren't you so glad to know that even if your world turns upside down, God is always the same? He is your rock (Psalm 18:2) and your strong tower (Proverbs 18:10), forever and always.

Immutable God, thank You for being constant and reliable in my life, no matter what is going on or changing around me. Amen.

Day 30

MORE ABOUT THE TRUTH

As Jesus said these things, many people put their trust in Him. He said to the Jews who believed, "If you keep and obey My Word, then you are My followers for sure. You will know the truth and the truth will make you free."
JOHN 8:30–32

Honesty and truth are so super important, especially in a world where they often seem harder and harder to find. Let God and the Bible be your number one source of truth, and let all of these scriptures grow you in wisdom about how important it is!

- "The honor of good people will lead them, but those who hurt others will be destroyed by their own false ways" (Proverbs 11:3).

- "A man who tells lies about someone will be punished. He who tells lies will be lost" (Proverbs 19:9).

- "Show me Your ways, O Lord. Teach me Your paths. Lead me in Your truth and teach me. For You are the God Who saves me" (Psalm 25:4–5).

- "Do your best to know that God is pleased with you. Be as a workman who has nothing to be ashamed of. Teach the words of truth in the right way. Do not listen to foolish talk about things that mean nothing. It only leads people farther away from God" (2 Timothy 2:15–16).

Dear God, You and Your Word are the ultimate truth! Help me to love You and the Bible more and more each day. Amen.

Day 31

THE BEST MASTER

I said to the LORD, "You are my Master!
Every good thing I have comes from you."
PSALM 16:2 NLT

Wouldn't it be incredible to find a magic lamp like Aladdin? It's fun to imagine that a genie would have to obey your commands and call you master! What would you wish for?

Do you know that you can call God *Adonai*, which means Master? Using it shows that you acknowledge that you serve and obey Him. Too many people think that's a bad thing, as if you're chained up and treated cruelly like a slave. But that's not true at all with our good and loving Adonai. Serving Him and calling Him Master is an honor and privilege because no one loves you or cares for you more than He does. Every command He wants you to obey that He gives you in His Word results in what is best for you and is full of blessings for you!

Adonai, I trust that You are the very best master and that You only want me to obey Your commands so that I can live the best life possible, the life You created me for. I choose to serve You, and I'm so blessed because of You! Amen.

Day 32

WISDOM WHEN YOU'RE WORRIED, PART 1

Give all your worries to Him because He cares for you.
1 PETER 5:7

The best and wisest thing you can do when you're feeling worried is remember that God wants to take those worries away from you. His Word says to give them all to Him. Not just the big and worst worries—but *all* of them. Now, if you're worried about your upcoming test at school, does that mean you should give the worry about it to God and then just skip studying? Of course not. Let the worry motivate you to do the good work of studying, but then give the worry over to God. If you know you've studied and prepared well, then you have no need to worry. Just go and take your test, trusting that God will help you recall the things you learned as you studied, and He will help you do your best.

Dear God, thank You that You care about my worries. Please let them motivate me to do the good things I need to while I give the stressful part of the worry over to You. Please replace it with Your peace. Thank You! Amen.

WISDOM WHEN YOU'RE WORRIED, PART 2

"Do not worry about your life. Do not worry about what you are going to eat and drink. Do not worry about what you are going to wear. Is not life more important than food? Is not the body more important than clothes? Look at the birds in the sky. They do not plant seeds. They do not gather grain. They do not put grain into a building to keep. Yet your Father in heaven feeds them! Are you not more important than the birds?"
MATTHEW 6:25–26

Maybe it's not a test you're worried about these days. Maybe it's much worse. Maybe you're worried about having enough money, food, and clothes because of a hard situation in your family. If that's the case, this scripture in Matthew can give you great peace. Read it over and over until it's stuck in your brain, so that you never forget that God takes care of you. No matter what happens in your life, He knows what you need and will provide for you.

Dear God, thank You for showing me how much I matter to You! Please give me the wisdom to remember that I never need to worry because You will always take care of me. Amen.

Day 34

WISDOM WHEN YOU'RE WORRIED, PART 3

"For God so loved the world that He gave His only Son. Whoever puts his trust in God's Son will not be lost but will have life that lasts forever."
JOHN 3:16

Maybe you're worried about sickness and death for a family member or friend, or even for yourself. And the hard truth is that every single one of us will die someday. That's why knowing Jesus as Savior is so important. Only He can promise us eternal life because only He rose to life again after dying for our sin. While death is so sad here on earth for those who are left behind to miss their loved one, Jesus gives hope. There is great joy and peace in trusting that every person who believes in Him as the one and only Savior will be in heaven forever in a perfect new body that will never, ever die again.

Dear God, thank You for the hope of heaven for all who trust in You. Please help me to share about You with others so more people know You as Savior and will have eternal life. Amen.

Day 35

JESUS, WHAT A WONDERFUL NAME

*His name shall be called Wonderful Counselor,
Mighty God, Everlasting Father, Prince of Peace.*
ISAIAH 9:6 ESV

A huge part of the fun of getting a new doll or stuffed animal—or better yet, a real, live pet—is to give it a name! In first grade, I had a hamster I named Reggie. I have no idea now why I picked that name; he just looked like a Reggie, I guess. Too bad I had to give Reggie back to the pet store because he bit me a lot. (That may or may not have had something to do with the fact that I liked to stick him in toilet paper tubes and turn him upside down.)

Ask your parents the story of deciding on your name. Did they know right away, or did it take them awhile to decide? What were some of their other favorites on their list when choosing your name?

When Mary gave birth to Jesus, she didn't name Him herself. His name came straight from God and had been foretold long before He was actually born. Isaiah 9:6 (NIV) prophesied about His name: "For to us a child is born, to us a son is given, and the government will be on his shoulders. And he will be called Wonderful Counselor, Mighty God, Everlasting Father, Prince of Peace." That's a lot of things to call Jesus, right? It helps show us how amazing He is!

---

*Jesus, I don't think I'll ever fully understand how awesome
You are, but I want to keep learning more about You
every day! Thank You for letting me! Amen.*

Day 36

WISDOM FROM
THE BOOK OF NUMBERS

*"If the Lord is pleased with us, then He will bring us into
this land and give it to us. It is a land which flows with
milk and honey. Only do not go against the Lord."*
NUMBERS 14:8–9

The book of Numbers starts out with God telling Moses to take a
census, which means a counting, of all the men ages twenty and older
of the nation of Israel. The total number was 603,550! The book goes
on to describe how the people of Israel wandered in the wilderness
after God delivered them from slavery in Egypt. They could have
reached the land God had promised to give them in just two weeks,
but because they had little faith in God and were very ungrateful
and whiny, God punished them. Much can be learned from the book
of Numbers, especially about being grateful and having great faith
in God, no matter what. He loves and wants to bless people, but
He will punish people who rebel and complain and don't trust Him.

---

*Dear God, thank You for the book of Numbers. Help me
as I read it and keep coming back to it in the future.
Teach me what You want me to learn from it to apply
to my life and to share with others. Amen.*

Day 37

GOD WITH US

"She will give birth to a son, and they will call him Immanuel, which means 'God is with us.'"
MATTHEW 1:23 NLT

Dreams are crazy things and can seem so very real! I hope yours are mostly good ones and never nightmares. Sometimes dreams aren't great or scary; they're just frustrating. I remember vividly dreaming as a kid that it was Christmas morning, but then I'd wake up and realize it was actually, like, the middle of March, with Christmas still soooo far away. Those dreams sure were mean little tricks my mind played on me, because I adore Christmastime! The presents and decorations and parties are all just so exciting and fun. Every year, though, I fall more in love with Christmas because of Immanuel. That's a name for Jesus that means "God is with us."

Remembering and celebrating the fact that Jesus came to be here on earth with us and knows firsthand our struggles and fears as human beings is so encouraging to my soul. God is with us. God is with *you*. Right now and every moment. No, we aren't alive during Jesus' time as a human on earth, but we trust that He was here and experienced a human life like we are now. And now we have His Word and the Holy Spirit to help us live for Him until our time on earth is up or He returns again, whichever comes first. That's sure a big reason to celebrate at Christmastime—and every other day of the year too!

Immanuel, You understand me because You came to be a human and lived in this world too. Please help me to trust You, depend on You, and relate to You more each day. Amen.

Day 38

BE HUMBLE, NOT PROUD

Let yourself be brought low before the Lord.
Then He will lift you up and help you.
JAMES 4:10

What is the story of your most embarrassing moment? Does it still make you cringe or turn red? It might make you feel so silly, but do you know that it's wise to be able to laugh at yourself? When you can laugh at yourself, it helps show that you are humble. Being humble is the opposite of being proud and thinking too highly of yourself. It's good to be confident and have good self-esteem, but it's not good to take that so far that you think you are better than others or can never make a mistake or that you have no need for God in your life. Being humble means that you know you mess up sometimes and need forgiveness and grace from God and from others. And being humble means that you know there are always ways you can learn and grow.

Dear God, please give me wisdom about knowing the difference between being proud and being humble. Help me to be humble and always know my need for Your grace and love!

Day 39

LOOK UP TO THE BEST

*For God knew his people in advance, and he
chose them to become like his Son.*
ROMANS 8:29 NLT

You probably have someone or several someones whom you look up to. Maybe a relative or older sibling or a certain athlete or musician or artist. What is it about them that you admire? It's great to have role models, but remember to keep your head on straight about them. You can respect others and want to have their qualities too, but there's always a good chance they'll let you down in some way, simply because no human being is perfect.

Only God is perfect, and He sent His Son, Jesus, to become a perfect human being among us. He alone is your only role model who will *never* let you down, and God is asking you to become more and more like Jesus every day. He's your example and guide for how God wants you to live and who He wants you to be like. God knows you can't be just like Jesus all on your own, but His grace covers you and encourages you to keep on striving to live a life like Jesus did, trusting that God sees you as perfect because Jesus took your sins away when you accepted Him as your Savior.

---

*Jesus, You are my best role model. I want to live
my life like You and for You! Amen.*

Day 40

PRAY ABOUT EVERYTHING

*Do not worry. Learn to pray about everything. Give thanks
to God as you ask Him for what you need. The peace of God
is much greater than the human mind can understand. This
peace will keep your hearts and minds through Christ Jesus.*

PHILIPPIANS 4:6–7

Instead of worrying, God wants you to pray about everything. As you pray and ask God for what you need, don't forget to focus on your blessings. List them in your head or out loud, or write them down on paper and thank God for them. (Maybe you have a fun, fuzzy-covered journal to write in like Jodi and Lilly do!) When you see the many ways God has already blessed you and provided for you, it helps you remember that you don't need to worry. He will always continue to bless you and provide for you. Thank Him and praise Him for who He is and all He has done as you pray, and let His amazing peace fill you up and chase away whatever worries you might have.

*Dear God, thank You for everything! Please chase away every
worry and fill me with Your incredible peace. Amen.*

Day 41

OUR ROCK

The Rock was Christ.
1 CORINTHIANS 10:4 ESV

There's a cool place in Florida called Bathtub Reef Beach. Doesn't that sound like you should bring your rubber ducky to swim with? To get there, you drive on a road where at one point, you're driving on a strip of land that seems barely any wider than the two-lane road because there is a big stretch of intracoastal water on one side and the vast Atlantic Ocean on the other. Such a cool place! But I couldn't help but wonder how storms and hurricanes don't just easily wash it all completely underwater. There's even a building there called the House of Refuge that's been standing since 1876! It's still intact because the roads and buildings there are built on a rocky shoreline, not just sand. For any structure to endure, it has to be built on something solid—just like Jesus teaches in His parable of the wise and foolish builders (Matthew 7).

You can be sure you're never destroyed by the storms of difficult circumstances if you build your life on the firm foundation of Jesus! Isaiah 26:4 (CEV) says, "So always trust the LORD because he is forever our mighty rock."

Jesus, I want to build my life with stability on the firm foundation of You! Amen.

Day 42

WHY PRAY?

Come close to God and He will come close to you.
JAMES 4:8

Sometimes you might wonder why praying matters, especially when the Bible says God already knows everything you're going to say before you even say it (Psalm 139:4; Matthew 6:8). But maybe you have a best friend who can almost seem to read your mind that way too. If she knows you so well, then why do you care about spending time with her? Because you love her and have so much fun being together and doing things together, right? That's the way God wants to be your absolute best, best friend. He loves you and knows you more than any person ever possibly could, and He hopes you will simply want to spend time with Him and be included in the good things He is doing.

Dear God, I want to be close to You through prayer and through reading Your Word. Help me to look forward to spending time with You as my very best friend of all. Amen.

Day 43

THE HOLY SPIRIT

You know the Spirit, who is with you and will keep on living in you.
JOHN 14:17 CEV

It's hard when family members and friends live far away. But at least it's easy to keep in touch these days. Jodi, Lilly, and I were talking recently about how in the old days if you missed someone you didn't live close to, you could only send them a letter—and who knows how long it would take to get to them and then get a response back? Sometimes months! Now we have phones, texting, email, FaceTime, and much faster mail service to keep in touch with people we love when we can't be near them.

Wouldn't it be nice to be able to call, text, email, and FaceTime back and forth with Jesus in heaven? When Jesus was ending His time on earth, He knew we all would miss Him and wish we could communicate directly with Him, and He said, "I will ask the Father to send you the Holy Spirit who will help you and always be with you. The Spirit will show you what is true" (John 14:16–17 CEV).

Until we get to heaven, Jesus did not leave us alone. The Holy Spirit, who is fully God, is here with us. In the Bible, He is called our helper and comforter and advocate.

Holy Spirit, I believe You are right here, right now.
Please remind me of Your presence constantly and help
me to learn to depend on You for everything. Amen.

Day 44

WISDOM FROM THE BOOK OF DEUTERONOMY

"Love the Lord your God with all your heart and with all your soul and with all your strength. Keep these words in your heart that I am telling you today. Do your best to teach them to your children. Talk about them when you sit in your house and when you walk on the road and when you lie down and when you get up."
DEUTERONOMY 6:5–7

Moses wrote the book of Deuteronomy to remind the people of Israel about all God had done for them and provided for them and taught them. Moses reminded the people again about the Ten Commandments. God also wants you to remember regularly all He has done for you and provided for you and taught you. He doesn't want you to forget the good instructions He has given through His Word to obey Him and live the life He has created you for. He loves and disciplines and forgives and wants to bless His people, and that includes you!

Dear God, thank You for the book of Deuteronomy. Help me as I read it and keep coming back to it in the future. Teach me what You want me to learn from it to apply to my life and to share with others. Amen.

Day 45

GOOD WARNINGS

*"The Holy Spirit tells me in city after city
that jail and suffering lie ahead."*
ACTS 20:23 NLT

Do you ever get a bad feeling about something that you can't quite explain? I'm not talking about just a bad feeling that putting brussels sprouts in pudding is probably gross. I'm talking about times when you have a serious vibe that you need to avoid a situation. That can be the Holy Spirit warning you of danger or trouble, like He warned Luke in the book of Acts.

I've had several experiences in my life when I thought I should avoid a situation or a decision. Sometimes they didn't make much sense other than just kind of a sense that something wasn't quite right. Our world often just calls it a gut feeling, but the Bible shows that the Holy Spirit can sometimes be the source of those gut feelings. Ask God to help you have wisdom and discernment. Our world is full of so much confusion and sin and untrustworthy people that it's absolutely necessary for Christians to constantly be praying for the Holy Spirit's help in avoiding danger and making good choices.

---

*Holy Spirit, I need Your guidance all the time!
Please give me wisdom and discernment. Amen.*

BUSY IS NOT BETTER, PART 1

*As they went on their way, they came to a town where
a woman named Martha lived. She cared for Jesus in
her home. Martha had a sister named Mary. Mary sat at
the feet of Jesus and listened to all He said. Martha was
working hard getting the supper ready. She came to Jesus
and said, "Do You see that my sister is not helping me?
Tell her to help me." Jesus said to her, "Martha, Martha,
you are worried and troubled about many things. Only a
few things are important, even just one. Mary has chosen
the good thing. It will not be taken away from her."*

Luke 10:38–42

How cool to think of having Jesus over for supper, right? Martha and
Mary got to experience that, and their story can help us to be wise
with how we spend our time. Martha was keeping very busy doing
good things to make a nice meal and take care of Jesus. But she was
upset that her sister, Mary, wasn't helping enough. Can you relate?
Do you ever feel like you're the one doing all the work when others
are supposed to be helping you? It's frustrating, for sure! But in this
case, Jesus gently told Martha that Mary was doing the very best
thing—listening to His teaching.

---

*Dear God, please remind me that keeping busy doing things is never
more important than listening to what You want to teach me. Amen.*

Day 47

BUSY IS NOT BETTER, PART 2

Obey the Word of God. If you hear only and do not act, you are only fooling yourself. Anyone who hears the Word of God and does not obey is like a man looking at his face in a mirror. After he sees himself and goes away, he forgets what he looks like. But the one who keeps looking into God's perfect Law and does not forget it will do what it says and be happy as he does it. God's Word makes men free.

JAMES 1:22–25

We could take that story of Martha and Mary too far and use it as an excuse for laziness, saying things like "Well, I guess Jesus said I don't ever need to clean my room. I'll just lie in my bed forever, reading my Bible." But that's not right! God created you to do good things, and that requires getting out of bed! With wisdom, we can understand there's a balance between hearing God's Word and *doing* what it says, and that balance can only happen if we put listening to and following Jesus at the top of our to-do list. Everything else we need to do should come after that number one priority!

Dear God, please help me always to find the right balance of listening to and following Your Word, plus doing the good things You have created me for. Amen.

Day 48

BEAUTIFUL BOLDNESS

After this prayer, the meeting place shook,
and they were all filled with the Holy Spirit.
Then they preached the word of God with boldness.
ACTS 4:31 NLT

If I could travel in a time machine, back to my younger self, I'd do it and I'd grab my own shoulders and shake them a little and say, "Be more confident!" I spent way too much brainpower worrying about messing up and what other people thought of me.

So much of my lack of confidence in my younger days probably came from fear of being made fun of and fearing the future wouldn't turn out well. But that means I was trusting too much in myself rather than in God. The Bible says that "the Spirit God gave us does not make us timid, but gives us power, love and self-discipline" (2 Timothy 1:7 NIV).

Don't let this world and your worries steal your confidence. Always remember that you are a daughter of the King of all kings! Let His Holy Spirit fill you and inspire you to be beautifully bold.

Dear God, help me to have confidence that is based on You. Amen.

Day 49

WISDOM FROM THE BOOK OF JOSHUA

*"This book of the Law must not leave your mouth.
Think about it day and night, so you may be careful to do
all that is written in it. Then all will go well with you. You will
receive many good things. Have I not told you? Be strong
and have strength of heart! Do not be afraid or lose faith.
For the Lord your God is with you anywhere you go."*

JOSHUA 1:8–9

The book of Joshua picks up where the book of Deuteronomy ended. Moses has died and Joshua is the new leader of the nation of Israel. He's ready to lead God's people into Canaan, the promised land. The first half of Joshua tells how the Israelites defeat any armies that stand in their way as they take over Canaan. The second half tells how the Israelites divided the land among their twelve tribes. One of our favorite stories in this book is of Rahab, a brave woman who helped God's people, and God protected her and her whole family because of her great faith and courage (Joshua 2; Hebrews 11:31; James 2:25).

Dear God, thank You for the book of Joshua. Help me as I read it and keep coming back to it in the future. Teach me what You want me to learn from it to apply to my life and to share with others. Amen.

Day 50

BOLD BUT NOT TOO BOLD

Not to us, O LORD, not to us, but to your name goes all the glory for your unfailing love and faithfulness.
PSALM 115:1 NLT

You do have to be careful with boldness. There is such a thing as too much, and that can cause some seriously obnoxious or annoying behavior. You have to balance boldness with being wise and humble—and wanting all glory and praise to go to God and not to yourself.

Nobody really likes to interact with people who seem to think they know everything. Sometimes people with too much boldness come across that way, and it's called arrogance. When I was in school, one of the most annoying things EVER was when one particular student raised their hand to answer every single question and pretty much never let anyone else have a chance to participate in class discussion. A good teacher will notice that and not let just one student overtake the class, but it's still annoying when they try.

Ask God to make you bold and outspoken when He wants you to be, and also ask Him to show you when it's better to just be quiet and listen to others. There are times for both.

God, I need Your help knowing when to speak out for You and when to just quietly listen to others whom I want to share Your love with. Help me be bold yet humble and do everything for Your glory. Amen.

FORGETFUL FOLKS

"But the Advocate, the Holy Spirit, whom the Father will send in my name, will teach you all things and will remind you of everything I have said to you."
JOHN 14:26 NIV

I am forever misplacing things around the house—especially forgetting where I last put my phone. One time I even put it in a basket of laundry I was carrying downstairs. . .and then I dumped the whole basket in the washing machine and washed my phone along with the load of whites. The bad news was it was totally dead; the good news was that it sure came out of the laundry squeaky clean!

Do you forget where you put things like I do? Or maybe you forget a certain chore you're supposed to do each day or the homework you leave in your backpack.

John 14:26 shows us that God understands that we are forgetful folks. He gave us the Holy Spirit to both teach us and remind us of all the things Jesus said. He knows we need constant encouragement and reminders of truth. How hard it would be to keep on track with God's Word in our culture today if we didn't have the Spirit constantly encouraging us to remember it!

Holy Spirit, thank You for teaching me and reminding me of all that Jesus said. It's so good to have You with me all the time. Amen.

Day 52

WISDOM FOR FRIENDSHIP

Don't fool yourselves. Bad friends will destroy you.
1 CORINTHIANS 15:33 CEV

Think about your favorite friends and why you love hanging out with them. We all need good friends in our lives, and we need to be good friends to others. But this verse makes it clear that we need a lot of wisdom about friendship too. If bad friends will destroy us, then we sure need to know how to figure out if a friend is a good friend or a bad friend. Your very best friend is Jesus as your Savior. The best kind of friends are those who love and follow Him too and try to be as much like Him as possible. A bad friend will want to lead you into trouble and away from following Jesus. Your whole life, you will need lots of wisdom and help from God to find good friends who care about you and also to avoid bad friends who will destroy you. Never stop asking God to show you every friend's true character and which friendships to keep and which ones to walk away from.

*Dear God, thank You for the gift of good friends,
and please give me lots and lots of wisdom about
friendship now and in the future. Amen.*

Day 53
TRUE OR FALSE?

*"And I will ask the Father, and he will give you another advocate
to help you and be with you forever—the Spirit of truth."*
JOHN 14:16–17 NIV

If you ever follow the news these days, you'll hear about fake news and false accusations and a constant need for fact-checkers. It seems like every day it gets harder and harder to know what's really true and which people are safe to trust! Thankfully, the Holy Spirit of God who is with us at all times is called the Spirit of truth. He can constantly help us determine what is true and what is false, whom we can trust and whom we need to be wary of.

John 16:13 (NIV) says, "But when he, the Spirit of truth, comes, he will guide you into all the truth." Don't let the world discourage you with so many lies. Trust completely that you have God's Spirit to show you truth in all things. Let Him guide and direct you every step of the way.

Spirit of truth, thank You for guiding me and showing me what to believe. I would be so lost in lies and confusion without You. Amen.

Day 54

KING SOLOMON'S REQUEST, PART 1

*Now Solomon loved the Lord. He walked
in the Laws of his father David.*
1 KINGS 3:3

King Solomon loved God and wanted to follow His ways, and so God wanted to bless him. First Kings 3:5 says, "The Lord came to Solomon in a special dream in Gibeon during the night. God said, 'Ask what you wish Me to give you.'" Solomon could have asked God for *anything* at all, but this is what he asked for: "Now, O Lord my God, You have made Your servant king in place of my father David. But I am only a little child. I do not know how to start or finish. Your servant is among Your people which You have chosen. They are many people. There are too many people to number. So give Your servant an understanding heart to judge Your people and know the difference between good and bad" (1 Kings 3:7–9). Wow, what a good and honorable choice! We should want to be like Solomon, recognizing that wisdom from God to know the difference between right and wrong is far more valuable than any treasure.

Dear God, please help me to learn from King Solomon's example and want wisdom from You more than earthly treasure. Amen.

KING SOLOMON'S REQUEST, PART 2

It pleased the Lord that Solomon had asked this.
1 KINGS 3:10

Because Solomon had chosen so well, God wanted to bless him *even more*. He said to Solomon, "You have asked this, and have not asked for a long life for yourself. You have not asked for riches, or for the life of those who hate you. But you have asked for understanding to know what is right. Because you have asked this, I have done what you said. See, I have given you a wise and understanding heart. No one has been like you before, and there will be no one like you in the future. I give you what you have not asked, also. I give you both riches and honor. So there will be no king like you all your days. And if you walk in My ways and keep My Laws and Word as your father David did, I will allow you to live a long time" (1 Kings 3:11–14).

When we choose to ask God for wisdom rather than riches, we please Him, just like Solomon did. He is our good heavenly Father who loves to bless us for choosing what's best.

Dear God, I trust that You love to bless me when I choose wisely. Lots of things seem good, but please help me to choose what's best in life. I want to please and honor You! Amen.

Day 56

DON'T GIVE UP ON OTHERS

*For it is God who works in you, both to will
and to work for his good pleasure.*
PHILIPPIANS 2:13 ESV

Do you have someone in your life you keep inviting to church, but they just won't come? Do you have someone in your life you keep praying for that they will want to know and love Jesus, but nothing seems to change?

Don't give up! It's your job to simply share the love and truth of Jesus as the Holy Spirit guides you. It's never your job to force someone to accept Jesus as their Savior. Only God can truly soften a person's heart to want to know Him. As you wait, keep praying and don't lose hope. Read Jeremiah 24:6–7 (NLT) and pray that God does the same for your loved ones who need to know Him as He said in that scripture: "I will watch over and care for them, and I will bring them back here again. I will build them up and not tear them down. I will plant them and not uproot them. I will give them hearts that recognize me as the LORD. They will be my people, and I will be their God, for they will return to me wholeheartedly."

---

*Dear God, please help my loved one want to know You.
Please care for and protect them and draw them close to You. Amen.*

Day 57

HAPPINESS OR JOY? PART 1

You will show me the way of life. Being with You is to be full of joy. In Your right hand there is happiness forever.
PSALM 16:11

Whatever makes you happy! That's a phrase you might hear a lot these days, but one we all need to be careful with—because if it's our constant goal just to be happy, we can truly ruin our lives. I'd probably be happy with a big plate of brownies to eat every single night, but that's sure not wise or good for me. I'd also really be happy if I got to go to the beach and Disney World every single week, but that's sure not wise or good for me either. Dessert and vacation can make us all really happy, but they have to be balanced wisely with healthy foods and times of work and learning. That's why joy is so much more important than happiness. Real joy is based on our relationship with Jesus and our hope of perfect heaven with Him forever, while happiness is usually just based on the situation we're in. When we focus on real joy and apply it to everything we do, that's when we can also find happiness in pretty much anything!

Dear God, please give me wisdom and keep me learning about how real joy in You is far better than just happiness. Amen.

HAPPINESS OR JOY? PART 2

"The joy of the Lord is your strength."
NEHEMIAH 8:10

We need to remember how quickly and easily our feelings change. Something that made you happy last year or even a month ago might seem totally boring to you now. That's another example of how real joy is so much better than happiness. Let these scriptures help teach and guide you all of your life with wisdom about knowing real joy:

- "I will give honor and thanks to the Lord, Who has told me what to do. Yes, even at night my mind teaches me. I have placed the Lord always in front of me. Because He is at my right hand, I will not be moved. And so my heart is glad. My soul is full of joy" (Psalm 16:7–9).

- "You have never seen Him but you love Him. You cannot see Him now but you are putting your trust in Him. And you have joy so great that words cannot tell about it. You will get what your faith is looking for, which is to be saved from the punishment of sin" (1 Peter 1:8–9).

Dear God, no matter what situation I'm in or what my emotions feel like, help me to remember that my true joy is always in You.

Day 59

GOD MAKES THE SEED GROW

*I planted the seed in your hearts, and Apollos
watered it, but it was God who made it grow.*
1 CORINTHIANS 3:6 NLT

As you keep praying for a friend or loved one to come to know Jesus, remember that God can use others in their lives to draw them close to Him too. Read what Paul says in 1 Corinthians 3: "Who is Apollos? Who is Paul? We are only God's servants through whom you believed the Good News. Each of us did the work the Lord gave us. I planted the seed in your hearts, and Apollos watered it, but it was God who made it grow. It's not important who does the planting, or who does the watering. What's important is that God makes the seed grow. The one who plants and the one who waters work together with the same purpose. And both will be rewarded for their own hard work" (1 Corinthians 3:5–8 NLT).

Have faith and confidence that it's never all just your job to lead others to Christ! It's your job to just keep walking closely to God and letting His light shine through you and His love be given through you. Ask Him each day how He wants you to do that.

---

*Dear God, thank You that all of us who love and serve You are
working together to share the gospel. I pray for my loved ones
who don't know You that they will receive the gospel! Amen.*

Day 60

NO SECRETS, PART 1

*O Lord, You have looked through me and have known me.
You know when I sit down and when I get up. You understand
my thoughts from far away. You look over my path and my lying
down. You know all my ways very well. Even before I speak a
word, O Lord, You know it all. You have closed me in from behind
and in front. And You have laid Your hand upon me. All You know
is too great for me. It is too much for me to understand.*
PSALM 139:1–6

You can gain wisdom from understanding that you can never keep a secret from God. Not ever. He knows absolutely everything. Even before you say a word, God knows you're going to say it. He knows every single one of your thoughts and always knows exactly what you're doing and where and when. To some people that might seem creepy, but for those who love God and want a good relationship with Him through Jesus, it never has to be. God loves you! And because He sees and knows everything about you, you should feel greatly loved and protected and cared for.

*Dear God, thank You for loving me so much that You
know absolutely everything about me! Amen.*

Day 61

NO SECRETS, PART 2

*The eyes of the Lord are in every place,
watching the bad and the good.*
Proverbs 15:3

Sometimes we might think we can hide doing the things we know are wrong, but it's just not true. In those times, we need to remember that we can keep no secrets from God. Remembering that truth can help us not to sin. God is going to see our sin, and there will be consequences. Thankfully, God loves to forgive us, like 1 John 1:9 says: "If we tell Him our sins, He is faithful and we can depend on Him to forgive us of our sins. He will make our lives clean from all sin."

Dear God, especially when I am tempted to sin and try to hide it from You, remind me that nothing is a secret from You. Help me to love that You are always watching me because You care about me and You want to keep me out of trouble. Thank You! Amen.

Day 62
UNIQUE GIFTS

There are different kinds of spiritual gifts, but the same Spirit is the source of them all. There are different kinds of service, but we serve the same Lord. God works in different ways, but it is the same God who does the work in all of us.
1 CORINTHIANS 12:4–6 NLT

I bet your friends have a lot of the same interests as you, but I bet you're very different too. That's part of the fun of being friends. You learn and grow and enjoy one another because of differences. How dull our world would be if everyone were all the same!

The Bible talks about how God's Holy Spirit gives different gifts to each of His people, different ways to serve Him, different ways to help one another. God has blessed us all with unique talents and individual abilities to do what He asks us to do. How cool is that? It's so important to never compare and expect other Christians to be exactly like you. God purposefully made you and every other person different, with tasks specifically designed for you. Let Him show you what they are, and then do them for His glory!

God, thank You for my unique gifts. Help me to know how and when to use them like You want me to. Amen.

Day 63

HELPING YOUR FRIENDS

Just as iron sharpens iron, friends sharpen the minds of each other.
PROVERBS 27:17 CEV

Think of some ways you and your friends help each other. Maybe you're a pro at math but a friend gets easily confused by it, so you try to help her understand it. Maybe you feel like you stink at writing essays but you have a friend who is an awesome writer, and she gives you pointers to improve. Kindness and help among friends are wonderful! And they also require wisdom—because what if your friend suddenly asked you to do all of her math homework for her? That would no longer be helping but would actually hurt her. It's okay if she needs *some* help, but it's not okay for her to expect someone else to do her own work for her. And you should never expect that either. As you share kindness with your friends, always keep asking God to give you wisdom about when to step in and when to step back when they need to do things on their own to learn and grow.

Dear God, please give me wisdom to know when to step in and help a friend and when to step back and be a bigger help by letting her do things on her own to learn and grow. Amen.

ONE WITH MANY

*The human body has many parts, but the many parts
make up one whole body. So it is with the body of Christ.
Some of us are Jews, some are Gentiles, some are slaves,
and some are free. But we have all been baptized into one
body by one Spirit, and we all share the same Spirit.*
1 CORINTHIANS 12:12–13 NLT

The human body is incredibly fascinating! Do you enjoy learning about it in your science classes? God is an amazing Creator. It's mind-boggling to think about how so many different parts work together so well to make you a living, breathing, thinking, feeling, loving, active, working, talented, creative human being! But when all our different body parts don't work together in the way they're supposed to, that's when an illness or disease results.

Now, think about how Paul describes God's people, the church, as one body with many parts. We have to realize and appreciate that we're all very different, with unique spiritual gifts and jobs to do. If we don't do that, the church gets sick and doesn't function well, either. We have to be willing to celebrate the differences and work together in unity like a healthy human body.

Dear God, please help me to appreciate all the differences in Your people and help me work toward unity in Your church. Amen.

Day 65

WISDOM FROM THE
BOOK OF JUDGES

Then the people of Israel sinned in the eyes of the Lord.
JUDGES 2:11

The book of Judges tells the stories of 13 judges who led the nation of Israel over about 350 years, including the only female judge of Israel, Deborah. You've probably heard of the strongman Samson, who was one of the judges. And Gideon is also one of the most well-known. Judges contains a lot of rough and violent stories showing how when God's people didn't care about following Him, they suffered greatly for it. But when they cried out to God, He delivered them. When we read Judges, we should be reminded to want to follow God's ways always. And we can remember that through all kinds of ups and downs, good choices and bad, blessing and suffering, God still dearly loves and never abandons His people.

Dear God, thank You for the book of Judges. Help me as I read it and keep coming back to it in the future. Teach me what You want me to learn from it to apply to my life and to share with others. Amen.

Day 66

POWER IN WEAKNESS

Be strong in the Lord and in his mighty power.
Ephesians 6:10 NLT

You have unique strengths and talents, and you have unique weaknesses too—things that are harder for you than they might be for other people. We all do, and we shouldn't be ashamed of them. Did you know the Bible says you should actually be happy about them? Sounds a little crazy, I know, but it's true, and here's why: When you're really good at something, you don't have to ask for help with it, right? But if you can admit you can't do something on your own, you know you need help. If you realize that you need to depend on God in those areas where you struggle, then you'll get closer to God because you'll keep asking Him for His help. He'll be so happy to assist, and you'll grow closer and closer to Him as He gives you the strength and ability you need! Second Corinthians 12:9–10 (NLT) says: " 'My grace is all you need. My power works best in weakness.' So now I am glad to boast about my weaknesses, so that the power of Christ can work through me. That's why I take pleasure in my weaknesses, and in the insults, hardships, persecutions, and troubles that I suffer for Christ. For when I am weak, then I am strong."

Dear God, no matter what weaknesses I have, remind me that You have the power to help me with anything! Amen.

Day 67

WISDOM WHEN YOU GET PUNISHED

There is no joy while we are being punished. It is hard to take, but later we can see that good came from it.
HEBREWS 12:11

What happened the last time you got in trouble? Did you instantly think of your punishment as something to be grateful for? Probably not. We get it. That's never been our instant reaction either. But actually, if you use God's wisdom during punishment, you can choose to see the good in it. Your parents and other grown-ups in your life are truly helping you when they punish or discipline you in wise ways for things you've done wrong. They're trying to teach you never to do the same bad thing again. They're trying to teach you things like safety and honesty and respect and responsibility. Ask God to help you appreciate punishment and discipline, even if they feel awful at first. Choose to learn from them and ask God to show you how He is maturing and teaching you because of them.

Dear God, please give me wisdom when I've done something wrong and then have to face the consequences. Even though I don't enjoy it, help me see the good in wise punishment and discipline, both now and in the future. Amen.

Day 68

SHEEP IN WOLF CLOTHES

Many false prophets have already gone out into the world,
and you can know which ones come from God.
1 JOHN 4:1–2 CEV

There are some *seriously* confusing kinds of differences among churches and people who call themselves Christians. Some differences are no big deal because they're just a matter of traditions and different tastes. But some differences result from churches and teachers and preachers going against the Word of God. Second Corinthians 11:13 (CEV) says these false teachers "only pretend to be apostles of Christ."

God is not surprised by these false teachers and churches. The Bible warns us again and again about them. But we don't have to be afraid. Plant yourself firmly in Jesus, and through the Holy Spirit, He will help you discern or figure out the false teachers and churches from the ones that truly know, love, and serve Him and that preach the whole Word of God. It's all about their fruit! Matthew 7:15–20 (CEV) says, "Watch out for false prophets! They dress up like sheep, but inside they are wolves who have come to attack you. You can tell what they are by what they do. No one picks grapes or figs from thornbushes. A good tree produces good fruit, and a bad tree produces bad fruit. A good tree cannot produce bad fruit, and a bad tree cannot produce good fruit. Every tree that produces bad fruit will be chopped down and burned. You can tell who the false prophets are by their deeds."

Holy Spirit, I want to hear what You want to teach me,
straight from Your Word and Your leading! Amen.

Day 69

SERVING JESUS HIMSELF

"'Lord, when did we see You hungry and feed You? When did we see You thirsty and give You a drink? When did we see You a stranger and give You a room? When did we see You had no clothes and we gave You clothes? And when did we see You sick or in prison and we came to You?' Then the King will say, '. . .because you did it to one of the least of My brothers, you have done it to Me.'"
MATTHEW 25:37–40

Sometimes I feel frustrated that I can't sit down with Jesus in person. Those who lived when Jesus did were so blessed to get to know Him and His love and learn His wisdom face-to-face. But we have God's Word and the Holy Spirit, and those are incredible gifts to us! We also have the instruction on how to be extra close and serve Jesus—by serving others in need. Jesus said in Matthew 25 that whatever we do for others, it's like we're actually doing it for Him. So ask Jesus to show you the people in need whom He wants you to serve. And as you do, ask Him to teach you the wisdom He wants you to learn through the experience.

Dear Jesus, I want to be close to You and learn from You by serving others in need. Please guide me and give me a loving, giving heart for others like You have. Amen.

Day 70

DON'T JAM IN THE JUNK

For a time is coming when people will no longer listen to sound and wholesome teaching. They will follow their own desires and will look for teachers who will tell them whatever their itching ears want to hear. They will reject the truth and chase after myths. But you should keep a clear mind in every situation.
2 Timothy 4:3–5 nlt

Back in Bible times, I'm guessing they didn't have Doritos and Kit-Kats and Sourpatch Kids and Skittles. We have a lot more junk food these days that we have to be very careful not to fill our bodies with. We also have a lot more junk for our brains available everywhere we go. Movies, books, television shows, music, magazines, a zillion different websites and blogs. There's a lot of good stuff out there in the media. . .and a lot of really awful stuff too.

I think people make it harder and harder to listen to the Holy Spirit by filling their minds so much with the junky things of this world. I know I'm guilty sometimes! That's why in such a confusing world with so many false teachers, it's more important than ever to be extra, extra, *extra* careful what we watch, read, and listen to, and what activities we participate in. God is always so near through His Holy Spirit, but how much do we tune Him out by the junk we keep jamming into our brains?

Dear God, help me empty my mind of the things that aren't good for me. I want to keep my mind clear so that I can easily hear from You. Amen.

Day 71

TRUE BEAUTY

Your beauty should come from the inside. It should come from the heart. This is the kind that lasts.
1 PETER 3:4

We love to shop (especially for good deals!) and find cute clothes to wear and fun accessories to go with them. How about you? Whether you do or not, everyone needs wisdom when we choose our clothes and styles and when we look in the mirror. Does real beauty come from the outside? Definitely not. You might know someone who always wears the coolest clothes and looks super pretty but doesn't act very nice or treat others kindly. Does that seem truly beautiful to you? It definitely should not. And maybe you know someone who never has the latest fashions and who doesn't ever follow the latest trends in hair and makeup, but they have kindness and honesty and love overflowing out of them for others. Does that seem truly beautiful to you? It totally should!

Dear God, please always help me to have the right idea in my mind about what true beauty is. People look at the outside, but You look at the heart (1 Samuel 16:7), and that's how I want to think of what beauty is too. Amen.

Day 72

His Follower First

*So don't boast about following a particular human
leader. For everything belongs to you—whether Paul or
Apollos or Peter, or the world, or life and death, or the
present and the future. Everything belongs to you, and
you belong to Christ, and Christ belongs to God.*

1 CORINTHIANS 3:21–23 NLT

You definitely need leaders in your life who help you grow and
mature. Your parents are your first leaders, and as you get older,
more people come into your life to help teach you and guide you.
You might have favorite teachers or coaches or music instructors.
Your most important leaders are the ones who point you to a good
relationship with Jesus Christ and help you grow in it. The Bible warns
about never boasting about following any of these leaders, though.
You have to be careful to never hold them up too high because any
human is able to fall from a position of good leadership. Let Jesus
alone be your one best leader whom you're always looking up to and
getting guidance from in His Word and through the Holy Spirit. Yes,
you have parents and teachers and others who want to help you and
teach you good things, and you need to listen to them and obey.
But most of all you belong to Jesus. You are His follower first and
foremost! He knows you better than anyone else and wants to lead
you in the very best kind of life!

*Dear Lord, You are my very best leader,
and I never want to stop following You! Amen.*

Day 73

TAKE GOOD CARE, PART 1

Growing strong in body is all right but growing in God-like living is more important. It will not only help you in this life now but in the next life also.
1 TIMOTHY 4:8

One way many people become too obsessed with outer appearance these days is in working out and getting in shape. Those are awesome goals to be healthy, and 1 Corinthians 6:19–20 tells us we should want to take good care of our bodies and honor God with them. But physical fitness goals aren't awesome if people take them too far and give them too much attention. Our focus should be on God most of all. First Timothy 4:8 reminds us that growing in healthy relationship with Him so that we do our best to live like Jesus matters not just for life on earth, which is temporary, but for life in heaven, which is forever!

Dear God, please give me wisdom for keeping my body healthy and strong, and even more importantly, for keeping my heart, mind, and spirit in a healthy and strong relationship with You!

Day 74

TAKE GOOD CARE, PART 2

Do you not know that your body is a house of God where the Holy Spirit lives? God gave you His Holy Spirit. Now you belong to God. You do not belong to yourselves. God bought you with a great price. So honor God with your body. You belong to Him.
1 CORINTHIANS 6:19–20

This scripture can inspire you your whole life to take good care of your body—it's a house for the Holy Spirit of God, who loves you like no one else does. You should want to keep your body healthy and special and able to do the good things God has planned for you. You can do that while you're young by keeping yourself clean and choosing more healthy foods than junk foods and being active to keep your body moving and all its parts working well. As you get older, you can continue all those things plus make wise choices about what you do with your body and what you put in it. Keep asking God to help you every day of your life!

Dear God, please remind me every day that my body is a house for Your Holy Spirit. Thank You that You are so close to me. You have given me this body to do the good things You have planned for me here on earth, and I want to take good care of it and honor You with it! Amen.

HELP FOR THE FIGHT

You, dear children, are from God and have overcome them, because the one who is in you is greater than the one who is in the world.
1 JOHN 4:4 NIV

No doubt, we have enemies in this world. The Bible says, "Your enemy, the devil, is like a roaring lion, sneaking around to find someone to attack" (1 Peter 5:8 CEV). He is the god of this world, but he is nothing like the one true God with a capital G! We don't ever have to fear, for within us is God's Holy Spirit, and as 1 John 4:4 says, He is greater than the one in the world. The Holy Spirit gives us the power to overcome the devil and any enemy or hard circumstance that comes against us.

Dear God, You are great and mighty—so much greater than the devil and all the evil of this world! You are with me and You protect me. I have nothing to fear because with You I can overcome anything Satan and this world throw at me. Amen.

Day 76

WISDOM WITH SOCIAL MEDIA

*So be careful how you live. Live as men who are wise
and not foolish. Make the best use of your time.*
Ephesians 5:15–16

Social media is a big deal these days, and although it can be fun, it can also be really bad for you. It's important to have wisdom not to get too caught up in it. Do you have friends who are already totally obsessed with it? Or maybe you're starting to be obsessed with it yourself. If that's the case, you need to let grown-ups help you set limits, and you need to train yourself to set limits. Choose to put down your phone and tablet and do things without a screen involved. And help encourage your friends to do so as well. Read books. Play actual board games. Get involved in sports and activities. Spend time talking in person and just hanging out doing silly good stuff together. Challenge yourself to see how much fun you can have with no social media involved—and if you still want it and it's okay with Mom and Dad, then just be super-duper wise about using it in small amounts of time.

---

*Dear God, it's not cool to ask You for help with limits on social
media, but I am asking anyway. I want to be wise about this and
make the best use of my time like Your Word tells me to. Amen.*

MORE WISDOM WITH SOCIAL MEDIA

Whatever you say or do, do it in the name of the Lord Jesus.
Give thanks to God the Father through the Lord Jesus.
COLOSSIANS 3:17

You might hear a lot about people being mean and bullying and arguing in nasty ways on social media—or sharing things that are definitely not kid or family friendly, things that would make God sad. Hopefully, if you ever do choose to be on social media, you will want absolutely no part of that. None! Make a promise that you will only use it in positive ways that encourage and help others. The world has enough mean and awful stuff going on; no one needs to spread around any extra!

Dear God, show me ways to use social media for good, to encourage others and share Your truth and love. Please help me always to stay far away from the awful stuff on social media. Thank You! Amen.

Day 78
HOW TO PRAY

Likewise the Spirit helps us in our weakness. For we do not know what to pray for as we ought, but the Spirit himself intercedes for us with groanings too deep for words.
ROMANS 8:26 ESV

Do you ever just feel like you're stuck with a mouth full of Laffy Taffy when you're trying to pray? You don't ever have to feel bad about that! It also doesn't mean you should just stop praying. God definitely wants to hear from you, and He wants you to tell Him your every worry and need, for others and for yourself, but the Bible says you won't always know what to pray for as you should. Thankfully, the Holy Spirit intercedes, or does it for you, with groanings that are too deep for words. That means the way the Holy Spirit communicates our prayers is in a way that is just too much for us to fully understand. But God understands! He sees all and knows all, and nothing surprises Him. He cares about your every need.

Holy Spirit, thank You that when I'm not sure how or what to pray, You are doing it for me. Amen.

WISDOM FROM THE BOOK OF RUTH

"May the Lord show kindness to you."
RUTH 1:8

The book of Ruth tells a story about a special woman who lived during the time when judges led the nation of Israel. Ruth and her mother-in-law, Naomi, and sister-in-law, Orpah, all lost their husbands, and it was dangerous in Bible times for a woman not to have a man to take care of her. So Naomi urged the younger women to leave her and go back to their homelands and their people there. But Ruth loved her mother-in-law and wanted to stay with her no matter what. She said, "Do not beg me to leave you or turn away from following you. I will go where you go. I will live where you live. Your people will be my people. And your God will be my God" (Ruth 1:16). Ruth wanted to have faith in the one true God of Israel. And if you read the whole story in the book of Ruth in the Bible, you'll see that because of her loyalty, love, and faith, God blessed Ruth far more than she ever thought possible. We should all want to have the same kind of loyalty, love, and faith as Ruth.

Dear God, thank You for the book of Ruth. Help me as I read it and keep coming back to it in the future. Teach me what You want me to learn from it to apply to my life and to share with others. Amen.

Day 80

THE LORD'S WAY

"Our Father in heaven. . ."
MATTHEW 6:9 ESV

Jesus gave us some clear instructions on how to pray. You've probably heard of the Lord's Prayer. It comes from the scripture in Matthew 6:7-13 (NLT). "'When you pray, don't babble on and on as the Gentiles do. They think their prayers are answered merely by repeating their words again and again. Don't be like them, for your Father knows exactly what you need even before you ask him! Pray like this: Our Father in heaven, may your name be kept holy. May your Kingdom come soon. May your will be done on earth, as it is in heaven. Give us today the food we need, and forgive us our sins, as we have forgiven those who sin against us. And don't let us yield to temptation, but rescue us from the evil one.'"

That's some very straightforward instruction from Jesus! It's a great idea to memorize this prayer and keep in mind its guidelines. When you pray:

- Praise God.
- Pray for His will to be done.
- Ask God for what you need.
- Ask for forgiveness and help in forgiving others.
- Ask for protection from temptation and from the enemy.

Lord, thank You for understanding I need help with knowing how to pray and for teaching me in Your Word! Amen.

Day 81

WISDOM FROM CHURCH

*Let us hold on to the hope we say we have and not be
changed. We can trust God that He will do what He promised.
Let us help each other to love others and to do good.
Let us not stay away from church meetings. . . . Comfort
each other as you see the day of His return coming near.*
HEBREWS 10:23–25

We hope you have a church you love going to where all of God's
Word is taught and where the love and salvation of Jesus are shared
and where others are helped to know Jesus and follow Him. And we
hope you love being active in that church. Church should never be
just a thing you do here and there, when it feels like a good idea,
especially around holidays or when you have a new outfit to wear.
Now and your whole life, you should want to be a part of a Bible-
teaching church to help you grow in wisdom as you learn and give
and serve and gain encouragement. The church is made up of all
believers in Jesus all around the world, and when you join in a group
of believers in a local church near you, you help to spread God's
great big kingdom, both now and forever!

---

*Dear God, in every stage of my life, help me to find
the church where You want me to grow in wisdom
from You and in love for others! Amen.*

Day 82

LEAVE IT UP TO HIM!

"But you will receive power when the Holy Spirit has come upon you, and you will be my witnesses in Jerusalem and in all Judea and Samaria, and to the end of the earth."

ACTS 1:8 ESV

You want to tell others about Jesus and His love, but it can be scary sometimes, right? Just remember that you know the hope of the world, the best news EVER that Jesus loves people and died and rose again to give us eternal life. And don't worry about when and how you will share with people. Just keep close to God and leave it up to Him! Keep praying for His will to be done in your life and tell Him you are willing and able to share His love with others whenever He wants you to. Then let Him show you how and when He wants you to share with others about His wonderful love and salvation. God's Holy Spirit will give you the words and actions you need if you are walking closely to Him and are staying sensitive to His leading.

Holy Spirit, please keep me constantly aware of Your presence, and help me pay attention for the times when You want me to share with others about Jesus' love and grace. Please use me for Your will. I know You will help me with everything You ask me to do. Amen.

WORKING WISELY, PART 1

Whatever work you do, do it with all your heart. Do it for the Lord and not for men. Remember that you will get your reward from the Lord. He will give you what you should receive. You are working for the Lord Christ.

COLOSSIANS 3:23–24

This scripture gives you wisdom about how to do your work—whether schoolwork or chores—with all your heart! That means doing your very best with a great attitude. But that's not always easy, is it? Some school subjects are super hard or just plain boring. Some chores seem to take forever when you'd rather be having fun. So, it's very important to remember the boss you're working for—yes, you might be working for your teacher who assigned the homework and will give you the grade, and you might be working for your parents who told you what chores to do. But above and beyond those bosses is your ultimate boss. That's God, and He loves you like crazy. He wants to reward you in all kinds of ways, here on earth and in heaven, when you do any kind of work with your best effort and best attitude in a way that brings honor to Him.

Dear God, please don't let me forget that You are my boss and You're the very best boss ever. Help me to do my very best and have a good attitude with any kind of work I have to do. Amen.

Day 84

WORKING WISELY, PART 2

*Call out with joy to the Lord, all the earth. Be glad as you
serve the Lord. Come before Him with songs of joy.*
PSALM 100:1–2

Here's a great way to work with a good attitude, doing your best—keep
nearly constant praise songs going in your head. Turn up the worship
music (if you're allowed) while you do chores, and if you can't actually
turn up the music, then just keep singing the praise songs you know
inside your mind. Remind yourself what a blessing it is to be able
to do work and to learn, and thank God for that blessing. There are
some people in the world who would love to go to school and to a
job but who don't have the abilities or opportunities. Choosing to
praise God while you work brings glory to Him and puts your mind in
the right place to give you the best kind of attitude, all while getting
good things done. That's a win-win-win!

---

*Dear God, thank You for the blessing of being able to work
and to learn. When I might be feeling grumpy about the
work I need to do, please help me to remember to start
singing praise to You with a grateful heart! Amen.*

WORKING WISELY, PART 3

For we are God's masterpiece. He has created us anew in Christ Jesus, so we can do the good things he planned for us long ago.
EPHESIANS 2:10 NLT

Hopefully, you already have some ideas of the job you want to have and the work you want to do when you grow up. It's good to start dreaming and thinking of the things you're already good at and how those talents might fit into jobs and goals in the future. Most important as you think and dream is to keep asking God to show you the good works He created you to do. The best jobs for you that will make you the happiest and feel the most rewarding will be the ones God has specifically designed you for. He's given you just the right natural talent—and if you let Him lead you, He'll guide you to all the right learning and people and places that He wants for you.

Dear God, thank You for the talents and abilities You have given me. As I keep learning about what I'm good at and growing in knowledge and wisdom, please show me all the good things You have planned for me to do in my life. Amen.

Day 86

PLAIN AND SIMPLE

*Always be prepared to give an answer to everyone who
asks you to give the reason for the hope that you have.*
1 PETER 3:15 NIV

I like big words, but I'm glad the Bible tells us we don't *have* to know them. It does tell us we always need to be ready to share with others about why we have hope (1 Peter 3:15), but it doesn't say we have to do that using elaborate speech with a bunch of big vocab. In fact, the apostle Paul talked about how he purposefully did *not* use fancy words sometimes when teaching people about Jesus, and he even talks about how he was super nervous and trembling with fear at first! (That makes me feel so much better because I'm such a big chicken about speaking in front of big groups of people!)

Read what Paul said in 1 Corinthians 2:1–5 (CEV): "Friends, when I came and told you the mystery that God had shared with us, I didn't use big words or try to sound wise. In fact, while I was with you, I made up my mind to speak only about Jesus Christ, who had been nailed to a cross. At first, I was weak and trembling with fear. When I talked with you or preached, I didn't try to prove anything by sounding wise. I simply let God's Spirit show his power. That way you would have faith because of God's power and not because of human wisdom."

---

*Dear Jesus, help me to just share simply and
honestly about how awesome You are! Amen.*

Day 87

WISDOM FROM THE BOOKS OF 1 AND 2 SAMUEL

Hannah prayed and said, "My heart is happy in the Lord. My strength is honored in the Lord."
1 SAMUEL 2:1

The book of 1 Samuel starts out telling about brave Hannah's prayer for a son and her promise and her faithfulness to God. The book goes on to tell about the life of her son named Samuel who became a prophet of God. Then it tells about bad King Saul's life. And then in 2 Samuel, David becomes king of Israel. He's known as the nation's greatest king, even though he started out as a lowly shepherd boy! But he was very brave (you've probably heard how he defeated the giant Goliath!), and most importantly he loved and had great faith in God. And even though he made lots of mistakes, he was called a man after God's heart. We should make it our goal to be described as girls and women after God's heart!

Dear God, thank You for the books of 1 and 2 Samuel. Help me as I read them and keep coming back to them in the future. Teach me what You want me to learn from them to apply to my life and to share with others. Amen.

Day 88

THE WORD

*In the beginning was the Word, and the Word
was with God, and the Word was God.*
JOHN 1:1 NIV

God is constantly with you through His Word, the Bible. He didn't physically write it Himself, but He used regular people to record the inspired words He gave them. Second Peter 1:20–21 (NLT) says, "Above all, you must realize that no prophecy in Scripture ever came from the prophet's own understanding, or from human initiative. No, those prophets were moved by the Holy Spirit, and they spoke from God."

Why can you trust the Bible as God's Word? If you took time to study the origin of the Bible, you would find that scholars and archaeologists have discovered time and time again that the Bible is accurate and consistent throughout history. Not to mention all the people throughout history whose lives have been transformed because of the Bible! And most importantly, there were so many eyewitnesses to the miracles of Jesus and to the fact that Jesus died on the cross then rose back to life! He is worthy of your trust and so is the Bible.

---

*Dear God, thank You for Your Word that I can trust and
read anytime I want to hear from You! Amen.*

Day 89

WISDOM ABOUT YOUR SAFEST PLACE

My being safe and my honor rest with God. My safe place is in God, the rock of my strength. Trust in Him at all times, O people. Pour out your heart before Him. God is a safe place for us.
PSALM 62:7–8

If you think of your safe place, do you think of the place where you feel most comfortable and relaxed and understood? We feel that way at home with each other, especially on cozy family movie and game nights. Or maybe you think of your safe place as with your best friend you can talk to about anything. Those are good safe places, but we also have to be careful we don't let anything take the place of our very best safe place—God! When we depend too much on other things for safety and comfort, we forget that God is the strongest and most protective, and He should be first in our lives. He is your rock solid, strongest safe place! He is with you anytime and anywhere. Talk to Him, cry out to Him, depend on Him, and trust Him for everything you need.

Dear God, You are my solid rock and safe place everywhere I go, in every situation. Thank You for giving me comfort and safety, and please help me to think only of You as my very best safe place. Amen.

BiG DECiSiONS

All Scripture is inspired by God and is useful to teach us what is true and to make us realize what is wrong in our lives. It corrects us when we are wrong and teaches us to do what is right.
2 TIMOTHY 3:16 NLT

Do you ever hear people say, "I just wish God would tell me exactly what to do!" when they are struggling with a big decision to make? I know I've said that before myself. Maybe you have too! We wish God would speak to us directly whenever we need Him to. The thing is, He does speak to us all the time, through His Word. If you spend consistent time learning about Him and reading the Bible, He gives you everything You need to know to live a good life and make wise decisions. You have to keep the whole Bible in mind, though, not just the parts of it you like best or that sound the nicest. That's why it's so important to keep God first in your life, make it a major priority to go to church where the Bible is studied and preached thoroughly and accurately, and not just hear the Word but *do* it—live it out! Those are the ways God best communicates to His children, and you are one of His treasured children!

Dear God, I want to listen well to Your Word. Please help me understand when it seems confusing. Please help me to be consistent in learning more about You and Your Word! Amen.

Day 91

WISDOM FROM THE BOOKS OF 1 AND 2 KINGS

The Lord told Israel and Judah of the danger, through all His men who told what would happen in the future. He said, "Turn from your sinful ways and obey My Laws. Keep all the Laws which I gave your fathers, and which I gave to you through My servants and men of God." But they did not listen.
2 KINGS 17:13–14

In 1 and 2 Kings, King David's son Solomon became king over the nation of Israel. God blessed him greatly for wanting to be faithful and have wisdom to know God's ways of right and wrong. But by the end of his reign, Solomon made bad choices and did not lead well. When his son took over as king, Israel soon split apart into two different nations, Israel and Judah. Throughout the years and rise and fall of kings, God spoke to the people through the prophets, especially Elijah and Elisha, who performed amazing miracles. But the nations of Israel and Judah did not listen well to the prophets from God, and by the end of 2 Kings both nations were defeated and held captive by other nations.

Dear God, thank You for the books of 1 and 2 Kings. Help me as I read them and keep coming back to them in the future. Teach me what You want me to learn from them to apply to my life and to share with others. Amen.

Day 92

OUR GOOD SHEPHERD

*"I am the good shepherd. I know my own and my own
know me, just as the Father knows me and I know the
Father; and I lay down my life for the sheep."*
JOHN 10:14–15 ESV

Have you ever watched the show *Dirty Jobs* with Mike Rowe? He needs to travel back in time and do an episode with the shepherds in the Bible. They sure didn't have a glamorous job! It was dirty and smelly and seriously hard work. Yet Jesus called Himself our Good Shepherd. He is certainly no arrogant, fancy-pants master of His people. He's our King of all kings and the Lord of all lords, yet He didn't demand a palace or anything special during His time here on earth. No, He is humble and so good to us, walking with the poorest of people and healing and performing miracles to show us the way to God. He put our needs before His own. He is our leader, yet He serves and cares for us too. That's the very best kind of leader. He's such a good shepherd that He gave His life for His sheep. He gave His life for *you* to be saved.

*My Good Shepherd, You lead and care for me
so well. I will always follow You! Amen.*

Day 93

WISDOM ABOUT BAPTISM

Jesus came and said to them, ". . .Go and make followers of all the nations. Baptize them in the name of the Father and of the Son and of the Holy Spirit. Teach them to do all the things I have told you."
MATTHEW 28:18–20

If you have accepted Jesus as your Savior, you can choose to be baptized to show other people that you love and follow Jesus. It's not something you absolutely *have* to do to be saved and go to heaven forever. The man who died next to Jesus when He died on the cross never had a chance to be baptized, and Jesus promised the man he would be with Him that day in paradise (Luke 23:42–43). But if you do have a chance, it is right to obey God's Word and follow Jesus' example. Baptism is a symbol with water to represent washing away your sin and choosing new life with Jesus. It's a way to show that you want to obey God and be like Jesus and that you are saved from sin and are His follower! Christians who get baptized help inspire others to trust in Jesus as Savior too.

Dear God, please give me wisdom about baptism. If it's Your will for me, help me to be brave to choose baptism. I want to show others how much I love and want to follow You! Amen.

LIGHT AGAINST DARKNESS

God is light, and in him is no darkness at all.
1 JOHN 1:5 ESV

Jodi, Lilly, and I attended a stargazing event at a nature center in Florida recently. We got to peer through some big telescopes and learn about several different constellations, and we saw the planet Venus shining very brightly. God's creation of all the stars and galaxies is beyond amazing! Of course, it had to be dark outside in order to see the stars. The darker the better, actually.

Sometimes when I get discouraged about how dark our world seems to be getting with sin growing so popular and being flaunted all around us, I remember that light shines brighter in darkness. And Jesus said, "I am the light of the world. Whoever follows me will not walk in darkness, but will have the light of life" (John 8:12 ESV). When we know Jesus as our Savior and we have the Holy Spirit with us, we are shining His light on a very dark world. And when we learn and live by and share God's Word, we spread God's light too, for the Bible is a lamp for our feet and a light to all our paths (Psalm 119:105). So don't get discouraged by darkness. Use it for opportunities to shine God's light in your life brighter than ever before!

Dear Lord, please help me to shine brightly
for You in a dark world. Amen.

WISDOM FROM THE BOOKS OF 1 AND 2 CHRONICLES

"If My people who are called by My name put away their pride and pray, and look for My face, and turn from their sinful ways, then I will hear from heaven. I will forgive their sin, and will heal their land."
2 CHRONICLES 7:14

The books of 1 and 2 Chronicles tell about a lot of the same history as in 1 and 2 Samuel and 1 and 2 Kings, but they focus more on the good lessons to learn in that history about loving and following and worshipping God. It's especially cool to learn more about the youngest king of Israel, Josiah. He wasn't even ten years old! From 2 Chronicles 34, we learn that "Josiah. . .ruled thirty-one years in Jerusalem. He did what was right in the eyes of the Lord, and walked in the ways of his father David" (vv. 1–2). That's pretty cool that such a young kid knew how important it was to follow God. He did many great things to help his nation to love and obey only the one true God of Israel. We should want to be a lot like King Josiah!

Dear God, thank You for the books of 1 and 2 Chronicles. Help me as I read them and keep coming back to them in the future. Teach me what You want me to learn from them to apply to my life and to share with others. Amen.

Day 96

NEVER ALONE

I am with you. Don't tremble with fear. I am your God. I will make you strong, as I protect you with my arm and give you victories.
ISAIAH 41:10 CEV

You go for years as a baby and then a little girl when it's not safe to be alone because you don't quite know enough to take care of yourself. No one should leave a little child all by herself before she's ready! And then suddenly you reach the age (maybe you're there or are almost there) when now you do know enough about safety rules and such that you can be left alone at home for certain lengths of time. Maybe you love that kind of independence or maybe it scares you a little—or maybe even a lot. If it scares you, be encouraged that God promises time and time again that He is always with you and is protecting you according to His perfect will. Call out to Him for comfort when you feel lonely and afraid. Talk to Him at any time, out loud even when you're home alone. Treat Him like He is right there in the room with you, because He always is! And if you enjoy the independence and it doesn't scare you at all, still never forget that He is with you. Enjoy the time alone when you can better focus your thoughts on God's constant presence with you!

God, remind me that You are here with me
every moment of every day. Amen.

Day 97

WISDOM WHEN YOU'RE ANGRY, PART 1

If you are angry, do not let it become sin.
Get over your anger before the day is finished.
EPHESIANS 4:26

We definitely get angry with each other in our family sometimes, and we don't always handle our anger well. We sure need God's help and wisdom! The Bible doesn't say anger is always bad; God knows we will and should be angry sometimes. But the Bible does say not to sin when we are angry. That's super hard to obey sometimes! The moment we feel anger start to rise up inside our hearts and minds, we need to train ourselves to take big deep breaths and slow down, then pray and ask God how we should react. Proverbs 14:29 says, "He who is slow to get angry has great understanding, but he who has a quick temper makes his foolish way look right." And James 1:19 (NIV) says, "Everyone should be quick to listen, slow to speak and slow to become angry."

Dear God, please help me slow down when I start to feel angry. Help me to stop and pray to You for wisdom on how to handle it. I don't want to sin when I am angry; I want to deal with it in ways that honor You and share Your love. Amen.

WISDOM WHEN YOU'RE ANGRY, PART 2

*God has chosen you. You are holy and loved by Him.
Because of this, your new life should be full of loving-pity.
You should be kind to others and have no pride. Be gentle and
be willing to wait for others. Try to understand other people.
Forgive each other. If you have something against someone,
forgive him. That is the way the Lord forgave you. And to all
these things, you must add love. Love holds everything and
everybody together and makes all these good things perfect.*
COLOSSIANS 3:12–14

Think of specific things that have made you angry, and then think of
ways you could replace the anger with something good. What if a
sibling or friend acts mean and picks a fight with you for no reason?
You could choose to keep a fight going, or you could choose to be
a peacemaker and suggest something fun to do together instead of
fighting. If the sibling or friend won't stop, then you can choose to
walk away and/or calmly get a grown-up to help. Let God help you
with all kinds of situations that make you angry. He can help you
find a way to turn them into something good.

*Dear God, please help me when I'm mad. I want to
make the situation better, not worse. Amen.*

WHEN YOU'RE NOT ALONE BUT LONELY

Do what is right and good in the LORD's sight.
DEUTERONOMY 6:18 NIV

Sometimes the worst kind of loneliness isn't when you're truly all alone; it's when you're surrounded by people but you feel like you just don't fit in and maybe you're afraid of being teased or laughed at. Or maybe you took a stand among a group of friends to avoid something you feel is wrong, and the rest of your friends chose to participate anyway. I know exactly what that's like, but I look back now and I'm thankful for those times. That seems crazy when you're young to be thankful for awkward social situations where you feel like no one understands you and you have no one to talk to and no one to stand up with you for what you believe in. But if you let those hard moments make you stronger friends with Jesus and hold tighter to His Word, then that's the part to celebrate!

In a world where so many people go along with anything just because that's what the group is doing, be the one who doesn't! Be unique! Be bold! Have confidence in your convictions! Hold fast to your beliefs! Some friends will come and go, but strengthening your friendship with Jesus will never disappoint you. Let Him show you how much He cares about you, especially in your loneliness when standing up for what is right. That's when His presence often seems the closest.

---

*Dear Lord, I want to do what is right in Your eyes,
no matter how lonely that feels sometimes. Please remind
me that You are my constant and best friend. Amen.*

WISDOM FROM THE BOOK OF EZRA

*Ezra had set his heart to learn the Law of the Lord,
to live by it, and to teach His Laws in Israel.*
EZRA 7:10

In the beginning of the book of Ezra, King Cyrus of Persia decided to allow the Jews who had been captive to return to their homeland in Israel. A group of them, led by a man named Zerubbabel, went back to Jerusalem to rebuild the temple, which had been destroyed seventy years earlier. In the last four chapters, the book of Ezra also tells about the life and ministry of a man named Ezra, who was a priest, or religious leader, who loved to learn and live by and teach God's Word. He is a great example of wisdom and faithfulness to God for all who choose to learn from his life.

Dear God, thank You for the book of Ezra. Help me as I read it and keep coming back to it in the future. Teach me what You want me to learn from it to apply to my life and to share with others. Amen.

Day 101

ALWAYS THERE

If I go up to heaven, you are there; if I go down to the grave, you are there. If I ride the wings of the morning, if I dwell by the farthest oceans, even there your hand will guide me, and your strength will support me.
PSALM 139:8–10 NLT

Jodi and Lilly love when I tell stories about college days. They think it's fun to hear about my times going to class, eating in a big cafeteria, and living in a dorm with lots of friends and fun times and, of course, some major challenges along the way too.

I graduated from Cedarville University, and my years there were truly some of the very best of my life. At times it was also some of the loneliest during my first couple of months when I didn't know many people and adjusting to a whole new life was really hard. But I look back now and remember how God pulled me closer to Him in those lonely times, and so now I'm so thankful for them! He taught me so much about how I am actually never alone at all. His Holy Spirit is with me and knows my every thought and emotion and need. Sometimes it's truly a blessing not to have anyone to hang out with or any fun event to go to—if you focus on the fact that God is with you and always wants to hang out with you, and if you spend the time with Him!

Dear God, remind me that You are my very best friend and know me better than anyone else and that You're always available to hang out! Amen.

WISDOM ABOUT GOD'S GRACE

*Are we to keep on sinning so that God will give us
more of His loving-favor? No, not at all!*
ROMANS 6:1–2

When we ask God for forgiveness from the things we do wrong, He is so good and loving! He forgives fully and well! So sometimes we might think it's no big deal to keep doing sinful things and then just ask for forgiveness. But that's not a good and wise way to think at all. If we truly love God, we want to obey Him and honor Him, not choose bad things again and again with a "who cares?" attitude. We are absolutely going to mess up and make bad choices sometimes, but we should feel sad about that and how it hurts God. Then we should do our best to avoid more sin in the future. Also, even while God always forgives when we ask, He doesn't always keep us from the consequences that go along with sin. Ask God to help you to keep running away from sin, not playing around with it like it doesn't matter.

---

*Dear God, I know You love me no matter what, but I don't
want to sin against You on purpose whenever I want and
pretend it's no big deal. Please help me to keep growing
in wisdom about Your wonderful grace. Amen.*

THINK ABOUT GOOD, NOT GARBAGE

Whatever is true, whatever is noble, whatever is right, whatever is pure, whatever is lovely, whatever is admirable—if anything is excellent or praiseworthy—think about such things.
PHILIPPIANS 4:8 NIV

I remember in high school joining some of my friends in watching popular horror movies and reading some scary books and going to haunted houses. Now I wish I hadn't. I wish I had followed the wisdom in this verse: "Don't copy the behavior and customs of this world, but let God transform you into a new person by changing the way you think. Then you will learn to know God's will for you, which is good and pleasing and perfect" (Romans 12:2 NLT). Years later, I still remember some of the awful scenes that can't seem to escape my brain. I don't care who calls me a big chicken—I'm now a big NON-fan of scary movies or haunted, gory houses and such. I believe it's very unwise to fill our minds with dark and evil things "just for the fun of it," even if they are just pretend. The Bible tells us, "When a good person gives in to the wicked, it's like dumping garbage in a stream of clear water" (Proverbs 25:26 CEV). I don't know about you, but I want my mind to be clear and free from garbage!

Dear God, please give me wisdom and good judgment to keep my mind free from evil things. Amen.

WISDOM FROM THE BOOK OF NEHEMIAH

*"O Lord, hear the prayer of Your servant and the prayer
of Your servants who are happy to fear Your name."*
NEHEMIAH 1:11

In the book of Nehemiah, we learn a lot about a Jewish man named Nehemiah who served as the cupbearer for the Persian king Artaxerxes. His job was to taste all the king's food and drink before the king did to make sure no one was trying to poison the king with it. The king liked Nehemiah, so when Nehemiah wanted to go back to his homeland and help build the walls around Jerusalem, the king let him. Nehemiah organized and led a team of builders, and within fifty-two days they were able to rebuild the city's walls. That was incredibly fast for such a big job, and it showed how God's power was clearly at work. Nehemiah loved and respected God with all of his heart, and he continued to help the Jewish people want to honor and obey Him in all things.

---

*Dear God, thank You for the book of Nehemiah.
Help me as I read it and keep coming back to it in the
future. Teach me what You want me to learn from it to
apply to my life and to share with others. Amen.*

Day 105

OUT OF DARKNESS, INTO LIGHT

He called you out of the darkness into his wonderful light.
1 Peter 2:9 nlt

Since we live in a world that gets darker every day with sin, it's important to let the light that is in us because of Jesus Christ shine so brightly that others might turn from darkness and come to know Him too. We need to show others that we are different from the dark world around us. Ephesians 4:17–24 (cev) states it with some pretty strong words: "As a follower of the Lord, I order you to stop living like stupid, godless people. Their minds are in the dark, and they are stubborn and ignorant and have missed out on the life that comes from God. They no longer have any feelings about what is right, and they are so greedy that they do all kinds of indecent things. But that isn't what you were taught about Jesus Christ. He is the truth, and you heard about him and learned about him. You were told that your foolish desires will destroy you and that you must give up your old way of life with all its bad habits. Let the Spirit change your way of thinking and make you into a new person. You were created to be like God, and so you must please him and be truly holy."

Dear God, please help me to turn from anything that is of the darkness and live in Your wonderful light. I know You only want what's best for me. Amen.

Day 106

WISDOM ABOUT THE ONE TRUE RELIGION

We need such a Religious Leader Who made the way for man to go to God. Jesus is holy and has no guilt. He has never sinned and is different from sinful men. He has the place of honor above the heavens. Christ. . .gave one gift on the altar and that gift was Himself. It was done once and it was for all time.
HEBREWS 7:26–27

You might hear people say that all religions are the same, and you need wisdom about that, because it's just not true. Belief in Jesus as God and our one and only Savior is the truth. Jesus was the only human being to live on earth who was holy and without any sin. He gave His own life to die once for all people of all time to save them from their sin—and then He rose again to show His power over death and offer eternal life to all who trust in Him. No other religion offers that kind of gift and love and miracle! To know Jesus as Savior is simply to believe in Him and accept the awesome gift of grace and eternal life he gave when He took our sins away by dying on the cross and rising to life again.

Dear Jesus, thank You for giving Your life to save everyone who believes in You! You are God and You are our one and only living Savior! Amen.

Day 107

BY GRACE ALONE

*We are made right with God by placing our faith in
Jesus Christ. And this is true for everyone who believes,
no matter who we are. For everyone has sinned; we all fall
short of God's glorious standard. Yet God, in his grace,
freely makes us right in his sight. He did this through Christ
Jesus when he freed us from the penalty for our sins.*
ROMANS 3:22–24 NLT

Some people believe it's the things you do and the way you follow rules that get you to heaven or a good eternal life. Not true! And how exhausting and stressful that would be! How could we ever do enough? Every major religion focuses on the deeds that must be done and the rules that must be followed to get to heaven—except true Christianity. Christianity focuses on what Jesus has already done and the fact that no one could ever possibly earn their way to heaven on their own. All that's required for a real relationship with God and for eternal life is faith in what Jesus has already done through His death and resurrection, and acceptance of His gift of grace. Ephesians 2:8–9 (NLT) says, "God saved you by his grace when you believed. And you can't take credit for this; it is a gift from God. Salvation is not a reward for the good things we have done, so none of us can boast about it."

---

*Lord , I believe in You and I need You as my Savior
from my sins. I'm so thankful for Your gift of grace,
through faith alone, that has saved me. Amen.*

WISDOM FROM THE BOOK OF ESTHER

*Queen Esther answered, "If I have found favor in
your eyes, O king, and if it please the king, I ask that
my life and the lives of my people be saved."*
ESTHER 7:3

In the book of Esther, we learn that when King Xerxes of Persia
began searching for a new queen, he liked Esther best. She was a
Jewish woman, but she had kept her family history a secret. A high
official in the land named Haman wanted all people to bow down
and honor him, but Esther's cousin Mordecai refused to bow down
to anyone but God. Because of this, Haman was filled with hate for
Jewish people, and he convinced King Xerxes to order a decree to
have them all killed. But Esther had great courage, and she asked the
king to have mercy on the Jews. When you read the whole account
in the Bible, you learn how Esther let God work through her to save
her entire nation of people.

---

*Dear God, thank You for the book of Esther. Help me as I read it and
keep coming back to it in the future. Teach me what You want me
to learn from it to apply to my life and to share with others. Amen.*

BE LIKE A TREE!

"Just as you can identify a tree by its fruit,
so you can identify people by their actions."
MATTHEW 7:20 NLT

When someone trusts Jesus as their Savior and has a true relationship with Him, they should be a bit like a good fruit tree. Just like a fruit tree is only healthy and growing correctly if it produces fruit, Christians are only healthy and growing correctly if they produce good fruit too—meaning the good deeds they do in their lives, the way they care for others, and the actions and habits that clearly show they love and follow Jesus and live by His Word. The good things you do are not what gain you salvation, but you were created by God to do good things for Him. As you trust and follow Him, He brings you opportunities to do the good things He has planned. The Bible tells us in Ephesians 2:10 (NIV), "For we are God's handiwork, created in Christ Jesus to do good works, which God prepared in advance for us to do."

Dear God, show me the good things You have planned for me
to do. There's nothing better I can do with my life. Amen.

Day 110

WISDOM TO CONQUER FEAR, PART 1

Show me Your loving-kindness, O God. . . .
When I am afraid, I will trust in You.
PSALM 56:1, 3

Can you think of a fear you used to have but then you got over it? What happened? How did God help you? Who were the people and things He provided to get you through it? It's wise to take time every once in a while to focus on things you used to be afraid of that now seem like no big deal. It helps you realize that whatever is making you scared or nervous today will probably one day be no big deal either. God never leaves you alone. He is right there with you in the middle of your fears, and you can call out for His help at any time. He will guide you through it to the other side where you can look back with relief and say, "Wow! Thanks, God! We conquered that together, and now I'm not afraid anymore!"

Dear God, please help me with these fears I have: ____.
I remember all the ways You have helped me conquer
fears in the past, and I am trusting that You will help
again now and always in the future too. Amen.

WiSDOM TO CONQUER FEAR, PART 2

*Wait for the Lord; be strong, and let your heart
take courage; wait for the Lord!*
PSALM 27:14 ESV

Sometimes you have to wait on God to help you conquer a fear. In those times, keep focusing on Him through scripture and prayer and praise. Read and memorize scripture about fear like these and repeat them, pray them, and sing them. When your mind is focused on God, it doesn't have time to focus on fear.

- ✻ "Even if I walk through the valley of the shadow of death, I will not be afraid of anything, because You are with me" (Psalm 23:4).

- ✻ "The Lord is my light and the One Who saves me. Whom should I fear? The Lord is the strength of my life. Of whom should I be afraid?" (Psalm 27:1).

- ✻ "God is our safe place and our strength. He is always our help when we are in trouble. So we will not be afraid, even if the earth is shaken and the mountains fall into the center of the sea, and even if its waters go wild with storm and the mountains shake with its action" (Psalm 46:1–3).

Dear God, please help me to keep my mind thinking about You, praying to You, and praising You when I feel afraid. I am waiting on You and trusting in You to help me conquer every fear. Amen.

WISDOM TO CONQUER FEAR, PART 3

*The Holy Writings say, "Because of belonging to Jesus,
we are in danger of being killed all day long. We are thought
of as sheep that are ready to be killed." But we have power
over all these things through Jesus Who loves us so much.*

ROMANS 8:36–37

Wow, that's quite a fear this scripture talks about—being afraid all day long of being killed! Hopefully, the fears you need to conquer are not quite that scary, but maybe they feel just as bad sometimes. If they do, be sure to keep reading in Romans 8, because that passage goes on to tell you exactly why you have power over anything that puts you in danger or scares you—it's because absolutely *nothing* can keep the love of God away from you! He will always be with you, taking care of you. Romans 8:38–39 says, "Death cannot! Life cannot! Angels cannot! Leaders cannot! Any other power cannot! Hard things now or in the future cannot! The world above or the world below cannot! Any other living thing cannot keep us away from the love of God which is ours through Christ Jesus our Lord."

*Dear God, I don't ever want to forget that absolutely nothing
can keep Your love away from me. Thank You so much for being
so powerful in me to overcome any kind of fear. Amen.*

Day 113

ON YOUR BEST BEHAVIOR

Always let others see you behaving properly.
1 PETER 2:12 CEV

It's not your good deeds that get you to heaven, but with the right attitude—knowing that it's grace through faith alone that begins your relationship with Jesus Christ and gives you eternal life—following rules and laws and doing good deeds is the smartest way to live. In fact, the Bible talks about living such a good life that no one can ever accuse you of doing anything wrong: "Dear friends, you are foreigners and strangers on this earth. So I beg you not to surrender to those desires that fight against you. Always let others see you behaving properly, even though they may still accuse you of doing wrong. Then on the day of judgment, they will honor God by telling the good things they saw you do. The Lord wants you to obey all human authorities, especially the Emperor, who rules over everyone. You must also obey governors, because they are sent by the Emperor to punish criminals and to praise good citizens. God wants you to silence stupid and ignorant people by doing right. You are free, but still you are God's servants, and you must not use your freedom as an excuse for doing wrong. Respect everyone and show special love for God's people. Honor God and respect the Emperor" (1 Peter 2:11–17 CEV).

Dear God, please help me to have good behavior,
because I want to honor You and point others to You. Amen.

Day 114

WHEN FEAR CAN BE A GOOD THING

Good thinking will keep you safe. Understanding will watch over you. You will be kept from the sinful man, and from the man who causes much trouble by what he says. You will be kept from the man who leaves the right way to walk in the ways of darkness.
PROVERBS 2:11–13

It's good to remember that sometimes fear can be good for you. It can keep you out of danger and trouble. You don't have to fear a backyard campfire, but you should fear fire in the sense that you know you should never play around with it and start a big out-of-control blaze. Also, you should fear what would happen if you listened to some friends who wanted to disobey the rules and sneak out of school sometime. That's a good fear to listen to, because you sure don't want to get in big trouble for that. God can use fear to direct you away from what would be harmful or foolish or troublesome for you, so keep on asking Him for wisdom to show you the times when it's good to listen to fear.

Dear God, please help me to know when fear is good for me because You're using it to keep me safe and out of trouble. Thank You for watching over me so well! Amen.

Day 115

NOTHING SEPARATES FROM GOD'S LOVE!

Nothing can ever separate us from God's love. Neither death nor life, neither angels nor demons, neither our fears for today nor our worries about tomorrow—not even the powers of hell can separate us from God's love. No power in the sky above or in the earth below—indeed, nothing in all creation will ever be able to separate us from the love of God that is revealed in Christ Jesus our Lord.
ROMANS 8:38–39 NLT

If you have specific fears either from things you imagine or from things that have happened to you, I encourage you to memorize the scripture above.

Of course, there are so many wonderful scriptures to memorize about God protecting us, so don't stop once you've memorized this one. Here are more to look up, read, and remember. God's Word is your best weapon to be brave in this world!

* Isaiah 41:10

* 1 Peter 5:7

* Psalm 56:3–4

* Ephesians 6:10–18

* Psalm 91

* Psalm 27

Heavenly Father, nothing can ever separate me from You, and because of that I have nothing to fear. Amen.

Day 116

WISDOM FROM THE BOOK OF JOB

"The Lord gave and the Lord has taken away.
Praise the name of the Lord."
JOB 1:21

The book of Job is a story about a very rich man from the land of Uz named Job. (His name rhymes with *robe*.) He was a very good man who had great faith in God. He had a wife and a large family and lots of livestock. He was called the greatest man among all the people of the East. But then God allowed our enemy, Satan, to take everything from Job, including his children, and cause him to suffer. Still, Job loved and praised and followed God. God reminded Job of His great power and goodness, and Job recognized his wrong thinking. Job was sorry and prayed for forgiveness, and God listened and forgave him—and then God restored to Job all he had lost plus much, much more! When we learn from Job's story, we gain wisdom to help us in our sufferings too.

Dear God, thank You for the book of Job. Help me as I read it and keep coming back to it in the future. Teach me what You want me to learn from it to apply to my life and to share with others. Amen.

Day 117

REAL BEAUTY

"People judge by outward appearance,
but the LORD looks at the heart."
1 SAMUEL 16:7 NLT

My heart hurts when I see countless magazine covers in stores that tell girls like you and women like me that beauty comes from the outside, from what our bodies and faces look like and what we wear. It's so not true! It's such a cruel lie that is pushed on you at pretty much every single turn in this world. Don't believe it, no matter how hard that is to do! There is nothing wrong with a nice outer appearance and clothes, of course, and a healthy body is certainly a good goal to honor our heavenly Father who gave us our bodies. But the appearance of your body never determines your worth and your real beauty. Your true beauty comes from the fact that you were created by God and made in His image. People look at the outward appearance, but God looks at your heart; and if you've accepted Jesus Christ as your Savior, then He sees you covered in His amazing grace and you are perfect in His sight.

God, help me to ignore the lies of the world that tell me that beauty means my reflection in the mirror has to match all the magazine covers. Help me to be confident that I am priceless and beautiful because You are awesome, and I am created by You! Amen.

Day 118

KEEP LOOKING TO JESUS

Let us put every thing out of our lives that keeps us from doing what we should. Let us keep running in the race that God has planned for us. Let us keep looking to Jesus. Our faith comes from Him and He is the One Who makes it perfect.
HEBREWS 12:1–2

There are so many cool things to do in life, but we sure can't do them all. It's just not possible! So we need wisdom from God to choose the best things He has for us in the midst of the many good things. And there are lots of bad things to stay far away from too. So the best way to live is to keep looking to Jesus, keep reading His Word, keep praying to Him and asking Him to show you the race God has mapped out specifically for you. Jesus is our example because He lived a perfect life and did exactly what God had planned for Him, and now He is sitting in the very best place in heaven forever!

Dear Jesus, I want to keep looking to You and following Your example for wisdom. Please keep showing me the good race God has mapped out for me. Amen.

Day 119

BEAUTY FROM WITHIN

Don't be concerned about the outward beauty of fancy hairstyles, expensive jewelry, or beautiful clothes. You should clothe yourselves instead with the beauty that comes from within, the unfading beauty of a gentle and quiet spirit, which is so precious to God.
1 PETER 3:3–4 NLT

God wants you to do your best to keep your body healthy. It's a temple for the Holy Spirit, after all! You should eat good-for-you foods and not too much candy and junk (but enjoying a little is fine!). You should climb and run and play outside, maybe join a sports team, or simply find the physical activities you love to do just for fun to get the exercise your body needs. You should keep yourself in good shape so that you're ready and able to do what God asks of you. But God never wants your outer appearance or physical shape to be top priority. In fact, He says beauty should come from within and "physical training is good, but training for godliness is much better, promising benefits in this life and in the life to come" (1 Timothy 4:8 NLT).

Dear God, how I love and serve You comes first because You look at my heart. Help me see my beauty like You do, from the inside out. Help me be spiritually healthy first of all and then physically fit. Amen.

WISDOM FROM THE BOOK OF PSALMS

Praise the Lord, all nations! Praise Him, all people!
For His loving-kindness toward us is great. And the
truth of the Lord lasts forever. Praise the Lord!
PSALM 117

The book of Psalms is the longest book of the Bible with 150 chapters! It's a big collection of songs and poems and writings in which the authors are praising and worshipping, praying and crying out to God with all kinds of emotions we can relate to. As we read them, they can lead us in good praise and worship and help guide us in our prayers and crying out to God too.

Dear God, thank You for the book of Psalms. Help me as I read it and keep coming back to it in the future. Teach me what You want me to learn from it to apply to my life and to share with others. Amen.

STOPPING THE SCREAM

A person without self-control is like a city with broken-down walls.
PROVERBS 25:28 NLT

Do you ever find yourself in a situation where you just want to SCREAM?!?! Sometimes it's so hard to hold it in! Without trying to gossip or complain about others, later you might just need to vent to someone you trust about the angry emotions you had and the way you wanted to act in response *but didn't*. That's the key, and that's what self-control is.

Our sinful nature gives us lots of emotions in response to situations and plenty of ideas of how to react that would not please God. What matters is what you do with those unhealthy responses. As hard as it is sometimes, you need to let them go and act according to God's Word—with patience, kindness, and love. That doesn't mean you always have to be a doormat, letting others walk all over you and never boldly stating your opinions or disagreeing. You can disagree and be firm but still be kind and compassionate. You never have to choose one of those over the other. You can disagree strongly with others and still be kind. You can practice self-control over your words and actions.

God, please help me to control my actions and reactions. Amen.

WISDOM FROM THE GREATEST COMMANDMENTS

"Teacher, which one is the greatest of the Laws?" Jesus said to him, "'You must love the Lord your God with all your heart and with all your soul and with all your mind.' This is the first and greatest of the Laws. The second is like it, 'You must love your neighbor as you love yourself.' All the Laws and the writings of the early preachers depend on these two most important Laws."
MATTHEW 22:36–40

Knowing and following the commandments that Jesus said are the most important to obey is definitely wise! He said the greatest command is to love God with all your heart, soul, and mind. And the second is to love your neighbor as yourself. If you put these things on the top of your list every moment of every day, you will automatically do other things well too. Because as you love God with all your heart, soul, and mind, you will be wanting to learn more and more about Him. And as you constantly learn about Him and grow closer to Him plus love others as you love yourself, you'll find yourself living the awesome life He has planned for you!

Dear God, I want wisdom about Your greatest commandments. Help me to follow them and love You and others more and more and more each day! Amen.

Day 123

MESS INTO A MESSAGE

*"Come now, let's settle this," says the LORD. "Though your
sins are like scarlet, I will make them as white as snow."*
ISAIAH 1:18 NLT

I don't like to clean up messes, yet I'm super good at making them!
What's your favorite kind of mess to make? Or do you always keep
things neat and tidy?

Messes make me think of the saying I've heard that "only God
can turn a mess into a message, a trial into a triumph, and a victim
into a victory." What an encouraging reminder! Our lives might look
kind of chaotic and untidy here on earth because we're constantly
slopping through the major muck that sin causes in our own lives and
the lives of everyone around us. But God is turning the messes into
messages. Because of grace, He pulls us out of our sin and mistakes
and helps us get back on track and work them out for good and His
glory so that we can share our stories with others and help them
see His grace too. Praise Him for that! He's the only one who can
take the ugliest, filthiest things and make them as white and clean
as fresh new snow!

*Dear Lord, I praise You for Your amazing grace You give time
and time and time again! Thank You for turning messes into
messages for others to know Your grace too. Amen.*

BE WISE AND BE KIND, PART 1

Your kindness will reward you, but your cruelty will destroy you.
PROVERBS 11:17 NLT

A girl who is wise knows that being mean to others never does any good. If you've ever acted like a mean girl, you need to admit your sin, apologize, and make it right and work toward doing better at choosing kindness. God loves and forgives you! Here's what God's Word says about kindness and doing good to others to help us:

- "Love is kind" (1 Corinthians 13:4).

- "Do not let yourselves get tired of doing good. If we do not give up, we will get what is coming to us at the right time. Because of this, we should do good to everyone. For sure, we should do good to those who belong to Christ" (Galatians 6:9–10).

- "We know what real love is because Jesus gave up his life for us. So we also ought to give up our lives for our brothers and sisters. If someone has enough money to live well and sees a brother or sister in need but shows no compassion—how can God's love be in that person? Dear children, let's not merely say that we love each other; let us show the truth by our actions" (1 John 3:16–18 NLT).

Dear God, help me always to be wise to know that being kind rewards me but being mean destroys me. Please fill me with Your real love and goodness to share with others. Amen.

BE WISE AND BE KIND, PART 2

We who have strong faith should help those who are weak. . . . Each of us should live to please his neighbor. This will help him grow in faith.
ROMANS 15:1–2

Being kind to others doesn't mean you have to be close friends with every person around you. That would be impossible! And even trying to be friends with every person is not wise, because if you did, you'd never have time for everyone and for the good things God has planned for you. Plus the Bible tells us there are people we should never want to be close friends with, like angry ones described in Proverbs 22:24–25.

Being kind to others also doesn't mean you have to agree with them about everything. You can agree to disagree and still show kindness and respect. When you focus on the fact that every single person in the world (no matter who they are or what they do or what their personality is like) is created and loved by God, He will help you to be kind and respectful to anyone who comes into your life. Ask God to help you grow in kindness, and He will help you share kindness in wise and loving ways.

Dear God, please help me to remember all people are so loved by You and to treat everyone kindly and respectfully. Give me wisdom about sharing kindness and love with those You have planned for me to. Amen.

TRIAL INTO TRIUMPH

My friends, be glad, even if you have a lot of trouble.
JAMES 1:2 CEV

Anyone who says the Christian life is easy and *only* full of blessing and prosperity is flat-out wrong. Jesus guarantees it Himself when He says in John 16:33 (NIV), "In this world you will have trouble. But take heart! I have overcome the world."

There are many more places in the Bible that talk about how to endure trials too. For example, God uses trials to test us (1 Peter 4:12–13) and to strengthen us in our faith (James 1:2–4) and to develop our endurance, character, and hope (Romans 5:3–5)!

Every trial will turn into triumph. Sometimes we'll see those triumphs in our lives here on earth, and some trials won't be fully resolved until heaven, but ultimately Jesus has triumphed over every kind of trouble because He has overcome the world!

Lord Jesus, please help me in all my troubles and those
of my loved ones too. Only You have the power to help us
overcome them because You overcame the whole world!
That is so cool, and I'm so thankful for You! Amen.

Day 127

WISDOM FROM THE BOOK OF PROVERBS

These are the wise sayings of Solomon, son of David, king of Israel: They show you how to know wisdom and teaching, to find the words of understanding. They help you learn about the ways of wisdom and what is right and fair. They give wisdom to the child-like, and much learning and wisdom to those who are young. A wise man will hear and grow in learning. A man of understanding will become able to understand a saying and a picture-story, the words of the wise and what they mean.

PROVERBS 1:1–6

The book of Proverbs is all about wisdom! It's a big collection of short sayings and thoughts and tips to help people of all ages in all kinds of situations choose right instead of wrong by following God's good ways. It's really neat how there are thirty-one chapters since most of our months have thirty-one days. It's super wise to read one chapter of Proverbs every day of the month and then start all over again the next month.

Dear God, thank You for the book of Proverbs. Help me as I read it and keep coming back to it in the future. Teach me what You want me to learn from it to apply to my life and to share with others. Amen.

VICTIM INTO VICTORY

*Joseph had a dream, and when he told his brothers
about it, they hated him more than ever.*
GENESIS 37:5 NLT

If you have siblings, I sure hope your relationship with them isn't anything like Joseph in the Bible. His brothers were SO nasty to him—first they wanted to kill him, but then they had a little mercy and sold him into slavery instead. Yikes! Such meanies!

Joseph was definitely the victim of some incredibly cruel treatment. (Read the whole story in Genesis 37:1–50:26.) My favorite lesson from Joseph's account is how he was faithful to God even through *years* of waiting and hardship and betrayal. And instead of being bitter and cruel to his brothers in return when he had the perfect opportunity, he said to them, "Don't be afraid of me. Am I God, that I can punish you? You intended to harm me, but God intended it all for good. He brought me to this position so I could save the lives of many people. No, don't be afraid. I will continue to take care of you and your children" (Genesis 50:19–21 NLT).

If you are ever the victim of someone treating you cruelly, keep faith in God to help you. Remember Joseph's words: "You intended to harm me, but God intended it all for good." Keep following God, and He will turn your suffering into awesome victory!

*Dear God, thank You for encouraging me with Joseph's
story. I want to be a lot like him. Amen.*

WISDOM ABOUT WEALTH

A God-like life gives us much when we are happy for what we have. We came into this world with nothing. For sure, when we die, we will take nothing with us. If we have food and clothing, let us be happy. But men who want lots of money are tempted. They are trapped into doing all kinds of foolish things and things which hurt them. These things drag them into sin and will destroy them. The love of money is the beginning of all kinds of sin. Some people have turned from the faith because of their love for money. They have made much pain for themselves because of this.

1 TIMOTHY 6:6–10

A lot of people make their goals in life based on what will help them gain more money, and that's not wise at all. Choose now while you are young not to make that your focus. Instead, trust God's Word that getting trapped in wanting lots of money can lead to all kinds of sin and foolish things. Let Him help you focus on goals that match up with His good plans for your life.

Dear God, please give me wisdom about wealth. I don't want my goals to be about money; I want them to be about serving You and doing the good things You have planned for me! Amen.

WHEN PEOPLE MOCK YOU

"So be strong and courageous!"
DEUTERONOMY 31:6 NLT

One night I was sitting in a café, and I overheard a group of teenagers saying nasty things about a classmate of theirs who was a Christian. I prayed for him, and I prayed for his mockers as well. And very soon, the Holy Spirit brought this scripture to my mind: " 'God blesses you when people mock you and persecute you and lie about you and say all sorts of evil things against you because you are my followers. Be happy about it! Be very glad! For a great reward awaits you in heaven' " (Matthew 5:11–12 NLT).

It's really hard to think of it as a blessing to get made fun of. But the Bible tells us to celebrate it! God hears each instance, He's keeping track, and He rewards loyalty and love for Him. The fact that this group even knew to tease their classmate for being a Christian shows that he wasn't hiding his faith, and God is pleased by that! If you're ever made fun of because you follow Jesus, remember this scripture. God knows and blesses every moment that you ever suffer for Him.

Dear Lord, help me to keep the right perspective if I'm made fun of for following You. I trust that You care and will bless me. Amen.

Day 131

WISDOM FROM THE BOOK OF ECCLESIASTES

The last word, after all has been heard, is: Honor God and obey His Laws. This is all that every person must do. For God will judge every act, even everything which is hidden, both good and bad.
ECCLESIASTES 12:13–14

The writer of the book of Ecclesiastes was most likely King Solomon, the king whom God was so happy with when he asked for wisdom. But remember that King Solomon didn't continue using wisdom later on in his life, and some Bible experts think he wrote Ecclesiastes to help teach other people the lessons he learned from his bad choices. We are wise when we listen to those who have made mistakes and learned from them, because hopefully we won't make the same mistakes!

Dear God, thank You for the book of Ecclesiastes. Help me as I read it and keep coming back to it in the future. Teach me what You want me to learn from it to apply to my life and to share with others. Amen.

Day 132

WILLING TO WAIT

*Wait for the LORD; be strong, and let your heart
take courage; wait for the LORD!*
PSALM 27:14 ESV

I used to be in 4-H when I was younger, and maybe you are now! I worked on dog obedience with my beautiful collie named Lad. I love dogs! It's so amazing to watch a well-trained pup! Even just the command to "Wait" when they see a yummy treat but are not allowed to get it right away is so cool! They want it so badly, but they're obedient to a good master because they know the reward of pleasing him or her is better than the instant pleasure of getting the treat immediately.

Sometimes I need to take lessons from furry friends who are trained well. I don't always like to wait on God. Too often I want to get things done or have what I need according to my own time frame, not someone else's. I find myself wishing all the time that He would hurry up already, both with answering prayer requests and just coming back again to make all things right in the world. But the Bible says that with God a day is like a thousand years, and a thousand years are like a day (2 Peter 3:8). I don't fully understand His ways or His timeline, but I trust that He is my good Master and I want to obey Him well, even while I'm waiting.

*Dear God, when I need to wait, please help me do it
with a good attitude and with faith in You! Amen.*

DON'T HOLD ON TO ANGER

Put out of your life all these things: bad feelings about other people, anger, temper, loud talk, bad talk which hurts other people, and bad feelings which hurt other people. You must be kind to each other. Think of the other person. Forgive other people just as God forgave you because of Christ's death on the cross.
EPHESIANS 4:31–32

Have you ever gotten angry when your parents promised something fun, but then plans had to change because of a stressful situation? Maybe your family had to cancel vacation because of illness or there was no money for the dance lessons you wanted because of a job loss for Dad or Mom. Of course you'll feel upset about those kinds of things, but you can hold on to anger, or you can be forgiving, understanding, and loving when your family is going through a hard time. The first choice will just make a bad situation worse, but the second will encourage and bless you and everyone around you.

Dear God, when I'm disappointed and angry that plans have to change, please help me to choose a good attitude, with forgiveness, understanding, and love. Amen.

Day 134

LISTEN AND DO

*But don't just listen to God's word. You must do what it says.
Otherwise, you are only fooling yourselves. For if you listen
to the word and don't obey, it is like glancing at your face in
a mirror. You see yourself, walk away, and forget what you
look like. But if you look carefully into the perfect law that
sets you free, and if you do what it says and don't forget
what you heard, then God will bless you for doing it.*
JAMES 1:22–25 NLT

Our family enjoys watching cooking shows on Netflix, but none of us are awesome cooks. We just don't often use what we learn from the shows in our kitchen. We seem to stick to the same old simple recipes we've been using for years. Hopefully, that will change and we'll start applying what we learn by trying some new recipes. . . .

We could watch a zillion more hours of cooking shows on television, and if we keep on just watching and never doing any of the things we see, then what good is it other than a bit of entertainment?

The Bible should never be thought of as some simple storybook for entertainment. It is living and active and sharper than any two-edged sword (Hebrews 4:12). It's our guide for life, and we cannot treat it like a cooking show we only watch for fun.

---

*Dear God, I don't want to just listen to Your Word; I want to
do it. I want to live out my faith for Your glory. Amen.*

WISDOM FROM THE BOOK OF SONG OF SOLOMON

The Song of Songs, the most beautiful of them all, which is Solomon's.
SONG OF SOLOMON 1:1

Song of Solomon, or Song of Songs as it's also called, is a book about the beauty of married love. Some Bible experts think it was written (either by Solomon or about him) as a way to compare married love with how much God loves His people. He loves us all far more than we can even imagine!

Dear God, thank You for the Song of Solomon. Help me as I read it and keep coming back to it in the future. Teach me what You want me to learn from it to apply to my life and to share with others. Amen.

CHOOSING GOOD FRIENDS

"Bad company corrupts good character."
1 CORINTHIANS 15:33 NLT

We love to eat apples, and there are so many yummy varieties—many with fun names. Pink Lady is a new favorite of ours. Ginger Gold and Gala and Golden Delicious are also top on our list of faves. We gobble them up, but sometimes when we stock up on a bunch at once, we have to be careful not to let one rotting spot on one apple spoil several more around and soon they're all bad!

Maybe you've heard the saying that "one bad apple spoils the whole barrel." Have you ever thought of that in regard to the types of friends you make?

The Bible says, "Bad company corrupts good character," or as another version puts it, "Bad friends will destroy you" (CEV). You can think about it like that one rotten apple ruining the ones around it. If one friend in a group enjoys doing disobedient and dangerous things and is constantly encouraging the rest of the group to do likewise, then the whole group can easily turn bad. Be careful, then, when choosing your friends and joining groups of friends. Bad can so easily rub off on you because peer pressure is so strong at your age. Resist bad company, run away from it, and then wait and watch how God rewards.

Dear God, please help me avoid bad company among my friends and peers. I know it will only lead me to trouble to hang out with people who enjoy doing bad things. Help me be strong against peer pressure. Amen.

Day 137

WISDOM ABOUT TROUBLES, PART 1

Troubles help us learn not to give up. When we have learned not to give up, it shows we have stood the test. When we have stood the test, it gives us hope. Hope never makes us ashamed because the love of God has come into our hearts through the Holy Spirit Who was given to us.
ROMANS 5:3–5

What would it look like to you if everything about life was always easy and fun? Would you always be on vacation with no homework or tests to take or chores to do, no fighting with siblings or friends, no bedtime, no sickness or death? All that sounds pretty great, but it's wise to know that a trouble-free life is sadly just not possible because of sin in the world. But the good news is, God is using the troubles for good, and His Word promises that "the little troubles we suffer now for a short time are making us ready for the great things God is going to give us forever. We do not look at the things that can be seen. We look at the things that cannot be seen. The things that can be seen will come to an end. But the things that cannot be seen will last forever" (2 Corinthians 4:17–18).

Dear God, please help me to expect troubles and learn from them as I trust that You are turning them into good things for me. Amen.

WISDOM ABOUT TROUBLES, PART 2

You are being kept by the power of God because you put your trust in Him and you will be saved from the punishment of sin at the end of the world. With this hope you can be happy even if you need to have sorrow and all kinds of tests for awhile. These tests have come to prove your faith and to show that it is good. Gold, which can be destroyed, is tested by fire. Your faith is worth much more than gold and it must be tested also. Then your faith will bring thanks and shining-greatness and honor to Jesus Christ when He comes again.

1 PETER 1:5–7

We can find all kinds of wisdom in the Bible to help us deal with troubles, like this wisdom in 1 Peter 1 that reminds us that how we react to our troubles helps prove our faith in God. If we say we have faith in God *only* when times are good, then that faith isn't real. But if we hold to our faith even when times are bad, we prove that we love and believe in God no matter what!

Dear God, please help me to remember that hard times prove whether I truly love and believe in You. I want to show You and everyone around me that my faith in You is real and strong! Amen.

Day 139
NO FUN

Why am I discouraged? Why is my heart so sad? I will put my
hope in God! I will praise him again—my Savior and my God!
PSALM 43:5 NLT

I don't know why the word *fun* is in the word *funk*, because a funk certainly isn't any fun. Do you ever feel like you're walking around with a gloomy gray rain cloud hovering just over your head—or worse, one that's black with an angry thunderstorm? Sometimes you can't even really explain why you feel depressed or angry, you just do. Or maybe your personal or family or school situations seem just too hard to deal with.

Let God shoo away the funky clouds and lift your spirit. He does not always take all the troubles or reasons for your funk away, but He will walk with you right through them. You can focus your eyes and your attitude on hoping in Him, trusting that He will work all things together for good (Romans 8:28).

Dear God, when I'm down in a funk,
please lift me up. My hope is in You. Amen.

Day 140

WISDOM FROM THE BOOK OF ISAIAH

For sure He took on Himself our troubles and carried our sorrows. Yet we thought of Him as being punished and hurt by God, and made to suffer. But He was hurt for our wrong-doing. He was crushed for our sins. He was punished so we would have peace. He was beaten so we would be healed. All of us like sheep have gone the wrong way. Each of us has turned to his own way. And the Lord has put on Him the sin of us all.
ISAIAH 53:4–6

The book of Isaiah is the first in a series of seventeen books written by prophets. They are books that warn about God's judgment and also give encouragement with the promises of God's salvation and forgiveness and the way He rescues when people turn back to Him. Isaiah is extra special among the prophetic books because it has more prophecies about our Savior Jesus than any of the others!

Dear God, thank You for the book of Isaiah. Help me as I read it and keep coming back to it in the future. Teach me what You want me to learn from it to apply to my life and to share with others. Amen.

COMFORT OTHERS

*God is our merciful Father and the source of all comfort.
He comforts us in all our troubles so that we can
comfort others. When they are troubled, we will be able
to give them the same comfort God has given us.*
2 CORINTHIANS 1:3–4 NLT

Our big dog Jasper is just about the cuddliest and nicest dog you could ever meet. (He even plays dress-up with us but is also a protective watchdog.) I wish I could let everyone in the world have some snuggle time with him when they're feeling sad. He's so soft and sweet to pet, and there's something so comforting about having him near when you're feeling sad.

The Bible tells us that God is the source of all comfort (I think good pets are part of His way of providing us comfort), and He comforts us so that we can comfort others. The more we need comfort, the more God gives, and the more we have to share with other people. And hopefully those people will want to know Jesus as their Savior because they've been shown much love in their hard times. God is working for good in every hard situation.

---

*Dear God, thank You for being near and comforting
me in hard times. And thank You for pets that help
comfort us too. Please help me share all the comfort
You give with others and point them to You. Amen.*

WISDOM FROM JESUS' STORIES

The followers of Jesus came to Him and said,
"Why do You speak to them in picture-stories?"
MATTHEW 13:10

When Jesus lived on earth and taught people about God, He often used parables, or "picture-stories." His followers asked Him why He taught people this way, and He said: "This is why I speak to them in picture-stories. They have eyes but they do not see. They have ears but they do not hear and they do not understand. It happened in their lives as Isaiah said it would happen. He said, 'You hear and hear but do not understand. You look and look but do not see. . . . They hear very little with their ears. They have closed their eyes. If they did not do this, they would see with their eyes and hear with their ears and understand with their hearts. Then they would be changed in their ways, and I would heal them' " (Matthew 13:13–15).

Remember this answer from Jesus and be praying for great wisdom and understanding as you study His stories and His example and all the writings in the whole Bible. We want to have eyes and ears and hearts that are open and paying attention to understand how God is trying to teach and guide and love us.

Dear God, please give me great wisdom and understanding
as I read Your Word and learn from Jesus. Help me and guide
me and change any of my ways that need changing. Amen.

Day 143

SO MUCH MORE

Now to him who is able to do immeasurably more than all we ask or imagine, according to his power that is at work within us, to him be glory in the church and in Christ Jesus throughout all generations, for ever and ever!
EPHESIANS 3:20–21 NIV

Do you like to give long and specific wish lists, you know, just so everyone has a good idea of what you'd like for Christmas and birthdays? ☺ God wants to hear your wish lists too. We can absolutely pray specifically about our needs, worries, fears, and even dreams and goals and things we want! As long as we are constantly asking with humility, knowing that God is sovereign and good over all things, and we are praying ultimately for God's will, God wants to hear about everything in our prayers, even the most specific. He wants us to depend on Him and trust Him. He wants a constant conversation with us. Remember, though, that it would be foolish to expect or even hope that God would answer every prayer exactly like we wish would happen. Why? Because He is able to do IMMEASURABLY more than anything we can dream up! There have been some amazing times in my life when I can look back and see when I prayed for something, was so SURE it was the very best thing, was so disappointed when it didn't work out, and then God did something SO much better than what I had asked to answer that prayer. I'm so glad God doesn't always do what I ask!

God, thank You for not always answering the way I want. Your ways are so much better than I can ever dream of! Amen.

Day 144

GOOD GROUND

"When anyone hears the Word about the holy nation and does not understand it, the devil comes and takes away what was put in his heart. He is like the seed that fell by the side of the road. The seed which fell between rocks is like the person who receives the Word with joy as soon as he hears it. Its root is not deep and it does not last long. When troubles and suffering come because of the Word, he gives up and falls away. The seed which fell among thorns is like the person who hears the Word but the cares of this life, and the love for money let the thorns come up and do not give the seed room to grow and give grain. The seed which fell on good ground is like the one who hears the Word and understands it. He gives much grain. Some seed gives one hundred times as much grain. Some gives sixty times as much grain. Some gives thirty times as much grain."

Matthew 13:18–23

This picture-story or parable from Jesus gives us wisdom about what happens among different types of people who hear God's truth from His Word. We should always want to be like the last kind of people described—those who hear God's Word and understand it so that we can grow more good things in our lives that honor God and spread even more of His truth and love.

Dear God, please help my heart and mind and my whole life be "good ground" where Your wisdom and truth grow and multiply! Amen.

Day 145

ENDLESS GRACE

In fact, I don't understand why I act the way I do.
I don't do what I know is right. I do the things I hate.
ROMANS 7:15 CEV

Sometimes I feel absolutely sure that God just might give up on me today, that I've messed up one too many times and now He won't forgive me. I wonder why on earth I keep messing up in the same ways over and over. My struggles especially come from not guarding the words I say as carefully as I should. But I quickly have to remember that thinking God won't forgive me is a total lie! God's grace is endless, and He forgives again and again and takes our sins as far as the east is from the west (Psalm 103:12). Oh, how thankful I am for that!

I'm encouraged by the fact that there was no perfect person other than Jesus in the Bible. God loves and saves and uses regular sinners just like you and me! David, who was called a man after God's own heart, had some seriously shady moments. And Paul, who wrote so much of the New Testament, was once a murderer of Christians. Yet God loved and saved and used them both for good. He turned them from their sins, just like He turns us from ours. Be sad for your sin (2 Corinthians 7:10) and let the sadness lead you to repentance (which means to ask for forgiveness), but then don't hold it against yourself anymore. God doesn't, so why on earth should you?

Dear God, I need Your amazing grace so much! Thank You
so much for forgiving my sin again and again and again.
I can't even describe how grateful I am. Amen.

WISDOM FROM THE BOOK OF JEREMIAH

The Word of the Lord came to me saying, "Before I started to put you together in your mother, I knew you. Before you were born, I set you apart as holy. I chose you to speak to the nations for Me." Then I said, "O, Lord God! I do not know how to speak. I am only a boy." But the Lord said to me, "Do not say, 'I am only a boy.' You must go everywhere I send you. And you must say whatever I tell you. Do not be afraid of them. For I am with you to take you out of trouble."

JEREMIAH 1:4–8

After King Josiah died, the nation of Judah had turned almost completely away from God. So in his book, the prophet Jeremiah warned the people of Judah of the punishment and suffering that was about to come their way because of their rejection of God and His good ways. The book reminds us never to reject God and His good ways. He always wants what is best for us!

Dear God, thank You for the book of Jeremiah. Help me as I read it and keep coming back to it in the future. Teach me what You want me to learn from it to apply to my life and to share with others. Amen.

WHERE GOD LEADS

We can make our plans, but the LORD determines our steps.
PROVERBS 16:9 NLT

Have you ever planned for something and then nothing went according to your plan? Sometimes what you expect to happen is so different from reality. Lilly remembers a particular birthday party for a friend where she had a plan in her mind of how things would go, but then the real party was nothing like what she had hoped for and expected. Still, she needed to make the best of it and focus on what was going right at the party (cupcakes, for one! Yum!) and the blessing of just being there. There are so many times in life when you will make a plan, but something will happen to change it. God is sovereign over everything, and He determines our actual steps. Make your plans but know that ultimately, your path will follow exactly where He leads.

Dear God, I just want to follow You because I know You lead me in exactly the right way. Help me to make wise plans but hold them loosely, knowing that You allow and direct changes to them according to Your perfect will! Amen.

Day 148

JESUS' WISDOM ABOUT LITTLE CHILDREN

[Jesus] said, "For sure, I tell you, unless you. . .become like a little child, you will not get into the holy nation of heaven. Whoever is without pride as this little child is the greatest in the holy nation of heaven. Whoever receives a little child because of Me receives Me."
MATTHEW 18:3–5

Jesus taught His followers about how much He loves and values little children and how we need to be like them. Then He went on to teach in a parable about the lost sheep to show that God loves His children and never wants even one to be lost: "For the Son of Man has come to save that which was lost. What do you think about this? A man has one hundred sheep and one of them is lost. Will he not leave the ninety-nine and go to the mountains to look for that one lost sheep? If he finds it, for sure, I tell you, he will have more joy over that one, than over the ninety-nine that were not lost. I tell you, My Father in heaven does not want one of these little children to be lost" (Matthew 18:11–14).

Dear Jesus, thank You for teaching Your wisdom about children and Your great love for us! Thank You for never wanting me or anyone to be lost! Amen.

GUARD AGAINST GREED

*"A person is a fool to store up earthly wealth but
not have a rich relationship with God."*
LUKE 12:21 NLT

Do you keep any collections like Shopkins, Beanie Boos, Num Noms, or Tsum Tsums? They're all adorable and so much fun! I admit I love them almost as much as Jodi and Lilly do! The Beanie Boos especially! I like to tease that their big glittery eyes are hypnotic and they make you want to buy them just by staring into them. "I'm so cute and sparkly! Take me home and love me," they seem to repeat over and over! But they just keep coming out with more cute characters and collections and extra-special, ultra-rare ones! Yikes, it's so hard to keep up!

It's fun to have toys and collections, as long as you don't get carried away. Remember to be thankful for what you already have, not just greedy for more. Jesus told the parable of the rich fool in Luke 12:15–21 and said, "Beware! Guard against every kind of greed. Life is not measured by how much you own" (v. 15 NLT).

---

*Dear God, thank You for my many blessings! I know it's
okay to play and enjoy things, just please give me wisdom
about them, and help me not to be greedy. Amen.*

WHY DO BAD THINGS HAPPEN?

We know that we belong to God, but the whole world is under the power of the devil. We know God's Son has come. He has given us the understanding to know Him Who is the true God. We are joined together with the true God through His Son, Jesus Christ. He is the true God and the life that lasts forever. My children, keep yourselves from false gods.
1 JOHN 5:19–21

You might wonder sometimes why bad things happen in this world, especially when you're in the middle of something bad happening to you. It's because the whole world is under the power of the devil. But for all of us who believe in Jesus as Savior, we belong to God and the devil can never defeat us. The devil can attack us and hurt us, but God gives us life that lasts forever, no matter what! We should never want to follow any other type of false god who will lead us into the ways of the devil. Only the one true God leads us to life that lasts forever.

Dear God, please give me extra love and wisdom when bad things happen and I don't totally understand. I trust that with Jesus as my Savior, no matter what happens to me, You give me life that lasts forever! Amen.

UNIQUELY BEAUTIFUL

*So God created man in his own image, in the image of God
he created him; male and female he created them.*
GENESIS 1:27 ESV

Maybe you enjoy playing with Barbies or maybe you don't, but I think it's pretty cool that they're making the dolls in a better variety of shapes and sizes. Even if the new dolls don't get it exactly right, they're at least helping more people appreciate that *all* girls are beautifully unique in height, weight, skin color, hair, and features.

No one else is exactly like you! Don't let the world get you down if you don't fit into a cookie-cutter idea of what's stylish and gorgeous. Be yourself and be comfortable; do your best to keep your body healthy; consider what the Bible says about modesty and how Christians should represent themselves in the clothing they wear; and then don't stress what the world says looks good or doesn't. The Bible says, "Charm can be deceiving, and beauty fades away, but a woman who honors the LORD deserves to be praised" (Proverbs 31:30 CEV).

I know this is a tough one that pretty much every girl struggles with in our world, but every day when you look in the mirror, try praying this scripture to God: "I praise you because I am fearfully and wonderfully made; your works are wonderful, I know that full well" (Psalm 139:14 NIV).

---

*Dear God, please help me to look in the mirror on both
good days and bad with confidence because I am created
beautifully in Your image and I am loved by You! Amen.*

WISDOM FROM THE BOOK OF LAMENTATIONS

*My eyes become weak from crying. My spirit is
very troubled. My heart is poured out in sorrow,
because my people have been destroyed.*

LAMENTATIONS 2:11

Lamentations, written by the prophet Jeremiah, is a super sad book. A lamentation is an expression of sorrow, such as a sad poem or song or journal entry. Sometimes when you feel sad about something, it can be really helpful to write down all your sad feelings as you tell God about them and let Him comfort you. You can share them with trusted loved ones in your life too. In the book of Lamentations, Jeremiah was writing down all of his sadness about the way the city of Jerusalem had been destroyed (just like God had told him to warn about in his first book) because the people had turned away from God.

---

*Dear God, thank You for the book of Lamentations.
Help me as I read it and keep coming back to it in the
future. Teach me what You want me to learn from it to
apply to my life and to share with others. Amen.*

Day 153

DEALING WITH THE DIFFICULT

Don't be hateful to people, just because they are hateful to you. Rather, be good to each other and to everyone else.
1 Thessalonians 5:15 cev

I'm sure you already know how hard it can be to deal with difficult people. It's sad to say, but you're going to have to deal with a lot of them in your life—in school, in activities, in your church, and in all sorts of ways later on in your life as a grown-up too. Many difficult people will make you want to give up and quit the area of your life that involves them, or they'll push you toward conflict.

The first thing to think about, though, is how you can often be a difficult person yourself and how you need so much grace; so ask God to help you give the same kind of grace that He constantly gives you. Then you have to pray for so much wisdom, for God to show you if you need to get out of a situation or if He wants you to stay in it and He'll help see you through it. And then you listen and wait for His answers, which are often so much better than you ever expected. God wants you to do your best to live at peace with everyone (Romans 12:18), and He will help you deal with difficult people in wise ways if you wait patiently for Him to show you.

Dear Lord, please help me to deal kindly and peacefully with people in my life who are so difficult to be around. Amen.

Day 154

LOVE FOR NEIGHBORS

He asked Jesus, "Who is my neighbor?"
Luke 10:29

Jesus taught wisdom about loving others in this parable:

"A man was going down from Jerusalem to the city of Jericho. Robbers. . .took his clothes off and beat him. . . leaving him almost dead. A religious leader. . .saw the man. But he went by. . . . A man from the family group of Levi. . . saw the man [and] kept on going on the other side of the road. Then a man from the country of Samaria came by. . . . As he saw him, he had loving-pity on him. He got down and put oil and wine on the places where he was hurt and put cloth around them. Then the man from Samaria put this man on his own donkey. He took him to a place where people stay for the night and cared for him. The next day the man from Samaria. . .gave the owner of that place two pieces of money to care for him. He said to him, 'Take care of this man. If you use more than this, I will give it to you when I come again.'

"Which of these three do you think was a neighbor to the man who was beaten by the robbers?" The man who knew the Law said, "The one who showed loving-pity on him." Then Jesus said, "Go and do the same." (Luke 10:30–37)

Dear Jesus, help me to love and care for others,
no matter who they are, just like You taught. Amen.

Day 155

BE A LITTLE CLUELESS

For the wisdom of this world is foolishness in God's sight.
1 CORINTHIANS 3:19 NIV

Have you ever been in a group of friends or classmates and you don't have a clue what everyone else is talking about because it's something you're not allowed to do or watch or read? I remember so well how terrible that feeling is. It can make you feel left out and like you want to sink through the floor with embarrassment—but only if you let it!

I know it's so hard to deal with the peer pressure to fit in and not get teased. I remember and totally get it. But I promise you, as you get older, it will get so much easier. If you stay confident in whose you are (God's!), who He made you to be, and how He wants you to live, and *don't* go along with the crowd just so that you don't feel clueless, you will reach a point where you look back and wonder why it EVER mattered.

The Bible says the wisdom of this world is foolishness in God's sight (1 Corinthians 3:19). That doesn't mean you shouldn't learn anything here on earth and you get to quit school. Nice try! ☺ But it does mean that it's totally okay to be a little clueless (or even a lot!) to the sinful things of this world. Satan is looking for all kinds of ways to destroy you. Pressuring you to go along with the harmful things that others are doing so that you don't feel left out is one of his favorite tricks—but you can fight back if you know that being clued in to God's Word and following it is far, far better than being clued in to the crowd.

Dear God, help me be totally clued in to You! Amen.

Day 156

WISDOM FROM THE BOOK OF EZEKIEL

"As I live," says the Lord God, "I am not pleased when sinful people die. But I am pleased when the sinful turn from their way and live. Turn! Turn from your sinful ways!"
EZEKIEL 33:11

Ezekiel was a prophet whose name means "strengthened by God." He preached to the people of his day about God's judgment and salvation. Sometimes God told Ezekiel to do some pretty weird-sounding things to demonstrate the warnings God wanted the people to hear. For example, when Ezekiel was told to lie on his left side for 390 days, that was to show the nation of Israel it would be punished for 390 years for turning away from God. However, as Ezekiel 33:11 shows us, God is never happy when people are punished for their sins. He wants people to turn away from them and let Him give them life, the best kind of life of faith in and obedience to Him.

Dear God, thank You for the book of Ezekiel. Help me as I read it and keep coming back to it in the future. Teach me what You want me to learn from it to apply to my life and to share with others. Amen.

GET OUT OF LINE!

*Don't copy the behavior and customs of this world,
but let God transform you into a new person by changing
the way you think. Then you will learn to know God's will
for you, which is good and pleasing and perfect.*
ROMANS 12:2 NLT

It seems so silly how our culture tells you to be unique and be yourself but then often pressures you into things just because everyone else is doing it. Sometimes that's no big deal, and sometimes it's extremely harmful. On an episode of *Brain Games* recently, Jodi learned and laughed about how many people do things just because they see others doing them, even when they have no idea why. One example was people forming a line in a city. . .so many people just joined right in without any clue what they were waiting for. How ridiculous, right? Not a big deal if it's for a free doughnut or something, but what if everyone's lining up to watch a movie you know is not good for you? Or to gossip about a classmate and plan a mean trick on her? In those cases, GET OUT OF LINE!

No friend should ever force you to go along with anything that makes you feel uncomfortable—that uncomfortable feeling could very well be because the Holy Spirit is whispering to you to stop and waving red flags of warning. And He's telling you to follow Him and His ways in the Bible instead.

*Dear God, help me be smart to never even join the lines of
people doing sinful things; but if I happen to get into one,
please give me the wisdom to quickly get out! Amen.*

Day 158

BUBBLE BRAIN, PART 1

Keep your minds thinking about whatever is true, whatever is respected, whatever is right, whatever is pure, whatever can be loved, and whatever is well thought of. If there is anything good and worth giving thanks for, think about these things.
PHILIPPIANS 4:8

This scripture is not always easy to obey. If we're honest, we often have thoughts in our mind that are the opposite of what is right, pure, lovely, good, and grateful. On grumpy days and when things go wrong or when someone is mean to you, your first thought isn't usually a happy, thankful one. But God wants you to try to get rid of bad thoughts and keep your mind thinking positively. When you focus on praise and gratitude to Him most of all and on the many things that are right and true in your life, you keep your thoughts in the best places. When negative and nasty thoughts try to take over your mind, think of popping them like a bubble to make them disappear. Then blow positive bubbles into your brain that are strong and healthy for you because they are full of God's goodness and love.

Dear God, please help me to keep my brain thinking about what is good for me—most of all You because You are so awesome! Amen.

Day 159

BUBBLE BRAIN, PART 2

*Do not act like the sinful people of the world. Let God
change your life. First of all, let Him give you a new mind.
Then you will know what God wants you to do. And the
things you do will be good and pleasing and perfect.*
ROMANS 12:2

God wants to give you a new mind full of good thoughts that are
focused on Him and are wise and right and true! Check out all these
verses that will help you want to train your brain to think about God
and what He wants for you more than anything else:

* ❋ "If your sinful old self is the boss over your mind, it
  leads to death. But if the Holy Spirit is the boss over
  your mind, it leads to life and peace" (Romans 8:6).

* ❋ "You will keep the man in perfect peace whose mind is
  kept on You, because he trusts in You" (Isaiah 26:3).

* ❋ "If then you have been raised with Christ, keep looking
  for the good things of heaven. This is where Christ is
  seated on the right side of God. Keep your minds thinking about things in heaven" (Colossians 3:1–2).

---

*Dear God, please be the boss over my mind through Your Holy Spirit.
Please keep me in perfect peace and on the good paths You have
for me because I want to think about You and follow You! Amen.*

Day 160
NOT ASHAMED!

*For I am not ashamed of this Good News about Christ.
It is the power of God at work, saving everyone who believes.*
Romans 1:16 nlt

Christianity is made fun of in so many ways and places in popular culture these days. Television shows, movies, books, and music love to make fun of being a Christian. That can be so discouraging, but it makes me focus on the fact that the devil is doing everything he can to keep people from believing in Jesus—and the devil has no reason to make others want to ridicule Jesus if Jesus is not the one and only hope of salvation. So, the more people are opposing and making fun of Christianity, the more it shows that Jesus absolutely is the Way, the Truth, and the Life and that no one gets to God except through Him (John 14:6)! He truly lived and died and rose again to save you from your sins. That's the good news, and there's nothing to make fun of about that amazing hope we have!

So when you encounter people laughing at Christianity, don't let it get you down or make you embarrassed or ashamed, and in fact let it strengthen your faith! Keep on loving people, sharing the Good News, and believing and following God's Word anyway—and say like Paul did: "I am not ashamed of this good news about Christ. It is the power of God at work, saving everyone who believes" (Romans 1:16 nlt).

*Dear God, please help me to not let the ridicule of You
by this world ever let me lose faith in You! Amen.*

Day 161

WISDOM FROM THE BOOK OF DANIEL

*God gave these four young men much learning
and understanding in all kinds of writings
and wisdom. Daniel even had understanding
in all kinds of special dreams.*
DANIEL 1:17

The book of Daniel has several amazing Bible stories you might recognize—like the account of Daniel being thrown into the den of lions because he refused to stop praying to God. And the account of Daniel's friends Shadrach, Meshach, and Abednego who were thrown into a fiery furnace because they would not bow down to a false god. These true accounts and others about faithfulness to God, even in the worst and scariest of situations, can help you to be strong and brave in your faith as well.

Dear God, thank You for the book of Daniel. Help me as I read it and keep coming back to it in the future. Teach me what You want me to learn from it to apply to my life and to share with others. Amen.

Day 162

LITTLE SUPERHEROES

Don't let anyone think less of you because you are young.
Be an example to all believers in what you say, in the way
you live, in your love, your faith, and your purity.
1 TIMOTHY 4:12 NLT

As the youngest of four kids, when I was little I sometimes felt like the least important one in the family. All my older siblings seemed to be doing much cooler things than I was allowed to do, and sometimes it felt like anything I was doing didn't really matter or everyone else had been there, done that.

But I stayed close to God, and He helped me see the blessing in 1 Timothy 4:12. And He helped me focus on the good plans He had for *me*. God has a unique story for everyone individually, and if we constantly try to compare or see if we're doing better or more important things than those around us, we lose the focus on pleasing God alone with what He's given us to do.

No matter your age or where you are in your lineup of siblings or if you're an only child or what anyone tells you about your worth, believe that you absolutely matter to God. You can be His little superhero when you believe in His plans for you and depend on His supernatural power.

Dear God, I know I matter to You, and that's what matters most about me! Help me to do Your will for my life. Amen.

Day 163

WHEN YOU'RE TEASED ABOUT YOUR FAITH

*If men speak bad of you because you are a Christian, you will
be happy because the Spirit of shining-greatness and of God
is in you. . . . But if a man suffers as a Christian, he should not
be ashamed. He should thank God that he is a Christian.*
1 PETER 4:14–16

If you are ever teased for being a Christian, you can think about it
with wisdom and be happy about it! Maybe that sounds silly, but
God's Word tells us we should not be ashamed; we should be thankful instead! It means God's Spirit is in you and that you are saved
forever, so don't worry about what anyone else might say to tease
you or be mean to you. Matthew 5:11–12 (NLT) says, "God blesses you
when people mock you and persecute you and lie about you and say
all sorts of evil things against you because you are my followers. Be
happy about it! Be very glad! For a great reward awaits you in heaven."

---

*Dear Jesus, help me not to get angry or ashamed if people tease
me or act mean because I love and follow You. Give me wisdom
about what the Bible says. Remind me to be happy because You
have saved me and my rewards will be great in heaven. Amen.*

LET GOD LIFT YOU

*How great is God's love for all who worship him? Greater than the
distance between heaven and earth! How far has the Lord taken
our sins from us? Farther than the distance from east to west!*
PSALM 103:11–12 CEV

If you're ever feeling down because you've messed up and you just
can't get things right, you need to follow the cure in this scripture
and let God lift you up: "So humble yourselves before God. Resist
the devil, and he will flee from you. Come close to God, and God
will come close to you. Wash your hands, you sinners; purify your
hearts, for your loyalty is divided between God and the world. Let
there be tears for what you have done. Let there be sorrow and deep
grief. Let there be sadness instead of laughter, and gloom instead
of joy. Humble yourselves before the Lord, and he will lift you up in
honor" (James 4:7–10 NLT).

Yes, be sad for a time over your mistakes. Admit them and ask for
forgiveness from God and from any people you need to. And then
when you have washed your hands and purified your heart of the sin
because of God's grace, you can be confident that God has taken your
sin away as far as the east is from the west. Praise and thank Him for
that! He's so good and loves you so much. He wants to cover you with
grace and lift you up in honor!

---

*Dear God, I'm so sorry and sad about my sin. Please help
me to turn completely away from it and from my enemy.
Please help me to ask forgiveness from others when I need
to. I need Your grace to cover my mistakes. I praise and
thank You that it does! I ask You to lift me up! Amen.*

WISDOM FROM THE BOOK OF HOSEA

"Come, let us return to the Lord. He has hurt us but He will heal us. He has cut us but He will cover the sore. After two days He will give us new life. He will raise us up on the third day, that we may live before Him. So keep on trying to know the Lord. His coming to us is as sure as the rising of the sun. He will come to us like the rain, like the spring rain giving water to the earth."

HOSEA 6:1–3

The book of Hosea tells how the prophet Hosea, whose name means "salvation," obeyed God's instructions to marry a woman named Gomer, who was not faithful to him. But God told Hosea to go win her back when she ran away. God used this to illustrate how even while the people of Israel were unfaithful to God, God still loved them and wanted to win them back to Him.

Dear God, thank You for the book of Hosea. Help me as I read it and keep coming back to it in the future. Teach me what You want me to learn from it to apply to my life and to share with others. Amen.

FRIENDS FOREVER

A friend loves at all times.
PROVERBS 17:17 ESV

If you ever need help on how to be a good friend, the Bible is the best source of advice for BFFs!

Here are some scriptures to read and put into practice:

* "Do to others as you would have them do to you" (Luke 6:31 NIV).

* "Just as iron sharpens iron, friends sharpen the minds of each other" (Proverbs 27:17 CEV).

* "God loves you and has chosen you as his own special people. So be gentle, kind, humble, meek, and patient. Put up with each other, and forgive anyone who does you wrong, just as Christ has forgiven you. Love is more important than anything else. It is what ties everything completely together" (Colossians 3:12–14 CEV).

* "My friends, you are spiritual. So if someone is trapped in sin, you should gently lead that person back to the right path. But watch out, and don't be tempted your-self. You obey the law of Christ when you offer each other a helping hand" (Galatians 6:1–2 CEV).

* "Don't use foul or abusive language. Let everything you say be good and helpful, so that your words will be an encouragement to those who hear them" (Ephesians 4:29 NLT).

---

*Dear God, please help me to have good
friends and be a good friend. Amen.*

JESUS' WISDOM ABOUT THE RICH MAN

"The fields of a rich man gave much grain. The rich man thought to himself, 'What will I do? I have no place to put the grain.' Then he said, 'I know what I will do. I will take down my grain building and I will build a bigger one. I will put all my grain and other things I own into it. And I will say to my soul, "Soul, you have many good things put away in your building. It will be all you need for many years to come. Now rest and eat and drink and have lots of fun."' But God said to him, 'You fool! Tonight your soul will be taken from you. Then who will have all the things you have put away?' It is the same with a man who puts away riches for himself and does not have the riches of God."
LUKE 12:16–21

Jesus shared this parable to teach us that when we have a lot, we should be willing to share it with others. No person has any idea exactly how many days they will live on this earth. It's far better to be generous to others than to store it all up selfishly. Our goal should be to have the riches of God, not the riches of this world.

Dear God, help me to remember Your wisdom and never be selfish with my money and possessions. Please give me a heart that loves to share. Amen.

WORKING HARD, DOING YOUR BEST

Whatever you do, do it all for the glory of God.
1 Corinthians 10:31 NIV

In school, it's easy to get distracted by what your classmates are doing. It's fun to chat and be silly, and there are times for that, but you know those things can get you in trouble if you're supposed to be working. Galatians 6:4–5 (NLT) says, "Pay careful attention to your own work, for then you will get the satisfaction of a job well done, and you won't need to compare yourself to anyone else. For we are each responsible for our own conduct."

Whether or not you find it hard to focus on your schoolwork sometimes, let God's Word inspire you to always do your best on it, not just to please your teacher or your parents but to worship God through it! Work hard and do your best for His glory! Praising and worshipping God is never just singing songs and saying nice things to and about Him. Those are great too, of course, but worship is so much of what we do and how we work with the abilities He has given us.

Dear God, please help me to focus on my work when I need to and focus on You at the same time! I want my work to make You happy and bring You praise because I'm doing my best with what You've given me! Amen.

Day 169

WISDOM FROM THE BOOK OF JOEL

"I will show powerful works in the heavens and on the earth, like blood and fire and clouds of smoke. The sun will turn dark and the moon will turn to blood before the day of the Lord. His coming will be a great and troubled day. It will be that whoever calls on the name of the Lord will be saved from the punishment of sin."

JOEL 2:30–32

In the book of Joel, God uses grasshoppers and His message through the prophet Joel to warn the nation of Israel to turn back to Him. Grasshoppers might seem like no big deal, but a huge swarm of them could ruin crops and cause famine and starvation and devastation for a whole nation of people. They were an example of God's judgment on sinful people and warning of how awful it would be if armies of men instead of grasshoppers invaded the land of Israel. God wanted His people to listen to the warning so He could save and bless them.

Dear God, thank You for the book of Joel. Help me as I read it and keep coming back to it in the future. Teach me what You want me to learn from it to apply to my life and to share with others. Amen.

WITHOUT GRUMBLING

Do everything without grumbling or arguing.
PHILIPPIANS 2:14 NIV

Think about your most hated chore or schoolwork assignment. It stinks, right? I have plenty of household chores and tasks that aren't my favorite, either. But time and time again when I have a bad attitude about them, I realize how much worse I make them, and they usually take me longer to do! And the times I'm smart and turn on some music or focus on blessings instead of complaining or, best yet, talk to God while I'm doing the task, everything goes so much better and faster too! Time flies when you're having fun, right? Try to make the tasks you hate fun in some way, or at least be positive about them if you just can't think of them as fun. ☺

The Bible says that in everything we do or say, we have the opportunity to represent Jesus in it! "And let the peace that comes from Christ rule in your hearts. For as members of one body you are called to live in peace. And always be thankful. Let the message about Christ, in all its richness, fill your lives. Teach and counsel each other with all the wisdom he gives. Sing psalms and hymns and spiritual songs to God with thankful hearts. And whatever you do or say, do it as a representative of the Lord Jesus, giving thanks through him to God the Father" (Colossians 3:15–17 NLT).

Dear Lord, remind me that grumbling just makes everything worse. When I'm doing a task I don't enjoy, please help me to remember that I represent You in everything I do and that I need to keep a good attitude and a grateful heart. Amen.

A BIG, GOOD GOAL

I will set no sinful thing in front of my eyes.
PSALM 101:3

Psalm 101:3 is a big promise to make and a difficult one to keep these days. With phones and Wi-Fi devices right in our pockets, we have many opportunities to put sinful things in front of our eyes. So it's extra wise to make this verse our goal. It means being super careful about what we read and watch and look at to make sure those things don't lead us to go against God's Word and into things that are full of harm and trouble. With God's constant help, we can rise to the challenge to make setting no sinful thing in front of our eyes our goal. We can ask Him to fill us with wisdom to choose and use the internet and social media in good ways instead of sinful ways. And if we do mess up, then we confess to God right away and ask for help from others in our life who want to help us keep away from sin too.

Dear God, please give me the wisdom I need to help me keep away from watching and reading sinful things. I want to obey You in this because I know You want to protect me from things that might seem like no big deal at first but can actually be really harmful to me. Amen.

Day 172

STOP WORRYING

*You will keep in perfect peace all who trust in
you, all whose thoughts are fixed on you!*
ISAIAH 26:3 NLT

Have you ever gotten a nasty sunburn and then put that cooling aloe gel on? Ahhhh, sweet relief! That's how I feel about this scripture every time I repeat it when I'm feeling anxious. I've lain awake at night, and all through some days too, focusing on this scripture. I pray it to God while I also pray that He helps me keep my focus on Him during times when everything feels so out of my control. He is our amazing, endless source of real peace! His Word says, "Don't worry about anything; instead, pray about everything. Tell God what you need, and thank him for all he has done. Then you will experience God's peace, which exceeds anything we can understand. His peace will guard your hearts and minds as you live in Christ Jesus" (Philippians 4:6–7 NLT).

Whether you're worried about a big test at school tomorrow or the health of a loved one or other major problems in your family's, your friend's, or your own life, tell God *all* of them and let Him give you peace that He knows, He cares, He's good, and He's working for your good in all things.

---

*Dear God, sometimes things in my life seem so out of control and
I'm filled with such anxious thoughts. Please help me to keep my
thoughts fixed on You. Fill my mind with Your goodness and truth
from Your Word, and give me unexplainable peace. Thank You! Amen.*

WHAT YOU LISTEN TO, SAY, AND DO

Let the teaching of Christ and His words keep on living in you. These make your lives rich and full of wisdom.
COLOSSIANS 3:16

We all need wisdom, not just for what we watch and look at, but for choosing what we listen to and say and do as well. Everything that we put into our minds through our eyes and ears affects what we say and do. So this scripture in Colossians 3 helps guide us. If we let all the teachings of Jesus and His words actively live in us—meaning we focus on, listen to, and obey them most of all as we try our best to live like Jesus did—we will have lives that are rich and full of wisdom. ("Rich" in this case doesn't necessarily mean a life full of lots of money, but it means a life full of all the goodness God wants to give us—especially the things money can never buy.) So even as you do something as simple as choosing your favorite music, you can ask yourself, *Does this help me to focus on God and following Jesus or not? If not, what could I choose instead that would help me focus on Him?*

Dear God, please help me to make even the smallest choices in my life with wisdom from You. Please help me to strive to do and say all things in ways that honor You! Amen.

SUPPLYING YOUR NEEDS

And this same God who takes care of me will supply all your needs
from his glorious riches, which have been given to us in Christ Jesus.
PHILIPPIANS 4:19 NLT

Maybe you have specific worries about your family having enough money for food, clothes, and shelter. If you do, read and remember Matthew 6:25–33 (NLT) where Jesus says: "That is why I tell you not to worry about everyday life—whether you have enough food and drink, or enough clothes to wear. Isn't life more than food, and your body more than clothing? Look at the birds. They don't plant or harvest or store food in barns, for your heavenly Father feeds them. And aren't you far more valuable to him than they are? Can all your worries add a single moment to your life? And why worry about your clothing? Look at the lilies of the field and how they grow. They don't work or make their clothing, yet Solomon in all his glory was not dressed as beautifully as they are. And if God cares so wonderfully for wildflowers that are here today and thrown into the fire tomorrow, he will certainly care for you. Why do you have so little faith? So don't worry about these things, saying, 'What will we eat? What will we drink? What will we wear?' These things dominate the thoughts of unbelievers, but your heavenly Father already knows all your needs. Seek the Kingdom of God above all else, and live righteously, and he will give you everything you need."

Dear God, help me to focus on following You and then
trust that You'll always give me everything I need.
You've promised that, and I believe You. Amen.

WISDOM FOR WHAT YOU SAY, PART 1

We make a horse go wherever we want it to go by a small bit in its mouth. We turn its whole body by this. Sailing ships are driven by strong winds. But a small rudder turns a large ship whatever way the man at the wheel wants the ship to go. The tongue is also a small part of the body, but it can speak big things. See how a very small fire can set many trees on fire. The tongue is a fire.

JAMES 3:3–6

I love remembering when Jodi and Lilly first started talking! Ask your parents what your first words were and see if they have any videos of them. When a baby starts talking, it's a big deal. And what we say never stops being a big deal. The Bible is clear about how powerful the words we say are, so we need to remember God's wisdom that we should be careful with them. Proverbs 21:23 says, "He who watches over his mouth and his tongue keeps his soul from troubles." And Ephesians 4:29 says, "Watch your talk! No bad words should be coming from your mouth. Say what is good. Your words should help others grow as Christians."

Dear God, please help me to remember that the words I say matter and they are powerful. Please help me to use my mouth wisely. Amen.

WISDOM FOR WHAT YOU SAY, PART 2

*If a person thinks he is religious, but does not keep
his tongue from speaking bad things, he is fooling
himself. His religion is worth nothing.*
JAMES 1:26

If we say we love and believe in and follow Jesus as our Savior, then
we need to care about what we are saying and the impact our words
have. And if we mess up and say bad things or lies, we need to confess
and correct that sin as quickly as possible. Here are more scriptures
that help us remember how powerful our mouths and tongues are:

- ✳ "A gentle answer turns away anger, but a sharp word
  causes anger. The tongue of the wise uses much learning in a good way, but the mouth of fools speaks in a
  foolish way" (Proverbs 15:1–2).

- ✳ "The one who talks much will for sure sin, but he who is
  careful what he says is wise" (Proverbs 10:19).

- ✳ "If you want joy in your life and have happy days, keep
  your tongue from saying bad things and your lips from
  talking bad about others. Turn away from what is sinful.
  Do what is good. Look for peace and go after it. The
  Lord watches over those who are right with Him. He
  hears their prayers. But the Lord is against those who
  sin" (1 Peter 3:10–12).

*Dear God, like Psalm 141:3 says, please "put a watch over my
mouth. Keep watch over the door of my lips." Thank You! Amen.*

DON'T PLAY FAVORITES

For God does not show favoritism.
ROMANS 2:11 NLT

Do you still have a very favorite stuffed animal or blanket that you always, always, *always* have to sleep with at night? I took a very favorite blanket that I couldn't sleep without *to college* with me, so I completely understand!

Sometimes showing favoritism is totally okay. Sometimes it's totally not, like when treating some people better than other people. James 2:1–4 (CEV) talks about it: "My friends, if you have faith in our glorious Lord Jesus Christ, you won't treat some people better than others. Suppose a rich person wearing fancy clothes and a gold ring comes to one of your meetings. And suppose a poor person dressed in worn-out clothes also comes. You must not give the best seat to the one in fancy clothes and tell the one who is poor to stand at the side or sit on the floor. That is the same as saying that some people are better than others, and you would be acting like a crooked judge."

In God's eyes, every single person is created equal and every single person is equally valuable. Acts 10:34–36 (NLT) says, "Peter replied, 'I see very clearly that God shows no favoritism. In every nation he accepts those who fear him and do what is right. This is the message of Good News for the people of Israel—that there is peace with God through Jesus Christ, who is Lord of all.' "

Dear God, please help me to never treat any person better than any other. Amen.

MATCHING WORDS AND ACTIONS

But to sinful people nothing is pure. Both their minds and their hearts are bad. They say they know God, but by the way they act, they show that they do not. They are sinful people. They will not obey and are of no use for any good work.

TITUS 1:15–16

Our words matter, and so do our actions. If we say all the right things but then not do what is right, our words mean nothing and we become a hypocrite—a person who says one thing but does the opposite. Maybe you've experienced someone like that at school—someone who says the right things to look good for the teacher, but behind the teacher's back that person is always breaking the rules or doing mean things. Hypocrites are dishonest and cannot be trusted, and we should never want to be like them. This scripture in Titus talks about people who say they know God but behave like they don't. We should always strive to make sure that what we say about loving and believing in God and following Jesus matches up with how we live our lives.

Dear God, please help me not just to say that I love and follow You but to show others that is true by what I do. Amen.

UNFAILING LOVE

Praise the LORD! He is good. God's love never fails.
Praise the God of all gods. God's love never fails.
Praise the Lord of lords. God's love never fails.
PSALM 136:1–3 CEV

One time when Lilly was about three or so, she told me, "I don't like it when Jodi gets in trouble. I love her!"

I told her that was sweet, but I also said to her (because she was in a tattling phase at that time), "Why do you tattle on her sometimes just to get her in trouble?"

Lilly tearfully replied, "Sometimes I forget my love."

What an honest answer from a tiny little girl, one that everyone can relate to! I know I forget my love for others sometimes when I let angry or frustrated or stressed-out emotions take over. I'm guessing you do too. We *all* do! Thankfully, we have God's grace to cover our mistakes and help us remember our love, ask for forgiveness, and restore the relationship. And thankfully, there is one source of love in our lives that is never forgotten and never leaves us—God's great love for us.

God's Word promises that "the steadfast love of the LORD never ceases; his mercies never come to an end; they are new every morning; great is your faithfulness" (Lamentations 3:22–23 ESV).

Heavenly Father, thank You that even though my love
for others fails sometimes, and so does theirs for me,
Your love never, ever fails. You never forget Your love
for me. Help me to be more like You! Amen.

Day 180

WISDOM FROM THE BOOK OF AMOS

The Lord says to the people of Israel, "Look for Me and live."
AMOS 5:4

Amos was a shepherd and a fruit picker, just a totally ordinary kind of guy who became a prophet for God. This reminds us that God can use anyone He chooses, no matter their background, to do His good works. Amos warned His people that even though things were going well for them overall, they would soon be judged for their sin they were holding on to. There are good lessons for us in the book of Amos to remind us that we should look for any sin we're holding on to underneath the good in our lives and confess that sin to God and ask for forgiveness. God loves to forgive and bless us when we turn back to Him.

Dear God, thank You for the book of Amos. Help me as I read it and keep coming back to it in the future. Teach me what You want me to learn from it to apply to my life and to share with others. Amen.

EVEN WITH THE LITTLE THINGS

"You are a good and faithful servant. I left you in charge of only a little, but now I will put you in charge of much more. Come and share in my happiness!"
MATTHEW 25:21 CEV

Just the other day, Jodi, Lilly, and I were buying a few things at the drugstore (including some Kit-Kats, yum!), and when we checked out, I was a little confused by the total. I knew it couldn't be right because I'd added up in my head an estimate of what the total should be and it was at least five dollars off. But the cashier had bagged up our items already and was telling us to have a good day. . . . I admit, a big voice in my brain was saying, "No big deal, you get to save five bucks today! It's not your fault the cashier didn't do his job right." But with God's grace, I was able to stop that voice. I knew that the cashier had accidentally put an item in my bag without my paying for it, and even though it wasn't on purpose, since I knew it had happened, it would be a form of stealing if I didn't say something about it. So I did say something, and the cashier thanked me for making it right. I was able to leave the store knowing I had done the honest and right thing. A clear conscience is worth far, far more than the five dollars I could have kept in my wallet.

Dear God, please help me to be honest even in the smallest kinds of things. I know You see everything, and I want to please You. I believe You bless me when You see I'm trustworthy. Amen.

WISDOM FROM THE BOOK OF OBADIAH

"For the day of the Lord is near for all nations.
As you have done, it will be done to you. What you
do will come back to you on your own head."
OBADIAH 15

The book of Obadiah has only twenty-one verses total! That's the shortest book in the Old Testament. In it, God's prophet Obadiah had a message for Edom, a not-so-nice neighbor nation of Israel. Edom would be destroyed because of how they celebrated when bad things happened to Israel and how they fought against Israel when they needed Edom's help. The book of Obadiah helps show us how protective God is of His people, and He wants to bring justice to those who mistreat them.

Dear God, thank You for the book of Obadiah. Help me
as I read it and keep coming back to it in the future.
Teach me what You want me to learn from it to apply
to my life and to share with others. Amen.

TRUST GOD'S TIMING

The LORD is a God of justice. Blessed are all who wait for him!
ISAIAH 30:18 NIV

Sometimes doing the right thing feels like it's getting you nowhere, and doing what's wrong seems to be getting some people you know all the good stuff. Maybe you've seen someone cheating at school and they never get caught and they keep getting good grades, but you're studying hard and refusing to cheat and you can't ever seem to get an A. I know it's so hard, but wait on God. Keep doing what you know is right. Stop comparing your blessings with the people around you and let God deal with them if they are gaining things dishonestly.

Galatians 6:7–9 (NLT) says, "Don't be misled—you cannot mock the justice of God. You will always harvest what you plant. Those who live only to satisfy their own sinful nature will harvest decay and death from that sinful nature. But those who live to please the Spirit will harvest everlasting life from the Spirit. So let's not get tired of doing what is good. At just the right time we will reap a harvest of blessing if we don't give up."

Remember that it says, "at just the right time" your blessings will come. Let God see that you trust His timing and will keep doing good no matter what!

Dear Lord, I need help waiting on You when I'm trying to do the right thing, but I feel like it's getting me nowhere. Help me to trust that You see and know, and bless me when I'm trying my best to live for You. Amen.

Day 184

WISDOM ABOUT PEER PRESSURE

Do not want to be like those who do wrong. . . . Trust in the Lord, and do good. So you will live in the land and will be fed. Be happy in the Lord. And He will give you the desires of your heart.
PSALM 37:1–4

It's not always easy to stay away from those who do wrong. Sometimes it seems fun and harmless to be like them and just go along with whatever seems popular, even if deep down you know that what is popular is wrong. So it takes courage to stay away from those doing wrong, especially if you're feeling pressure from people you thought were your friends. But God promises that if you trust Him and do good, you will have everything you need and He will give you the things that make you happy because first you are happy in Him!

Dear God, please help me to have wisdom and courage not to want to be like those who do wrong. I want to do what is wise and makes You happy. I trust that's the best way for me to be happy too. Amen.

TONGUE TAMING

*Indeed, we all make many mistakes. For if we could
control our tongues, we would be perfect and could
also control ourselves in every other way.*
JAMES 3:2 NLT

You know how you blow a BIG bubble-gum bubble (so fun!) and within an instant it pops and you chew it all back into your mouth? Sometimes I wish the things I said were like that bubble. God's Word talks about how powerful our tongues are and how hard it can be to control them. I'm thankful He knows what a struggle it is. Our emotions seem to overtake our tongues too quickly sometimes, and before we know it, mean words are hanging out there in the air for others to hear and be hurt by—and we can't chew them back in like a popped bubble-gum bubble.

No, you can never get back the unkind or discouraging words you've said, but you can trust that God's grace covers them when you're sorry for them. Apologize to the person who was the target of your mean words and ask for forgiveness, knowing that everybody struggles with this! Then ask God for supernatural help in making your tongue obey His way.

---

*Dear Lord, I pray like Psalm 141:3 that You take control of
what I say and guard my lips. Please and thank You! Amen.*

WISDOM FROM THE BOOK OF JONAH

The Word of the Lord came to Jonah the son of Amittai, saying,
"Get up and go to the large city of Nineveh, and preach against
it. For their sin has come up before Me." But Jonah ran away
from the Lord going toward Tarshish. He went down to Joppa and
found a ship which was going to Tarshish. Jonah paid money,
and got on the ship to go with them, to get away from the Lord.
JONAH 1:1–3

Jonah is one of the most well-known names in the Bible because of his time spent inside the belly of a big fish! What an incredible story that is! Jonah ended up inside that fish because he did not want to be God's prophet in Nineveh—and so he disobeyed. We can learn much wisdom from Jonah's story, especially that even if He must take extreme measures, God will show us what we've done wrong and help us to get back on the path He has planned for us.

Dear God, thank You for the book of Jonah. Help me as I read it and keep coming back to it in the future. Teach me what You want me to learn from it to apply to my life and to share with others. Amen.

NO TROUBLE LASTS FOREVER

When his people pray for help, he listens and rescues them from their troubles. The LORD is there to rescue all who are discouraged and have given up hope. The LORD's people may suffer a lot, but he will always bring them safely through.
PSALM 34:17–19 CEV

Think back to your worst *Alexander and the Terrible, Horrible, No Good, Very Bad Day* kind of day. We all have different stories of those kinds of days. Sadly, the older you get, the more kinds of bad days you have. But the more opportunity for all kinds of new *great* days too!

On the bad days, no matter what kind, remember this encouraging scripture from 2 Corinthians 4:17–18 (NLT): "For our present troubles are small and won't last very long. Yet they produce for us a glory that vastly outweighs them and will last forever! So we don't look at the troubles we can see now; rather, we fix our gaze on things that cannot be seen. For the things we see now will soon be gone, but the things we cannot see will last forever."

Dear God, I need to remember that no trouble lasts forever, but eternal life and blessing with You does! Right now, You see me and hear me and know what I need in the midst of these troubles. Help me to trust You more. Amen.

Day 188

WISDOM FROM THE BOOK OF MICAH

What should I bring to the Lord when I bow down before the God on high? Should I come to Him with burnt gifts, with calves a year old? Will the Lord be pleased with thousands of rams, or with 10,000 rivers of oil? Should I give my first-born to pay for not obeying? Should I give the fruit of my body for the sin of my soul? O man, He has told you what is good. What does the Lord ask of you but to do what is fair and to love kindness, and to walk without pride with your God?

MICAH 6:6–8

The nations of Judah and Israel were worshipping idols instead of God and were mistreating poor and needy people. Through the prophet Micah, God warned them that they would be destroyed for their bad behavior. Micah preached a message from God of both judgment and mercy, showing that God hates sin but never hates the people who sin. He wants each person to confess their sin, turn away from it, and turn back to Him for forgiveness and love. He wants us to honor Him with the ways we act fairly and kindly and humbly in our lives.

Dear God, thank You for the book of Micah. Help me as I read it and keep coming back to it in the future. Teach me what You want me to learn from it to apply to my life and to share with others. Amen.

Day 189

STAYING OUT OF THE TRASH

*Let us think of ways to motivate one another
to acts of love and good works.*
HEBREWS 10:24 NLT

Our dog Jasper is really good about staying out of the trash can—unless he's alone in the house and something smells really good to him in the trash can (so gross, right?). He's also good about never stealing food off the counter. . .unless we walk away and leave him alone near some kind of food lying out unwrapped. He gets overcome with temptation, and he just can't fight it when no one is around to help him remember the rules! He's tall when he stands on his hind legs, and one time I caught him when he'd just eaten half a loaf of delicious cranberry bread that I'd baked fresh and was letting cool on the kitchen counter. Bad dog, Jasper! Bad! (Good thing he's so sweet and cuddly and good most of the time!)

We can take a lesson from Jasper, that we all need people around to help us when we're tempted to do the wrong things. That's called having accountability. Our friends and family who love God can help keep us accountable to living according to His Word and doing our best not to sin when we're tempted.

---

*Dear God, please surround me with people who love
You and want to help me stay away from sin and on
track with living well to please You. Amen.*

WISDOM ABOUT SHARING THE GOOD NEWS

*I am not ashamed of the Good News. It is the power of God.
It is the way He saves men from the punishment of their sins if
they put their trust in Him. It is for the Jew first and for all other
people also. The Good News tells us we are made right with God
by faith in Him. Then, by faith we live that new life through Him.
The Holy Writings say, "A man right with God lives by faith."*

ROMANS 1:16–17

Even the wisest people have things here and there that they get embarrassed by or ashamed of. But no Christian should ever feel embarrassed or ashamed of Jesus. As the apostle Paul shared in Romans 1, we should all want to be able to say this—that we are not ashamed of the good news that Jesus came to earth to live a perfect life and teach us, then died on the cross to pay for our sins, and then rose to life again and offers us eternal life too. When we share this good news with others, we help spread God's power to save people from their sins.

---

*Dear God, please give me the wisdom I need never to be
ashamed to share the good news about Jesus! Thank You for
loving all people and wanting to save us from sin! Amen.*

Day 191

DELIGHTING IN DIFFERENCES

Always be humble and gentle. Patiently put up with each other and love each other. Try your best to let God's Spirit keep your hearts united. Do this by living at peace.
EPHESIANS 4:2–3 CEV

Not long ago, we were on a road trip and stopped at a Dairy Queen for some food and treats, and Jodi and Lilly got Dilly bars. Lilly ate hers the "normal" way, but we laughed so hard when we saw that Jodi took off little tiny chunks of the coating with her fingers and soon had this hilarious-looking naked Dilly bar.

Everyone does things a little differently, whether it's the way you eat your Dilly bar or the way you clean your room—and that's okay! We need to have patience with one another and give grace to one another, even when we sometimes wish others did things exactly the way we do. Sometimes we need to stop thinking that our way is *always* the best way of doing things. We can learn so much from others if we keep the right attitude of being humble and patient.

Dear God, help me to appreciate that You made everyone creative in their own ways. Remind me that I can learn so much from others when I'm humble, gentle, patient, and loving. Amen.

WISDOM IN THE HARD THINGS

When someone does something bad to you, do not do the same thing to him. When someone talks about you, do not talk about him. Instead, pray that good will come to him. You were called to do this so you might receive good things from God.

1 PETER 3:9

Even though being mistreated feels awful, you can choose to learn wisdom from the experience. You can learn good lessons when someone is mean or rude or does bad things to you—you can learn what *not* to do to someone else. You can learn to choose better or "take the high road." God wants us to take that higher road and not get revenge on others who mistreat us. In fact, He wants us to instead pray that good things will come to the people who do bad to us. That's sure not easy, but remember that God wants to bless you when you obey His wisdom on this. Ask Him to help you, and then see how He rewards you!

Dear God, I pray for those who treat me badly. Please help them to stop doing bad things and instead know You as Savior and want to share Your love. Please bless them with good things to fill their lives. Help me not want to get revenge. Instead, help me to trust in You to take care of everything. Amen.

DUNKIN' DOUGHNUTS

When I am afraid, I put my trust in you.
PSALM 56:3 ESV

When Jodi and Lilly were younger, they did not want to learn to swim. Not at all. They loved being in the water, but they hated getting their faces wet. So, I made a silly swimming game called Dunkin' Doughnuts. Whoever was "it" had to think of a type of doughnut, and everyone else had to guess. If you didn't guess right, you had to dunk your face in the water.

Little by little and lots of games of Dunkin' Doughnuts and pool time later, the girls are now swimming just fine, and they realize how much they were missing out on by being afraid to get their faces wet. It's so fun to jump in the pool and swim underwater! Maybe learning to swim never bothered you, or maybe you can relate to this. Trying new things can be scary, but as long as you know it's a safe something to do, you can really miss out on amazing fun by letting fear control you. Let God help you come up with ways to help you get over your fear. Think up silly games like we did or ask a family member or friend to help you. Get creative and trust that when you're leaving your comfort zone, God is going with you. In fact, out of your comfort zone is often where God grows your faith in Him the most!

Dear God, help me to put my trust in You when I'm afraid of trying new things! I know You can make me brave. Amen.

WISDOM FROM THE BOOK OF NAHUM

The Lord is good, a safe place in times of trouble.
And He knows those who come to Him to be safe. But He
will put an end to Nineveh by making a flood flow over it.
And He will drive those who hate Him into darkness.

NAHUM 1:7–9

Remember when God sent Jonah to preach to the people of Nineveh? (And Jonah finally made it there after spending a few days inside the big fish for disobeying at first!) The people of Nineveh did repent, and God had mercy on them, but one hundred years later they were back to doing bad things like they were in trouble for the first time! So God sent a message through the prophet Nahum that God was going to destroy Nineveh, and He did just that about fifty years after Nahum warned them. The book is a lesson that we must remember what a good, safe place God is for all who trust and follow Him. But He will destroy those who hate Him.

Dear God, thank You for the book of Nahum. Help me as I read it and keep coming back to it in the future. Teach me what You want me to learn from it to apply to my life and to share with others. Amen.

FRUIT-OF-THE-SPIRIT PERKS

But the Holy Spirit produces this kind of fruit in our lives: love, joy, peace, patience, kindness, goodness, faithfulness, gentleness, and self-control.
GALATIANS 5:22–23 NLT

It seems like every store and business has some kind of perk card you can carry with you to earn points toward free stuff. I have so many cards filling my wallet, it's hard to find the right one when I need it! I've noticed lately that in a world where so many people are impatient and rude over the slightest little thing, you often get a treat just for being patient and kind! Who even needs to carry those perk cards? For example, in just the past few months, the girls and I have gotten things like free ice cream, cookies, iced tea, and coffee at stores and restaurants just for using good manners and not being rude when we had to wait a little extra to be waited on or to pay. Because so many people don't use good manners anymore, employees of restaurants and stores are often majorly impressed by people who still use good manners.

Ask God to constantly grow the fruits of the Spirit in your life, and then watch and see how God blesses you when you use them with others. That's the very best kind of perk!

Dear God, please grow love, joy, peace, patience, kindness, goodness, faithfulness, gentleness, and self-control in me. Amen.

WISDOM ABOUT YOUR IDENTITY

*And God made man in His own likeness. In the likeness of
God He made him. He made both male and female.*
GENESIS 1:27

You might hear a lot these days about people trying to figure out their identity. If we look to God, that's where we find it! His Word is clear in Genesis 1 that God made us in His likeness. He has made boys and girls to grow up into men and women, and He has given us the Bible to guide us in how to live and love like He does. Here are more scriptures that help us have wisdom to know our identity is in God and we become new creations in Jesus when we accept Him as Savior.

* "Christ lives in me. The life I now live in this body, I live by putting my trust in the Son of God. He was the One Who loved me and gave Himself for me" (Galatians 2:20).

* "But you are a chosen group of people. You are the King's religious leaders. You are a holy nation. You belong to God. He has done this for you so you can tell others how God has called you out of darkness into His great light" (1 Peter 2:9).

---

*Dear God, please help me always to have wisdom that
my identity is found in You! Thank You for creating me
and saving me from sin! I live my life with trust in You,
following Jesus Christ, who lives in me! Amen.*

ALL THE LOVE

God is love.
1 JOHN 4:16 NLT

I think Valentine's Day is so much fun. Pretty cards, hearts and flowers, and yummy candy! A celebration of love is wonderful, especially if you know the real source of love—God. The Bible says, "We love because he first loved us" (1 John 4:19 NIV).

Our world has a lot of ideas about what real love is. Some are nice, but if they aren't inspired by God, then they aren't real love at all. The Bible says, "God is love, and all who live in love live in God, and God lives in them. And as we live in God, our love grows more perfect" (1 John 4:16–17 NLT). The only way to truly love one another is to keep walking with God and learning more about Him because He is love and the source of our love for others. Ask God to teach you more about real love each day and how to love others better with actions and not just words. First John 3:18–19 (NLT) says, "Dear children, let's not merely say that we love each other; let us show the truth by our actions. Our actions will show that we belong to the truth, so we will be confident when we stand before God."

Dear God, You are real love! Please help me to live in You and actively love others like You do. Amen.

Day 198

WISDOM ABOUT BEING PROUD

If anyone wants to be proud, he should be proud of what the Lord has done. It is not what a man thinks and says of himself that is important. It is what God thinks of him.
2 CORINTHIANS 10:17–18

Of course you feel happy when you accomplish something cool, right? And that's great! Just don't forget to give God credit for each good and cool thing you do. That's a great way to stay humble and never become full of pride in yourself rather than in God. He deserves every bit of praise and worship because He is the one who gives you your gifts and abilities.

Dear God, I want to be way prouder of You than I am of anything cool I do. You are the one who gives me my talents and abilities. Please help me to use them well in the ways You want me to, especially to share Your love and truth with others. Amen.

Day 199

ONE TRUE CREATOR

By faith we understand that the universe was created by the word of God, so that what is seen was not made out of things that are visible.
HEBREWS 11:3 ESV

These days it's far more popular to trust in science and Mother Nature than it is to believe there is one true God who is the Creator of our earth and the Creator of science itself. All the theories and formulas that scientists promote can make you start to doubt that God is for real. But simply look around at all the incredible trees and flowers and animals and humans! No scientist can explain how exactly they began growing and living and reproducing. Scientists have their theories, sure, but they don't have proof. And how could anything just begin here without a Creator creating it? Nothing else just appears that way. Everything that's made has to have a creator. Consider all these powerful scriptures on creation, and then praise our amazing God for His incredible handiwork!

* "Worthy are you, our Lord and God, to receive glory and honor and power, for you created all things, and by your will they existed and were created" (Revelation 4:11 ESV).

* In the beginning was the Word, and the Word was with God, and the Word was God. He was in the beginning with God. All things were made through him, and without him was not any thing made that was made" (John 1:1–3 ESV).

Dear God, I believe You are the one true Creator. Help my faith in You to grow each day, and show me more of You in Your creation. Amen.

Day 200

WISDOM FROM THE BOOK OF HABAKKUK

Even if the fig tree does not grow figs and there is no fruit on the vines, even if the olives do not grow and the fields give no food, even if there are no sheep within the fence and no cattle in the cattle-building, yet I will have joy in the Lord. I will be glad in the God Who saves me.
HABAKKUK 3:17–18

Habakkuk was a prophet of God who had lots of questions. He started out by writing, "O Lord, how long must I call for help before You will hear? I cry out to You, 'We are being hurt!' But You do not save us" (Habakkuk 1:2). We all can relate to asking God questions. We sometimes wonder why we must wait so long on Him or why He doesn't answer our prayers the way we want Him to. We can learn from Habakkuk that even though this prophet never got the exact answers he was hoping for from God, he got answers that reminded him of this: God is all powerful and all good, and He will work out His perfect plans in His perfect timing. We must always trust what Habakkuk learned in our own lives today too.

Dear God, thank You for the book of Habakkuk. Help me as I read it and keep coming back to it in the future. Teach me what You want me to learn from it to apply to my life and to share with others. Amen.

Day 201

MORE ABOUT CREATION

God saw all that he had made, and it was very good.
GENESIS 1:31 NIV

Here are more passages of scripture to encourage you to look at the world around you and believe that our God is a great and mighty Creator!

Job 12:7–10 (NIV) says, " 'But ask the animals, and they will teach you, or the birds in the sky, and they will tell you; or speak to the earth, and it will teach you, or let the fish in the sea inform you. Which of all these does not know that the hand of the LORD has done this? In his hand is the life of every creature and the breath of all mankind.' " I love this scripture because it reminds us that we humans are the ones with too many questions sometimes when clear answers are right there in front of us. The animals, even the fish and birds, know that God is our one true Creator! Studying all of earth's creatures should just give us more and more reason to trust and praise and learn more about God!

In Colossians 1:15–17 (CEV), we see again how Jesus is God Himself and also our Creator. He holds it all together! "Christ is exactly like God, who cannot be seen. He is the first-born Son, superior to all creation. Everything was created by him, everything in heaven and on earth, everything seen and unseen, including all forces and powers, and all rulers and authorities. All things were created by God's Son, and everything was made for him. God's Son was before all else, and by him everything is held together."

---

*Dear Jesus, I trust in You and I praise You for
all of Your awesome work! Amen.*

A PARABLE ABOUT PRAYER

Jesus. . .said, "There was a man in one of the cities who was head of the court. His work was to say if a person was guilty or not. This man was not afraid of God. He did not respect any man. In that city there was a woman whose husband had died. She kept coming to him and saying, 'Help me! There is someone who is working against me.' For awhile he would not help her. Then he began to think, '. . .I will see that this woman whose husband has died gets her rights because I get tired of her coming all the time.'" Then the Lord said, "Listen to the words of the sinful man who is head of the court. Will not God make the things that are right come to His chosen people who cry day and night to Him? Will He wait a long time to help them? . . . He will be quick to help them."

LUKE 18:1–8

Sometimes we feel like giving up when it seems like God isn't hearing us or is taking too long to answer. This picture-story from Jesus reminds us that we should "always pray and not give up." That is wonderful wisdom from Jesus that we should never, ever forget!

Dear Jesus, thank You that You taught me never to give up on prayer. Please help me when I do feel like giving up. Remind me of this story. Amen.

Day 203

BELIEVING WITHOUT SEEING

For we live by believing and not by seeing.
2 CORINTHIANS 5:7 NLT

Have you ever thought, *Sometimes I don't know if I believe Jesus is real or not because I can't see Him here*? At times it is really hard not to be able to see Jesus with our eyes and hear Him talk to us with our ears and touch Him and hug Him with our hands and arms. But Jesus said, "Have you believed because you have seen me? Blessed are those who have not seen and yet have believed" (John 20:29 ESV).

We don't have Jesus here with us right now, but we trust that He was here on earth in the past and that we do have the Holy Spirit with us now until Jesus comes back again. We can "see" the Holy Spirit, not with our eyes but with our faith in Him and in the ways we sense Him leading us and talking to us, especially through the Bible.

And when we're struggling in our belief, we can pray like the man in Mark 9:24 (NLT), who said to Jesus, "I do believe, but help me overcome my unbelief!"

Dear Jesus, I'm sorry for the times that I doubt You are real. Remind me of the many ways You have shown me You are here through Your Holy Spirit. I trust You, and when my faith is weakening, please quickly strengthen it again. Amen.

WISDOM FROM GREAT FAITH HEROES

*Faith makes us sure of what we hope for and gives
us proof of what we cannot see. It was their faith
that made our ancestors pleasing to God.*
Hebrews 11:1–2 cev

We can get a lot of wisdom from the lives of people with great faith who have gone before us. Hebrews 11 is a wonderful chapter of the Bible to help us remember a whole list of great faith heroes, people like Noah and Moses and Joseph and Sarah and Rahab, who continued to believe in God and His promises, even during the most difficult times. Like them, we should want to hold on to our faith, no matter what. Think about the people among your family and friends who have super strong faith in God, those who are still living and those who have passed away. Keep looking up to and honoring them and their example, now and every day of your life too!

---

*Dear God, please help me to remember everyone
who has gone before me who kept great faith in You.
I want to be so strong in my faith too. Amen.*

ALWAYS WATCHING

*Nothing in all creation is hidden from God.
Everything is naked and exposed before his eyes,
and he is the one to whom we are accountable.*
HEBREWS 4:13 NLT

We laugh every time at the part in *Monsters, Inc.* when Roz says, "I'm watching you. . .always watching." A creepy monster/secretary is not always watching you, but God always is! With Jesus as your Savior, that never needs to freak you out, either. Even though you still make mistakes sometimes and God sees those, they are covered by the grace of Jesus if you've accepted Him. Since you know the Holy Spirit is always with you and God is always watching, let that inspire you in your best behavior. But when you mess up, remember that He's there and quickly ask for forgiveness—and ask Him to help you make things right again. He's such a good God who loves you more than anyone ever has or ever will, and He only wants what's best for you. You never have to be afraid of His constant presence in your life.

---

*Dear God, I trust that You are with me and see and know everything
I'm thinking and doing. Because of Your grace, that's something
not to feel weird about but to feel thankful for! Amen.*

WISDOM ABOUT EQUALITY

*You are now children of God because you have put your
trust in Christ Jesus. All of you who have been baptized
to show you belong to Christ have become like Christ.
God does not see you as a Jew or as a Greek. He does not see
you as a servant or as a person free to work. He does not
see you as a man or as a woman. You are all one in Christ.*
GALATIANS 3:26–28

You might hear the word *equality* a lot these days, and it's so important to have wisdom about who alone gives real equality—Jesus! Because of sin in the world, people will never get equality exactly right. There will always be bad people trying to say some groups of people are better than others. But don't ever listen to or join them. In God's eyes, because of Jesus, every single person is the same in value. We all matter so much to God that He sent Jesus to die to save us from our sins. And when anyone trusts in Jesus, they become a child of the one true God, the King of all kings. That makes us all equally royal, and we should want to share that awesome truth with everyone we can!

*Dear God, You offer the only true equality through
Jesus. Thank You that anyone can be Your child by
trusting that only Jesus saves. Help me to share
Your love and truth and wisdom. Amen.*

Day 207

WINDING PATHS

How great is our Lord! His power is absolute!
His understanding is beyond comprehension!
PSALM 147:5 NLT

I didn't start geometry in school until the ninth grade, but it seems you kids are smarter these days and learning it much younger! So maybe you've already learned the geometry rule that the shortest distance between two points is a straight line. That rule always makes me think about how God definitely does not follow the ways of this world. Isaiah 55:8–9 (NLT) says, " 'My thoughts are nothing like your thoughts,' says the LORD. 'And my ways are far beyond anything you could imagine. For just as the heavens are higher than the earth, so my ways are higher than your ways and my thoughts higher than your thoughts.' "

I look back on my life and see how God has gotten me from point A to point B with a lot of curvy and sometimes complicated lines with lots of ups and downs. And there were often a lot of people on those paths whom I needed to meet and experiences I needed to grow through. And sometimes I stepped off the path God wanted for me and did my own thing and later needed to find my way back to God's way. Your life already likely hasn't been a series of perfect straight lines that go up and to the right; and if you're following closely to God, you'll see how He uses challenges and detours to draw you even closer to Him and to accomplish His will.

Dear God, keep me close, and help me to trust You
in all the winding paths of my life. Amen.

Day 208

WISDOM FROM THE BOOK OF ZEPHANIAH

"Do not let your hands lose their strength. The Lord your God is with you, a Powerful One Who wins the battle. He will have much joy over you. With His love He will give you new life. He will have joy over you with loud singing."
ZEPHANIAH 3:16–17

The prophet Zephaniah preached a scary message from God in the first chapter of his book about awful suffering and judgment for the nation of Judah and all nations who turn away from God. Then he begged the people to turn to God before it was too late. And in the last chapter, he preached that despite all the bad things that will happen to those who reject God, there is great hope in God's promises for all who love and trust and obey Him.

Dear God, thank You for the book of Zephaniah. Help me as I read it and keep coming back to it in the future. Teach me what You want me to learn from it to apply to my life and to share with others. Amen.

Day 209

TIME TRAVEL

"Remember how the LORD your God led you through the wilderness for these forty years, humbling you and testing you to prove your character, and to find out whether or not you would obey his commands."
DEUTERONOMY 8:2 NLT

Time travel really would be amazing, right? It's fun to think about where you would go and whom you would visit in what time periods of the past. Do you know that if you're struggling with something and wondering how God is going to help, it's really smart to do a little time travel in your mind? Go back in your memories and think about all the ways He's helped you and provided for you in the past. Praise and thank Him for those times, and let them inspire you to have great faith that He will surely help and provide for you again! He says in Isaiah 46:9 (NLT), "Remember the things I have done in the past. For I alone am God! I am God, and there is none like me."

Dear God, when I'm discouraged or worried about the future, help me to travel back in time in my mind. You've been here all my life, helping me and providing for me, and because I see Your work in the past, I will trust You for the future. Amen.

Day 210

WISDOM WHEN YOUR HEART IS BROKEN, PART 1

*Jesus said. . ."In the world you will have much trouble.
But take hope! I have power over the world!"*
JOHN 16:31–33

We wish it were true that our hearts would never break in this world, but sadly it's not. Awful things do happen to every single one of us. Loved ones die, parents get divorced, friends betray us. Houses burn down, favorite things get stolen. People get sick or injured. Friends and loved ones move far away. And even lesser things can make us feel heartbroken. In any of those situations, we have a very important choice to make about our relationship with God—do we get closer to Him or further away? Do we choose to let Him help and comfort us, or do we choose anger and blame God? The wise choice is to grow closer to God. Psalm 34:17–18 says, "Those who are right with the Lord cry, and He hears them. And He takes them from all their troubles. The Lord is near to those who have a broken heart."

*Dear God, please help me to choose wisely when my
heart feels broken. Help me not to turn away from You
in anger and blame. Help me to remember that You are
near and You want to heal my broken heart. Amen.*

WISDOM WHEN YOUR HEART IS BROKEN, PART 2

Praise the Lord! For it is good to sing praises to our God. . . . He heals those who have a broken heart.
PSALM 147:1–3

If you have a broken bone, you shouldn't run away screaming and angry from the doctors and nurses who can fix it. How silly, right? You might *wish* you could run away, because the process of fixing it is painful and scary and feels like it takes forever. But worse would be never fixing the broken bone at all. It's the same way with a broken heart. God is the only one who can truly heal it. Wisely choosing to get closer to Him even when your heart feels broken doesn't mean you instantly feel all better. You will still hurt for a long time and might feel all kinds of emotions, including anger and fear. But if you let God, He will comfort you and help you with those emotions. It does take time to heal your broken heart, though, just like a broken bone takes time to heal. Keep praying to God. Keep reading His Word. Keep going to church and letting other people who love God encourage you. God will show you His love and care in many different ways as He heals you.

Dear God, please help me to be patient as I let You comfort me and show me Your love in all kinds of ways. Amen.

WISDOM WHEN YOUR HEART IS BROKEN, PART 3

*I pray that you will be able to understand how wide and how
long and how high and how deep His love is. I pray that you will
know the love of Christ. His love goes beyond anything we can
understand. I pray that you will be filled with God Himself.*
EPHESIANS 3:18–19

When your heart feels broken from losing a loved one and you're
choosing to get closer to God, it's wise to write in a journal to keep
track of how you see God helping you. You might wish so much that
He would bring back the loved one who died, but if you keep track,
you will see how God is bringing love to you in other ways, through
other people. If you write down the many memories you have of a
loved one you have lost, you can focus on being thankful for all the
love and time you did have together. And if your loved one knew
Jesus as their Savior and you do too, you can write down all the things
you want to tell them and do with them when you spend forever
together in perfect heaven with God.

---

*Dear God, please help me to keep track of all the ways You help
me heal, and show me Your awesome love when my heart is broken.
I don't want to forget how well You take care of me. Amen.*

Day 213

WHAT OTHERS HAVE

It's healthy to be content, but envy can eat you up.
PROVERBS 14:30 CEV

If you have siblings, you know it can be so hard not to be jealous over things that they have that you don't or their accomplishments and talents. But you're going to make yourself miserable if you let yourself be overcome by the green-eyed monster. (Did you know that expression came from the famous writer William Shakespeare?) Not only now with your siblings but with others your entire life, there will be people everywhere who have things you do not—and that's okay!

Be grateful for what you have, and celebrate what others have too. Read and remember what James 3:13–16 (NLT) says: "If you are wise and understand God's ways, prove it by living an honorable life, doing good works with the humility that comes from wisdom. But if you are bitterly jealous and there is selfish ambition in your heart, don't cover up the truth with boasting and lying. For jealousy and selfishness are not God's kind of wisdom. Such things are earthly, unspiritual, and demonic. For wherever there is jealousy and selfish ambition, there you will find disorder and evil of every kind."

Dear God, please help me to get rid of any kind of jealousy in my heart. I want to be more thankful for what I have and celebrate with others what they have. Amen.

Day 214

WISDOM FROM THE BOOK OF HAGGAI

"'Be strong, all you people of the land,' says the Lord. 'Do the work, for I am with you,' says the Lord of All. 'As I promised you when you came out of Egypt, My Spirit is with you. Do not be afraid.'"
HAGGAI 2:4–5

The prophet Haggai had a message for God's people to get back to work rebuilding the temple in Jerusalem. At first they had a good plan and a good start, but then they got distracted and let the project sit for years. We do that kind of thing sometimes too, don't we? We get excited about good things God has asked us to do, and we enjoy them for a while, and then we get off track to do our own thing instead. The book of Haggai can be a great reminder to us to keep asking God what He wants us to do and then never give up on His good plans for us! If we do get off track, God is happy to help us get right back to good work.

Dear God, thank You for the book of Haggai. Help me as I read it and keep coming back to it in the future. Teach me what You want me to learn from it to apply to my life and to share with others. Amen.

Day 215

FIGHTING SELFISHNESS

Don't be selfish.
PHILIPPIANS 2:3 NLT

What's your earliest memory? It's strange how our brains work and we can't remember much of when we were babies. I guess we might just remember a bunch of crying and sleeping and smelly diapers anyway, right? We'd also probably recall how one of the very first things we had to learn was how to share. As soon as we started to roll and crawl, our parents had to be on our case not to take things from others and not to try to keep things from others.

Selfishness is just in us right from the start of our baby days. It's part of our sin nature, and we have to constantly fight the urge to keep everything to ourselves for our own gain and pleasure. It's hard, I know, but the way to keep it in perspective is to realize that the way to have plenty in life is to constantly give it away! Jesus said in Luke 6:38 (NLT), "Give, and you will receive. Your gift will return to you in full—pressed down, shaken together to make room for more, running over, and poured into your lap. The amount you give will determine the amount you get back."

Dear God, I sure need Your grace when it comes to my selfishness. Please help me to fight it and always be generous and willing to share. Amen.

Day 216

WISDOM FROM THE BOOK OF ZECHARIAH

"The Lord of All says, 'I am going to save My people from the land of the east and from the land of the west. I will bring them back and they will live in Jerusalem. They will be My people and I will be their God. I will be faithful and do what is right and good for them.'"
ZECHARIAH 8:7–8

Like Haggai, the prophet Zechariah also preached to the people of Judah to encourage them to finish the good work they had started of rebuilding the temple in Jerusalem. He told them it would one day be the home of the Messiah Himself (the Savior they were hoping for, whom we know is Jesus Christ)! Zechariah kept encouraging the people and told them about all the blessings that would come to the Jewish people once they had obeyed and finished their good work. We can read Zechariah's words and let them inspire and motivate us to do the good work God has for us too. When we do, we will be blessed, and we have already been so very blessed by the gift of Jesus Christ as our Savior from sin.

*Dear God, thank You for the book of Zechariah.
Help me as I read it and keep coming back to it in the
future. Teach me what You want me to learn from it to
apply to my life and to share with others. Amen.*

Day 217

STORING UP REAL TREASURE

Remind the rich to be generous and share what they have.
1 TIMOTHY 6:18 CEV

Think about your favorite toys, games, clothes, photos, and such! Think about how blessed you are! As much as you love your stuff (I love mine too!), remember that you didn't bring any of it into the world with you, and you won't take any of it out. First Timothy 6:7–9 (CEV) says, "We didn't bring anything into this world, and we won't take anything with us when we leave. So we should be satisfied just to have food and clothes. People who want to be rich fall into all sorts of temptations and traps. They are caught by foolish and harmful desires that drag them down and destroy them."

So, enjoy your stuff, but be content with just what you need, and always be willing to share your blessings and live by God's Word. When you do, you're storing up treasures in heaven that do last forever! Our minds can't even imagine how great they will be! Matthew 6:19–20 (CEV) says, "Don't store up treasures on earth! Moths and rust can destroy them, and thieves can break in and steal them. Instead, store up your treasures in heaven, where moths and rust cannot destroy them, and thieves cannot break in and steal them."

Dear God, thank You for all the cool stuff I'm blessed with. Please help me not to hold on to it too tightly, though. I want to live according to Your Word and store forever-treasures in heaven. Amen.

WISDOM WHEN WE MAKE BAD CHOICES, PART 1

And Jesus said, "There was a man who had two sons. The younger son said to his father, 'Father, let me have the part of the family riches that will be coming to me.' Then the father divided all that he owned between his two sons. Soon after that the younger son took all that had been given to him and went to another country far away. There he spent all he had on wild and foolish living. When all his money was spent, he was hungry. There was no food in the land. He went to work for a man in this far away country. His work was to feed pigs. He was so hungry he was ready to eat the outside part of the ears of the corn the pigs ate because no one gave him anything. He began to think about what he had done."
LUKE 15:11–17

In this parable, Jesus was teaching about God's great love for us, even when we make bad choices, just like the younger son in this story. If you've ever made bad choices, God wants you to think about what you've done and pray to Him about them.

Dear God, please help me to think about my choices and admit to You when I've sinned against You. Please forgive me and help me not to make the same bad choices again in the future. Amen.

Day 219

WISDOM WHEN WE MAKE BAD CHOICES, PART 2

*"I will get up and go to my father. I will say to him,
'Father, I have sinned against heaven and against you.'"*
LUKE 15:18

The parable from Jesus continues: "The son got up and went to his father. While he was yet a long way off, his father saw him. The father was full of loving-pity for him. He ran and threw his arms around him and kissed him. The son said to him, 'Father, I have sinned against heaven and against you. I am not good enough to be called your son.' But the father said to the workmen he owned, 'Hurry! Get the best coat and put it on him. Put a ring on his hand and shoes on his feet. Bring the calf that is fat and kill it. Let us eat and be glad. For my son was dead and now he is alive again. He was lost and now he is found. Let us eat and have a good time'" (Luke 15:20–24).

God loves us just like the father in the story loved his sons. He does not want to hold our sins against us. When we confess them to Him and come back to close relationship with Him, He feels like throwing us a big party too!

Dear God, thank You so much for Your amazing grace to forgive my sins. Thank You for celebrating me and loving me so much! Amen.

Day 220

BUBBLE UP!

A joyful heart is good medicine.
PROVERBS 17:22 ESV

Every once in a while, and the more often the better, everyone needs a good belly laugh that makes you giggle so hard you have tears coming out of the corners of your eyes and your tummy hurts! God wants you to have joy and good, happy thoughts! Especially when they are about Him! It's always okay to laugh and have fun because you have joy bubbling up inside you when you know that the source of all real joy is God Himself. Because you know He is your hope and salvation forever, you can always focus on that and feel happy, even if other things going on in your life are not so happy. First Peter 1:8–9 (NLT) says, "You love him even though you have never seen him. Though you do not see him now, you trust him; and you rejoice with a glorious, inexpressible joy. The reward for trusting him will be the salvation of your souls."

So don't ever stop having joy! Philippians 4:4 (NLT) says, "Always be full of joy in the Lord. I say it again—rejoice!" And no matter what's going on in your day, remember that "this is the day that the LORD has made; let us rejoice and be glad in it" (Psalm 118:24 ESV).

---

*Dear God, please fill me with Your supernatural
kind of joy all the time! Amen.*

Day 221

WISDOM WHEN SCHOOLWORK IS HARD

You should be happy when you have all kinds of tests.
You know these prove your faith. It helps you not to give up.
Learn well how to wait so you will be strong and complete and
in need of nothing. If you do not have wisdom, ask God for it.
JAMES 1:2–5

Have you ever struggled with a particular subject in school? Maybe when you were first learning fractions in math or different types of sentences in language arts? Life can feel so stressful when you're just not "getting it." In those times, pray for wisdom. Ask God to help you to continue to do your best and try your hardest while also being patient with yourself. Keep studying and practicing, and God might suddenly help you make the connections in your brain. Or He will lead you to the right tutor or friend who knows how to explain things in just the right way. The most important thing is not to give up. You might not understand *yet*, but eventually, with God's help, you will!

Dear God, please give me wisdom and understanding as I try to learn new and hard things. Help me not to give up until I've "got it"! Amen.

Day 222

GENTLE GIRL OF GRACE

Your gentleness made me great.
PSALM 18:35 ESV

When I was around your age, I had a cat that let me dress him up in baby clothes and put him in my doll stroller and push him around! How I loved that cat! Plus he would sit in the basket of my bike and ride as I pedaled lap after lap around our driveway.

Now, our dog Jasper lets Jodi, Lilly, and me dress him up in all kinds of costume clothes and hats. We have such good times taking funny pictures of him. Someday we might just have to make a calendar of all the hilarious photos.

People sometimes wonder how on earth we have a dog that is so patient and easygoing to let kids dress him up. Mainly it's about being gentle with him. He would never tolerate it if we treated him roughly while putting silly outfits on him!

Gentleness is important with our pets, and even more importantly, the Bible talks about gentleness toward people. Gentleness is a fruit of the Spirit (Galatians 5:22–23), and gentleness is necessary when telling others about our hope in Jesus and in having good relationships with others (Ephesians 4:2; 1 Peter 3:15; Proverbs 15:1). Ask God to help you be a gentle girl as He grows you in His grace.

*Dear God, please help me be gentle the way
Your Word teaches me to. Amen.*

Day 223

WISDOM TO REMEMBER WHEN

Moses said to the people, "Remember this day in which you went out of Egypt, out of the land where you were made to stay and work. For the Lord brought you out of this place by a powerful hand."
EXODUS 13:3

Sometimes we want to forget the bad things that have happened to us because they were awful and we're so glad they're over. But doing that isn't always wise. We do need to remember them in some ways so that we never forget how God helped us through them. Looking back and remembering grows our faith and helps us trust that God will always rescue us again in the future. Moses told the people of Israel to remember the amazing day that God finally brought them out of slavery in Egypt. Just as they did, we need to remember all the amazing ways God has delivered us from hard things too.

Dear God, every bit of help and rescue I have ever received ultimately comes from You, through so many ways and so many people! I don't ever want to forget, and I trust You to help and rescue me again and again! Amen.

PATIENCE AND PRAISE INSTEAD OF POUTING

Praise the LORD. Praise God in his sanctuary;
praise him in his mighty heavens. Praise him for his acts
of power; praise him for his surpassing greatness.
PSALM 150:1–2 NIV

I'm not so great at fixing very many things, but Jodi and Lilly's dad is. Their grandpa and papa are too. But sometimes when something breaks or needs a repair, we have to wait until Daddy, Grandpa, or Papa is home from work and available to help fix what's broken.

It's hard when a favorite toy breaks or your bike tire is flat and you can't do the things you planned to do. Waiting for a problem to be solved is usually no fun at all. Whatever you do, though, don't pout and complain. That never helps anything or anybody, and it will often just get you into trouble for a bad attitude. The Bible says, "Do everything without grumbling" (Philippians 2:14 NIV).

Instead, you can learn to praise God in the waiting times. Focus on the blessings that you do have. Praise God for how awesome He is and for all His goodness! Get creative in figuring out something good to do during the wait time. Show others that you can be pleasantly patient even when things aren't going your way. God often blesses that kind of attitude in a totally cool new way that you never even thought of!

Dear God, please help me to have a good attitude during
problems while I have to wait on the solutions. I want
to praise You and be patient while I wait. Amen.

Day 225

WISDOM FROM THE BOOK OF MALACHI

*The names of those who worshiped the Lord and honored
Him were written down before Him in a Book to be
remembered. "They will be Mine says the Lord of All,
on that day that I gather My special people."*
MALACHI 3:16–17

Malachi was a prophet of God who spoke a message to help bring
God's people back into close relationship with Him. God wants that
for us too. He is upset when we choose sin that hurts our relationship with Him, and He wants us to confess and turn away from it so
that we can be close with Him again. You know what that's like in
your own friendships. If you make a bad choice and hurt a friend's
feelings, the conflict you have caused makes it seem like you aren't
good friends at all. But when you ask forgiveness and your friend
forgives you, then you can get back to being BFFs again! Malachi
wanted to help God's people—and that includes you—to be even
closer than great BFFs with God!

---

*Dear God, thank You for the book of Malachi. Help me
as I read it and keep coming back to it in the future.
Teach me what You want me to learn from it to apply
to my life and to share with others. Amen.*

Day 226

NEVER FORGOTTEN

The LORD answered, "Could a mother forget a child who nurses at her breast? Could she fail to love an infant who came from her own body? Even if a mother could forget, I will never forget you."
ISAIAH 49:15 CEV

It's an awful feeling to be forgotten or left out. When life is really hard because of what you're going through, you might wonder if God has forgotten you. But the Bible promises that never happens. God never leaves you and constantly loves you, even if you can't always understand what He's doing or why He's not answering prayer the way you want Him to.

Isaiah 49:15 is talking about how difficult it would be for a good mom to forget a baby who is depending on her for everything. But if even she forgot, God would still never, ever forget. His love for you is greater and better than anyone else's love for you by far—and He doesn't make any mistakes.

Dear God, I know that You never forget me. You know and care about every single thing going on in my life. I trust You to help me deal with it in a good way! Amen.

BE READY FOR GOOD WORK

In a big house there are not only things made of gold and silver, but also of wood and clay. Some are of more use than others. Some are used every day. If a man lives a clean life, he will be like a dish made of gold. He will be respected and set apart for good use by the owner of the house. Turn away from the sinful things young people want to do. Go after what is right. Have a desire for faith and love and peace. Do this with those who pray to God from a clean heart.
2 TIMOTHY 2:20–22

This scripture helps you think about how you want God to use your life. Do you want to be just like regular everyday wood and clay, or do you want to be like shining gold used for the coolest purposes? With wisdom to live a clean life, as far away from sin as possible, God can use you for the very best things He has planned.

Dear God, please constantly show me what areas of my life need to be cleaned up. Help me to stay far away from things that are bad for me. I want You to use me in the wonderful ways You created me for. Amen.

Day 228

AMAZING HANDIWORK

*When I look at your heavens, the work of your fingers, the moon
and the stars, which you have set in place, what is man that you
are mindful of him, and the son of man that you care for him?*
PSALM 8:3–4 ESV

Not long ago, our family got to see the full moon rise up over the
ocean on a clear night. While we sat on the beach, we also saw
a shooting star. Wow! What a fascinating and beautiful sight! It's
mind-boggling to consider how God created such beauty in the
night sky! We will have so many cool things to learn when we spend
forever with Him in heaven!

As God grows you as His girl of grace, make it your habit to look
at the world around you both day and night and to praise Him when
you see such amazing, unexplainable things in nature. The world wants
you to praise science and research, and while those things are great
and much needed, always give credit to God for His amazing work!
He is the reason we have science to study!

---

*God, I praise You for all Your amazing creation in the skies.
Your handiwork is wonderful and beautiful! Amen.*

Day 229

WISDOM FROM CREATION

Men know about God. He has made it plain to them. Men cannot say they do not know about God. From the beginning of the world, men could see what God is like through the things He has made. This shows His power that lasts forever. It shows that He is God.
ROMANS 1:19–20

What are your favorite things about nature and science? My girls and I especially love spending time at the ocean and studying the sky at night. Do you know that we gain wisdom simply by looking around and appreciating nature and science and the whole beautiful world God created? God has shown Himself through everything He has made in creation. So no person can say they know nothing about God. Anyone can know that He is real by the tiny details of a pretty flower or in the highest peaks of a rocky mountain range. Anyone can see Him in the intricate ways our human bodies are designed and in the ways animals know how to hunt for their food or build themselves a home. Our creator God is awesome, and He deserves all of our worship and praise!

Dear God, I love looking at Your work in all the things You have made. Thank You for making Yourself known through Your amazing creation! Amen.

Day 230

SUPER COOL SCIENCE

*"Worthy are you, our Lord and God, to receive glory
and honor and power, for you created all things,
and by your will they existed and were created."*
REVELATION 4:11 ESV

It's incredible how scientists do experiments and study how things work and build and engineer machines and solve problems and cure diseases and injuries, and on and on! No doubt, science is super cool, and it's interesting how recently there's a great emphasis on encouraging more girls to be scientists, like with Goldieblox toys and television shows like *SciGirls* and *Project MC²*. Maybe you have dreams of being a scientist when you're all grown up!

I wonder how much better our scientific progress for healing illnesses and creating new things to help people in this world would be if more scientists gave credit to the one true God as the Creator of all science? There are some amazing Christian scientists doing great work today, but what do you think might happen if even more scientists respected God and studied His Word along with studying science in the world He created? What might He reveal to them, and what breakthroughs might there be? That's something to pray for and something to consider for your life too, if you love science!

---

*Dear God, I pray for more scientists to acknowledge
You as the Creator of all science, and I ask You to
work through them to help our world. Amen.*

WISDOM FROM THE BOOK OF MATTHEW

He said to them, "But who do you say that I am?" Simon Peter said, "You are the Christ, the Son of the living God." Jesus said to him, "Simon, son of Jonah, you are happy because you did not learn this from man. My Father in heaven has shown you this."
MATTHEW 16:15–17

The book of Matthew is the first book of the New Testament in the Bible. Four hundred years passed from the time between the last book in the Old Testament, Malachi, until the time of the book of Matthew. It's one of the four Gospels—books that tell about the arrival and life and ministry of Jesus Christ. He's the star because He was (and is!) the Messiah, which means "chosen one," whom the Jewish people were eagerly waiting for. He had been promised by the prophets of God. Jesus said, "Do not think that I have come to do away with the Law of Moses or the writings of the early preachers. I have not come to do away with them but to complete them" (Matthew 5:17).

Dear God, thank You for the book of Matthew. Help me as I read it and keep coming back to it in the future. Teach me what You want me to learn from it to apply to my life and to share with others. Amen.

LOVING ENEMIES

"You have heard the law that says, 'Love your neighbor' and hate your enemy. But I say, love your enemies! Pray for those who persecute you! In that way, you will be acting as true children of your Father in heaven. For he gives his sunlight to both the evil and the good, and he sends rain on the just and the unjust alike."
MATTHEW 5:43–45 NLT

Wow, Matthew 5:43–45 is not a fun scripture to read, right? It sure doesn't make you feel good. Anyone who thinks the Bible only has warm and fuzzy things to say to keep us comfortable doesn't know much at all about the Bible. It's hard to think of anything more *un*comfortable than showing love to and praying for people who don't like us and who mistreat us. And yet that's exactly what Jesus tells us to do in this scripture.

Is there someone who is being mean to you? Someone who lies about you and turns other people against you? Whatever the situation is, get help from a grown-up to make sure you're safe in a situation and start praying like crazy for the person mistreating you. Ask God to show you exactly how He wants you to show love. Proverbs 25:21–22 (NLT) gives some advice too: "If your enemies are hungry, give them food to eat. If they are thirsty, give them water to drink. You will heap burning coals of shame on their heads, and the LORD will reward you."

Dear God, it's way too hard on my own to love people who are mean to me. Please show me how and exactly what to do. I trust You! Amen.

Day 233

WISDOM ABOUT GOD'S PROTECTION

*At my first trial no one helped me. Everyone left me. I hope this
will not be held against them. But the Lord was with me. He gave
me power to preach the Good News so all the people who do
not know God might hear. I was taken from the mouth of the
lion. The Lord will look after me and will keep me from every
sinful plan they have. He will bring me safe into His holy nation
of heaven. May He have all the shining-greatness forever.*
2 Timothy 4:16–18

Maybe you've had times when you felt alone with no one to help you
or protect you. In those times, you can read and remember these
words that Paul wrote in the Bible. Even with no one else there to
help, God Himself was with Paul and protected him and gave him
power. And Paul trusted that God would keep away every bad plan
that people might have against him. Paul also knew that no matter
what happened on earth, God would someday bring him into heaven
forever. Paul wrote this in his letter to Timothy to give him wisdom
about God's protection, but all of it is true for you to trust today.

*Dear God, thank You for Your protection. I trust that no
matter what happens here in this world, You will ultimately
always keep me safe, because someday You are going to
bring me into perfect paradise in heaven with You! Amen.*

Day 234

SLOW DOWN

But you, O Lord, are a God of compassion and mercy, slow to get angry and filled with unfailing love and faithfulness.
Psalm 86:15 nlt

In the movie *Inside Out*, it's hilarious when the character Anger takes over. Usually his hot temper creates some kind of funny situation we can all relate to. But that's just a fiction story, and in real life, anger is not often very good for us. Anger is not always bad, but the Bible talks about being very slow to get angry. God is not quick to get angry, and if He were, we'd be in a lot of trouble! Imagine how upset He would constantly be with people and our many mistakes!

When you're in a situation that makes you mad, literally take a deep breath and count to ten or take a little walk or scream into your pillow for a minute. Ecclesiastes 7:9 (nlt) says, "Control your temper, for anger labels you a fool." And James 1:19–20 (niv) says, "Everyone should be quick to listen, slow to speak and slow to become angry, because human anger does not produce the righteousness that God desires."

As you work to control anger, think about mistakes you have made and be grateful that God has been slow to anger with you. Pray and thank God, and then let Him help you be slow to anger with others.

Dear God, it's really hard not to get too upset sometimes. Please help me to be like You in slowing down anger when I feel it rising up in me. Amen.

Day 235

WISDOM ABOUT STUFF

*"Do not gather together for yourself riches of this earth. They will
be eaten by bugs and become rusted. Men can break in and steal
them. Gather together riches in heaven where they will not be
eaten by bugs or become rusted. Men cannot break in and steal
them. For wherever your riches are, your heart will be there also."*
MATTHEW 6:19–21

We're always needing to sort through and get rid of stuff in our
house—the things we have that seem to pile up quickly, the things
we buy that we don't really need but want for fun. Maybe you have a
big collection of toys or stuffed animals or games or movies or extra
clothes. Or maybe you wish you did. Whatever the case, we all need
wisdom about this. Jesus taught us to be careful because we should
be storing up riches for ourselves in heaven, not on earth. We can't
take any of our stuff with us from earth to heaven, so we shouldn't
get too caught up in having it here on earth. And what does it mean
to gather riches in heaven? It means that God will be rewarding us
with blessings that last forever there based on the good things we
are doing to bring praise to Him here on earth.

---

*Dear God, please help me to have lots of wisdom about
stuff. Help me to want treasure in heaven much more than
any collection of treasures here on earth. Amen.*

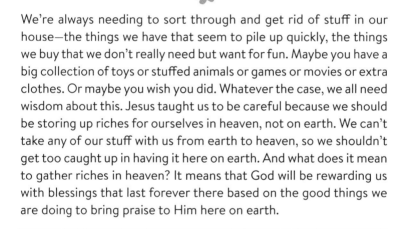

Day 236

LEARN GOD FIRST

Don't be impressed with your own wisdom.
Instead, fear the LORD and turn away from evil.
PROVERBS 3:7 NLT

I'm guessing you enjoy learning new things and telling others about what you've learned, even if you don't always love doing your schoolwork. But does Proverbs 3:7 mean a girl of grace gets a pass on ever doing lessons and homework and studying anything new? Sorry, but no! There's a healthy balance in fearing the Lord, which means respecting Him first, and letting true knowledge and wisdom result from your relationship with Him.

The Bible says in Proverbs 9:10 (NLT), "Fear of the LORD is the foundation of wisdom. Knowledge of the Holy One results in good judgment." God is the very beginning of all wisdom and knowledge. Respecting Him first is the only way to really know anything at all. It makes perfect sense that the source of learning about the world around us is the one who created it all in the first place! So rather than just being proud of yourself for learning new things, be thankful for new knowledge, proud of God for giving you the ability to learn, and grateful for who He is and what He has done!

God, You are the source for knowing and understanding anything about our world because You created it all! I praise You and thank You! Please help me grow in You first and gain my knowledge and wisdom from my relationship with You. Amen.

Day 237

WISDOM FROM THE BOOK OF MARK

"He came to care for others. He came to give His life so that many could be bought by His blood and be made free from sin."
Mark 10:45

Mark wrote the shortest of the four Gospels that tell about the life and ministry of Jesus. There are similarities and differences among all four of the Gospels because they are written by four different authors with four different personalities and perspectives. (If you and three friends wrote about the same topic, none of you would write it in exactly the same way, right? And that's a good thing! We learn more when multiple authors write about the same thing!) But the Gospels are similar in all the ways that matter most to tell us about the teaching and miracles and death and resurrection of Jesus and how He fulfilled what the prophets had preached in the Old Testament.

Dear God, thank You for the book of Mark. Help me as I read it and keep coming back to it in the future. Teach me what You want me to learn from it to apply to my life and to share with others. Amen.

A HEALTHY VIEW OF YOURSELF

*Don't think you are better than you really are.
Be honest in your evaluation of yourselves, measuring
yourselves by the faith God has given us.*
ROMANS 12:3 NLT

I hope you have amazing goals and dreams for your future, and I hope you look in the mirror and love the precious girl you see there—*you*! You are amazing and matter so much to God, no matter what you do! Our world talks a lot about pride in your own accomplishments and being a great and successful person. But the Bible talks very differently about how to view yourself. God doesn't ever want you to think you are worthless. He thinks you are so valuable that He sent His Son to die to save you, so obviously your worth is priceless! But a healthy perspective is to realize that *real* and lasting self-worth comes from your identity in Christ and the purposes He has created you for.

In this world, yes, it's possible to live without Jesus as Lord of your life, but no one can ever be truly fulfilled that way. They can make it look good from the outside, of course, but they will always be hollow inside without Jesus Christ. Ultimately, this world will seem like the briefest blink of an eye compared to eternity, and your value and status for eternity is based 100 percent on Jesus.

Dear God, help me to see myself as You do and do the things You have planned for me. I know You love me and value me more than anyone else ever does, ever has, ever will! Thank You! Amen.

WISDOM TO WANT GOOD CHARACTER

A good name is to be chosen instead of many riches. Favor is better than silver and gold. The rich and the poor meet together. The Lord is the maker of them all. A wise man sees sin and hides himself, but the foolish go on, and are punished for it. The reward for not having pride and having the fear of the Lord is riches, honor and life.

PROVERBS 22:1–4

A good name means a good reputation and good character, and it takes wisdom to want that for yourself. When people hear your name, do you want them to think of you in good ways or bad ways? Do you want to be known for things like laziness or lying or rudeness or getting into trouble? Or do you want to be known for things like doing your best and being honest, fair, kind, and worthy of respect? Choose now while you are young to do your very best to have excellent character your whole life. It doesn't mean you will always be perfect, but it means you will live for God and obey His ways of love and fairness and honesty—and you will quickly want to make things right when you make a mistake and do wrong.

Dear God, I want to be known for good character and a good name because I obey You. Please give me wisdom and keep me on the right paths following You. Amen.

TREASURE TROVE

Fear God and obey his commands, for this is everyone's
duty. God will judge us for everything we do, including
every secret thing, whether good or bad.
ECCLESIASTES 12:13–14 NLT

No matter what your dream job is for the future, God has already given you a job for every day of your life. It doesn't pay in dollars and cents here on earth, but it's building up a treasure trove of blessings waiting in heaven for you. And who doesn't want their own treasure trove, right?

Our job and purpose in life is the fear of (or respect for) God and obedience to His commandments. This is "everyone's duty," says Solomon in the book of Ecclesiastes. The Bible has the simple yet profound and perfect answer to all of life's questions—the *only* answer that can ever genuinely fulfill, if only people will believe it and test it! Yet so many people try *anything but* the Bible for answers; they keep trying and working—and coming up empty.

The only really satisfying job you can ever find is to do what your Creator intended specifically for you, to obey Him in what He has designed and prepared. Ephesians 2:10 (NIV) says, "For we are God's handiwork, created in Christ Jesus to do good works, which God prepared in advance for us to do."

Dear God, please help me to respect You and Your commandments
and to obey them. I need Your good guidance to show me all
the good things You have planned for me to do! Amen.

Day 241

WISDOM FROM THE BOOK OF LUKE

Many people have written about the things that have happened among us. Those who saw everything. . .and helped teach the Good News have passed these things on to us. . . . I have decided it would be good to write them to you one after the other the way they happened. Then you can be sure you know the truth about the things you have been taught.

LUKE 1:1–4

The Gospel that Luke wrote tells us the most about Jesus' parents and His birth and childhood. It gives us the most detail for our Christmas celebrations of Jesus. Luke wrote to show how Jesus was both human like us but also fully God and totally perfect without sin. Jesus was the only one who could pay the price of sin for us by dying on the cross. And because He took our sin on Himself, He made a way for us to have a good relationship with God. Luke wanted to make sure that everyone reading his Gospel understood that any person at all, no matter who they are or where they come from, could accept Jesus Christ as Savior and have a relationship with God and forever life in heaven.

Dear God, thank You for the book of Luke. Help me as I read it and keep coming back to it in the future. Teach me what You want me to learn from it to apply to my life and to share with others. Amen.

Day 242

OBEY AND BE BLESSED

"If you are willing and obedient, you will eat the good things of the land."
Isaiah 1:19 niv

The Bible promises that obedience equals blessings. That sounds like a great math equation! Think about the verse above and also these:

- "Blessed are those who fear the Lord, who find great delight in his commands. Their children will be mighty in the land; the generation of the upright will be blessed. Wealth and riches are in their houses, and their righteousness endures forever" (Psalm 112:1–3 niv).

- "When the Lord takes pleasure in anyone's way, he causes their enemies to make peace with them" (Proverbs 16:7 niv).

The thing is, sometimes the world's idea of blessings confuses believers. Obeying God does not mean total riches and fun and constant good health and always happy times here on earth. It certainly can mean those things, but ultimately it means all these things and more in your *eternal* awesome home that God is creating.

It also means God's guidance and peace for any hard thing here in this sinful world as you obey His commands, no matter the circumstances or temptations to ignore them. Obedience to God means His constant, loving presence in your life. "Those who obey God's commandments remain in fellowship with him, and he with them," says 1 John 3:24 (nlt).

Dear God, please help me to obey You the best I can in all situations. Amen.

Day 243

WISDOM ABOUT WORSHIP

Call out with joy to the Lord, all the earth. Be glad as you serve the Lord. Come before Him with songs of joy. Know that the Lord is God. It is He Who made us, and not we ourselves. We are His people and the sheep of His field. Go into His gates giving thanks and into His holy place with praise. Give thanks to Him. Honor His name. For the Lord is good. His loving-kindness lasts forever. And He is faithful to all people and to all their children-to-come.

PSALM 100

Do you have favorite worship songs you love to sing at church? We hope you sing them all throughout the week too! Sometimes we forget how important it is to sing to God every day, but the psalms are so good to remind us. When we sing praise songs to God, we put our focus where it needs to be—on God!—with beautiful music and words reminding us of His awesome character and love and power.

Dear God, please help me to remember to sing to You every day, no matter what I'm going through. I know songs of praise to You can fill me with joy and peace because of focusing on how awesome You are and how much You love me. Amen.

Day 244

REAL-DEAL SERVANT OF GOD

For God is working in you, giving you the desire
and the power to do what pleases him.
PHILIPPIANS 2:13 NLT

Have you ever had a classmate in school who acts perfectly obedient and sweet in front of the teacher, but whenever Teacher turns away or it's time for recess, this classmate is mean and breaks every rule but just sneakily keeps out of trouble?

God doesn't want the kind of obedience that is just for show or for selfish rewards. He wants obedience that comes from a willing heart—a heart that loves Him and His Word and wants to produce the good fruit He has planned for those who follow Him. He wants obedience that is looking to please Him alone, no matter what people around you think or say.

A question to ask yourself regularly as God grows you to be a girl of grace is the one Paul asks in Galatians: "Am I now trying to win the approval of human beings, or of God? Or am I trying to please people? If I were still trying to please people, I would not be a servant of Christ" (Galatians 1:10 NIV).

Be a real-deal servant of Christ first of all, and then let Him help you serve others as He directs.

Dear God, I want to please You above all, no matter
what. I want to be a real-deal servant of You! Amen.

Day 245

WISDOM FROM THE BOOK OF JOHN

*These are written so you may believe that Jesus is the
Christ, the Son of God. When you put your trust in Him,
you will have life that lasts forever through His name.*
JOHN 20:31

The book of John is the last of the four Gospels about the life and ministry of Jesus. The book of John doesn't give any detail at all about Jesus' life as a child, but it focuses a lot on the final days of Jesus' life on earth. Over half of the book is about the events and Jesus' teaching during His last week on earth. Some of His last earthly words to His disciples were "Do not let your heart be troubled. You have put your trust in God, put your trust in Me also. There are many rooms in My Father's house. If it were not so, I would have told you. I am going away to make a place for you. After I go and make a place for you, I will come back and take you with Me" (John 14:1–3). These words are meant to encourage us today too!

Dear God, thank You for the book of John. Help me as I read it and keep coming back to it in the future. Teach me what You want me to learn from it to apply to my life and to share with others. Amen.

FAMILY FEUDS

*A wise woman builds her home, but a foolish
woman tears it down with her own hands.*
PROVERBS 14:1 NLT

No one ever fights in our house! Ha! Just kidding. We absolutely fight and yell and stomp and slam doors sometimes. We're not proud of that, but we all know that families have their stressful times. Family feuds are impossible to avoid. The people you're related to and spend the most time with are bound to get on your nerves, and you'll drive them crazy sometimes too! It's just part of being a family. But with God's grace, family members can always work through the conflicts and never give up on one another. First Timothy 5:8 (NLT) makes it clear that Christian families are meant to take care of one another when it says, "But those who won't care for their relatives, especially those in their own household, have denied the true faith. Such people are worse than unbelievers."

Sure it can be hard, but Romans 12:15-18 (NLT) offers some good advice for keeping peace and keeping families together: "Be happy with those who are happy, and weep with those who weep. Live in harmony with each other. Don't be too proud to enjoy the company of ordinary people. And don't think you know it all! Never pay back evil with more evil. Do things in such a way that everyone can see you are honorable. Do all that you can to live in peace with everyone."

---

*Dear God, please help me to work out conflicts
among family members quickly. I know You want
us to take good care of one another. Amen.*

Day 247

REST WELL, PART 1

*On the seventh day God ended His work which He had done.
And He rested on the seventh day from all His work which He
had done. Then God honored the seventh day and made it holy,
because in it He rested from all His work which He had done.*
GENESIS 2:2–3

You might feel annoyed by your parents setting bedtimes and always trying to make sure you get enough sleep. *What's the big deal?* you might think. But getting enough rest really is a big deal. God thought it was such a big deal, He set aside an entire day of the week for it! So you should actually feel super grateful to God and to your parents for caring so much about you that they want you to rest. It's good for your physical health in many ways, and it's good for your spiritual health too. God intends rest for both actual sleeping and for time simply spent with Him, relaxing while you focus on how great He is and how much He loves you!

---

*Dear God, please help me to be thankful for rest
time rather than annoyed by it. You designed it,
and it's so good for me. Thank You! Amen.*

REST WELL, PART 2

"Come to Me, all of you who work and have heavy loads. I will give you rest. Follow My teachings and learn from Me. I am gentle and do not have pride. You will have rest for your souls. For My way of carrying a load is easy and My load is not heavy."
MATTHEW 11:28–30

Let these scriptures help you learn even more about how important good rest is to God. He doesn't want you to be constantly busy and stressed and exhausted. He wants you to be full of His peace, and for that you need plenty of actual sleep and plenty of time spent learning from Him, worshipping Him, and praying to Him.

- "The followers of Jesus came back to Him. They told Jesus all they had done and taught. He said to them, 'Come away from the people. Be by yourselves and rest' " (Mark 6:30–31).

- "Be quiet and know that I am God. I will be honored among the nations. I will be honored in the earth. The Lord of All is with us. The God of Jacob is our strong place" (Psalm 46:10–11).

Dear God, please help these verses stick in my mind forever to remind me of how important it is to rest well and especially to rest in You! Amen.

Day 249

FOR YOUR OWN GOOD

Praise the LORD! Blessed is the man who fears the LORD,
who greatly delights in his commandments!
PSALM 112:1 ESV

Obedience and *discipline* are probably not words that make you want to do a happy dance, but a girl of grace knows that when done right, they are for her own good. We first learn to obey our parents, and then we learn that ultimately we are to obey God. And God is not a killjoy just trying to ruin all the fun! The commands He wants us to obey are never just to rain on our parades and stop our joy. He longs for us to obey Him so that He can protect us from sin in the world plus let us receive many blessings. First John 5:3 (ESV) says, "For this is the love of God, that we keep his commandments. And his commandments are not burdensome."

And we need discipline to get us back on track when we don't obey, so that we'll remember why we need to obey in the first place. Proverbs 3:11–12 (NLT) says, "My child, don't reject the LORD's discipline, and don't be upset when he corrects you. For the LORD corrects those he loves, just as a father corrects a child in whom he delights."

Dear God, please help me to obey You in all things and
to appreciate discipline when I need it. I know that You
love me and just want what is best for me. Amen.

Day 250

WISDOM FROM THE BOOK OF ACTS

"You will receive power when the Holy Spirit comes into your life. You will tell about Me in the city of Jerusalem and over all the countries of Judea and Samaria and to the ends of the earth."

ACTS 1:8

At the end of the Gospels, Jesus had risen from the dead and appeared to various people to prove that He was alive. The book of Acts picks up right where the Gospel of Luke left off (and is written by the same doctor, Luke!) and soon Jesus went up to heaven to be with God the Father. But He didn't want to leave people alone without Him on earth. He promised to send the Holy Spirit in His place. The book of Acts tells about how that promise came true and how the group of believers in Jesus, called the *church*, started out with 120 people and then grew and grew and grew as those believers kept spreading the good news about our Savior Jesus and more and more people believed in Him.

Dear God, thank You for the book of Acts. Help me as I read it and keep coming back to it in the future. Teach me what You want me to learn from it to apply to my life and to share with others. Amen.

Day 251

BE CHILDISH

*When Jesus saw what was happening, he was angry
with his disciples. He said to them, "Let the children
come to me. Don't stop them! For the Kingdom of God
belongs to those who are like these children."*
MARK 10:14 NLT

Maybe you don't like being called a child because it makes you feel immature. Or you just can't wait to be a grown-up and make your own decisions. Of course growing in wisdom and maturity is a good thing, but don't ever let people make you feel bad or useless for being young. A real sign of maturity is being confident in the age you are and the abilities you have that come with that age. Trying to act older than your actual age totally backfires because those who are mature can recognize that kind of behavior as a sure sign of immaturity.

Consider what the Bible says about kids and being young. In Mark 10:14, Jesus was unhappy with the disciples for keeping kids away from them and said the kingdom of God belongs to those who have faith like children. Also, Matthew 18:10 (NLT) says, "Beware that you don't look down on any of these little ones. For I tell you that in heaven their angels are always in the presence of my heavenly Father." And 1 Timothy 4:12 (NLT) says, "Don't let anyone think less of you because you are young. Be an example to all believers in what you say, in the way you live, in your love, your faith, and your purity."

---

*Dear God, You love children and young people and want to grow
us and bless us in Your wisdom and love. Thank You! Amen.*

LOOKING UP TO OTHERS, PART 1

*The one who says he belongs to Christ should
live the same kind of life Christ lived.*
1 JOHN 2:6

Think of your favorite famous people. Are they athletes, actors, artists, and/or musicians? What are all the things you know about them, and why are you their fan? Have you been to their games or concerts or shows? All of that is so fun when we also use wisdom about celebrities as we look up to them. We should never become so obsessed with them to the point we practically worship them. They are never perfect, and we must never forget that. Jesus is the one and only perfect famous person, and He alone should be worshipped. Only He should be the one we try to live like.

Dear God, help me to have wisdom about looking up to famous people. I want Jesus to be my first and favorite person I look up to. I want to worship Him alone and live my life like Him. Amen.

Day 253

LOOKING UP TO OTHERS, PART 2

Follow my way of thinking as I follow Christ.
1 CORINTHIANS 11:1

Far more important than having celebrities you look up to is having mentors you look up to. These are people who have lived longer than you who can help you through the stages of life ahead since they have already been there, done that. Your parents are naturally your mentors, and sometimes a great mentor can be an older sibling or grandparent or cousin or aunt or uncle. Or you can find a mentor among older friends you know through your church or activities or community. They should definitely be people who love and follow Jesus so that they teach you more about loving and following Him too. Odds are, you will never build a relationship with a famous celebrity, but you can definitely build a relationship with great personal mentors who will be far more valuable to you. They can actually be a part of your life to help you learn and grow.

Dear God, please send me the right mentors into my life who love You and who will help teach and guide me to live like Jesus. Thank You! Amen.

Day 254

GIVE AND TAKE

*And he said, "Naked I came from my mother's womb,
and naked shall I return. The Lord gave, and the Lord
has taken away; blessed be the name of the Lord."*

Job 1:21 esv

I love the contemporary worship song called "Blessed Be Your Name." It's based on Job 1:21.

You've likely heard the story about Job. What a roller coaster his life was of blessings and then total loss and despair and finally blessings again. Through it all, he was faithful to God. Job had no "entitlement" problems like we hear of people having today. Some people these days feel like they're guaranteed certain blessings and opportunities in life. But Job knew that every person comes into the world with absolutely nothing, with no guarantees of what this life will be like, and with no way to take anything from this world into eternity. God alone is all-powerful, and He gives and takes away. We can choose to ignore or be angry with Him, or we can lean in close to Him and get to know Him better through His Word and His Spirit and praise Him through the times of both blessing and loss.

As God grows you to be a girl of grace, you will experience both good times and hard times. Choose to praise God in all things, no matter how difficult that might be, and then patiently wait while He changes you and makes His plans to bless you unimaginably for eternity.

Dear God, even when life is hard, I want to praise Your name! Amen.

Day 255

BE A WISE YOUNG LEADER

*In all things show them how to live by your life and by right teaching.
You should be wise in what you say. Then the one who is against you
will be ashamed and will not be able to say anything bad about you.*
Titus 2:7–8

Even while you're young, you can be a leader to others. At school, at church, in your community, and in your activities, there will always be younger kids who look up to you. Ask God to help you find opportunities to lead and mentor them intentionally. Maybe you can be a helper in a Sunday school class or at VBS or in a dance class or with a sports team. And you can simply show the younger kids in your life how much you care about them and want to get to know them. As you build friendships with kids younger than you, you can become a great mentor to them as you keep following Jesus and they look up to and follow you.

---

*Dear God, as I look up to and follow good and wise leaders
and mentors who love You, help me to be a good leader
and mentor to others too. Show me the people You want
me to help and grow me in wisdom to lead well. Amen.*

KNOWING GOD'S WILL

Always be joyful. Never stop praying.
Be thankful in all circumstances, for this is God's
will for you who belong to Christ Jesus.
1 THESSALONIANS 5:16–18 NLT

"I'm just not sure what God's will is." Maybe you've heard other Christians say this, and maybe you've said it yourself. Well, 1 Thessalonians 5:16–18 tells you what God's will is in every kind of situation. He wants you to have joy. He wants you to keep praying. He wants you to be thankful. Sounds simple, right? Well, sure, unless your situation is a really tough one—and who can avoid tough situations? We all struggle with all kinds of things, with all kinds of heartache and difficulty—and in those awful situations 1 Thessalonians 5:16–18 is sure a lot easier said than done.

Like anything you want to be great at, doing God's will takes practice. Again and again you must choose joy in your bad situation, remembering that real joy is not based on your circumstances but on the fact that God is with you and loves you. Choose to keep praying about every single thing, no matter how big or small, because the Bible says to cast ALL your anxiety on Him. And choose to give thanks for each of your blessings, listing them in your conversations with God.

Dear God, help me to remember that Your Word shows
me Your will for me in all things. Help me to constantly
have joy, talk to You, and give You thanks. Amen.

Day 257

WISDOM FROM THE BOOK OF ROMANS

Jesus died for our sins. He was raised from the dead to make us right with God. Now that we have been made right with God by putting our trust in Him, we have peace with Him. It is because of what our Lord Jesus Christ did for us.
ROMANS 4:25–5:1

The book of Romans is the first in a series of books that are kind of like reading someone else's mail. You should never do that without permission, but you absolutely have permission to read the letters (or *epistles* as they're sometimes called, which is just a fancy name for letters) included in the Bible. God wants you to read and learn from them. The book of Romans was a letter written by the apostle (that's another fancy word that means a follower of Jesus) Paul. The story of how his life was totally transformed by Jesus is in Acts. Paul wrote to the group of believers in the city of Rome to explain to them fully what it means to have salvation by trusting in Jesus as the sacrifice for sin.

Dear God, thank You for the book of Romans. Help me as I read it and keep coming back to it in the future. Teach me what You want me to learn from it to apply to my life and to share with others. Amen.

Day 258

WIDE, HIGH, LONG, DEEP

*And may you have the power to understand, as all God's
people should, how wide, how long, how high, and how deep
his love is. May you experience the love of Christ, though it is
too great to understand fully. Then you will be made complete
with all the fullness of life and power that comes from God.*
EPHESIANS 3:18–19 NLT

Do you ever have days when you just don't feel very lovable? Days
when you feel sure that God just might give up on you because
you keep making the same kinds of mistakes over and over? I do.
It's on those days that Ephesians 3:18–19 is so encouraging to me,
and I hope it is for you too. In it, the author Paul, inspired by God, is
praying for believers to realize how wide, long, high, and deep God's
love is for us. It's a love that is far too great to understand fully, but
that doesn't mean we shouldn't try! God wants us to keep talking
to Him and spending time hearing from Him in His Word to better
understand His love every single day.

God's love reaches so much farther than any distance or measure
we can imagine, even past our doubts that make us wonder if there
is a time that God might finally get fed up and stop loving us—never!
He will *never* do that. God loves you unconditionally, even on the
days you feel most unlovable!

*Dear God, help me, each and every day, to understand more about
Your great love for me. I'm so grateful for Your endless love! Amen.*

Day 259

WISDOM FOR TOUGH SCHOOL DAYS

*Open your heart to teaching, and your
ears to words of much learning.*
PROVERBS 23:12

Throughout your school years, you're going to have some teachers who are a lot of fun and easy to learn from, and some who totally aren't. Maybe right now you can think of a particular teacher who is just so hard to be in class with. Maybe his or her rules and assignments seem over-the-top too much and very frustrating. But if the teacher is just strict and tough, you might be able to learn a whole lot if you simply cooperate and show respect. God cares about your situation. Pray for wisdom and ask God to help things get better in class. Let Him show you how to communicate with the teacher well as you do your best in a tough situation.

---

*Dear God, please help me make it through this class
[or this school year] with [name of teacher]. Help me to
do my best and show respect, even when I don't feel like
it. Please help things to get better and make me stronger
and wiser because of this tough situation. Amen.*

WILLING TO WORK

Work willingly at whatever you do, as though you were
working for the Lord rather than for people.
COLOSSIANS 3:23 NLT

One of my favorite memories of fifth grade is that I got to work in the school cafeteria. It was considered a privilege and a reward to get asked to work there. And it was so much fun, plus we earned a free lunch that day. We left class a little early, and the teacher trusted that we'd make up any work that we missed. We got to help serve food or put silverware on each tray, and when everyone was done, we sometimes helped wash trays. My favorite task was scooping corn, and something about our school cafeteria corn was so much better than any corn I've ever tasted elsewhere!

Our world is changing quite a bit. Too many people seem to be forgetting that the ability to work is a good thing, a blessing! Did you know that every little thing you do, even if it's just scooping out corn onto a cafeteria tray, can be a way to worship God? It is when you do it with a good attitude, as if God is your boss—because He is! He's the best boss ever who loves and wants to bless you like no other.

Dear God, help me to remember that the ability to work is a blessing and that every act of work I do can be a form of praise to You! Amen.

Day 261

WISDOM FROM THE BOOKS OF 1 AND 2 CORINTHIANS

This letter is from Paul. I have been chosen by God to be a missionary of Jesus Christ. Sosthenes, a Christian brother, writes also. I write to God's church in the city of Corinth. I write to those who belong to Christ Jesus and to those who are set apart by Him and made holy. I write to all the Christians everywhere who call on the name of Jesus Christ. He is our Lord and their Lord also. May you have loving-favor and peace from God our Father and from the Lord Jesus Christ.

1 CORINTHIANS 1:1–3

The books of 1 and 2 Corinthians are more letters from the apostle Paul, this time to a church in the city of Corinth in Greece. Paul had heard that the Christians in the Corinthian church were not living as they should or treating each other as well as they should. His letters were meant to correct their wrongs and encourage them to do right, according to God's good ways. We can read these letters and let them help us correct our wrongs and do what is right according to God's good ways too!

Dear God, thank You for the books of 1 and 2 Corinthians. Help me as I read them and keep coming back to them in the future. Teach me what You want me to learn from them to apply to my life and to share with others. Amen.

Day 262

PICK UP!

"Call to me and I will answer you."
JEREMIAH 33:3 ESV

Have you ever really wanted to talk to a particular person, but their phone just kept ringing and they didn't pick up? When Jodi and Lilly spent the night at their grandparents' recently, they tried to call me to say good night, but I didn't realize my phone was turned off, and we were all sad that we didn't get the chance to say good night to one another.

It's frustrating when we can't get through to someone we're trying to communicate with. Thankfully, we never have to beg God to "pick up!" and hear our requests. Through the Holy Spirit, God is listening to us all the time, every moment! God's Word encourages us to "pray in the Spirit at all times and on every occasion. Stay alert and be persistent in your prayers for all believers everywhere" (Ephesians 6:18 NLT). And even when we're not sure what to pray, that's totally okay because "the Holy Spirit helps us in our weakness. For example, we don't know what God wants us to pray for. But the Holy Spirit prays for us with groanings that cannot be expressed in words" (Romans 8:26 NLT).

Dear Lord, remind me that You constantly hear me, You constantly want me to tell You my thoughts, and You constantly want to help with my needs and the needs of others. Thank You! Amen.

Day 263

WISDOM ABOUT ENDURANCE

We are pressed on every side, but we still have room to move. We are often in much trouble, but we never give up. People make it hard for us, but we are not left alone. We are knocked down, but we are not destroyed.
2 CORINTHIANS 4:8–9

Endurance means not to give up but to keep on going even when things are hard. Think of a time when you've needed great endurance. Maybe during a sport or activity like cross country or dance. Or maybe during a really hard test at school when you felt super stressed and wanted to give up but didn't. The Bible talks about how we will sometimes have so much trouble in our lives that it feels like we are almost totally defeated. But God will always help us have just enough new strength and energy not to give up. He will hold us up and keep us going!

Dear God, I trust that You keep giving me more strength and energy and endurance exactly when I feel like giving up. I never have to give up when I know You are helping me! Amen.

Day 264

POWERFUL AND EFFECTIVE

The prayer of a righteous person is powerful and effective.
JAMES 5:16 NIV

You never have to read this verse and think, *Well, I'm not good enough and I don't have the best behavior all the time, so there's no way my prayer is powerful and effective.* If you have asked Jesus Christ to remove your sin and be your Savior, then you are a righteous person. Anyone who has accepted Jesus has become perfect in God's sight, because Jesus paid the cost for our sin when He died on the cross.

So keep in mind every single time you pray that you are doing something powerful and effective like the Bible promises! Believe it! Then make a habit of constantly praying to God about all things, and watch what God does in your life and the lives of those you're praying for!

These verses on prayer will help motivate you to trust in the power of prayer more too:

* "The righteous cry out, and the LORD hears them; he delivers them from all their troubles" (Psalm 34:17 NIV).

* "And we are confident that he hears us whenever we ask for anything that pleases him. And since we know he hears us when we make our requests, we also know that he will give us what we ask for" (1 John 5:14–15 NLT).

Dear God, please remind me all the time how much You want to hear from me in prayer. Help me to trust how powerful and effective prayer is! Amen.

Day 265

WiSDOM FROM THE
BOOK OF GALATIANS

Christ made us free. Stay that way. Do not get chained all over again in the Law and its kind of religious worship.
GALATIANS 5:1

Think of the book of Galatians a little bit like the Fourth of July in the United States—a celebration of freedom! Paul wrote this letter to the churches in Galatia to correct them because he was upset that many people there were listening to some false teachers who taught that salvation in Jesus meant to believe in Him plus follow lots of Jewish customs and rules. But that's not true. Salvation in Jesus comes simply from believing in Him and accepting His gift of grace to pay for sin. Unmatched freedom and relief come from trusting that truth and realizing it's Jesus' work of dying on the cross that saves us and gives us eternal life, not any work we do or rules we follow. We should want to share that truth with *all* people so that they can have everlasting freedom in Jesus too!

Dear God, thank You for the book of Galatians. Help me as I read it and keep coming back to it in the future. Teach me what You want me to learn from it to apply to my life and to share with others. Amen.

Day 266

WISDOM, NOT WAVES

Blessed is the one who finds wisdom,
and the one who gets understanding.
PROVERBS 3:13 ESV

We think boogie boarding on calm waves is super fun, but bouncing around endlessly on really rough waves? Probably not so much. It must be so scary (and nauseating!) to be completely unsteady and tossed by wind and rough waters. God doesn't want your life to be like a turbulent ride on rough waves, either. You just need to ask God for His wisdom, trust that He gives it generously, and then believe in it! He is ready and willing to make your journey through life steady and sure. That doesn't mean you won't ever have hard times, but your life will always be anchored in Him, giving you stability even when everything in the world around you is chaotic and scary. James 1:5–8 (NLT) says, "If you need wisdom, ask our generous God, and he will give it to you. He will not rebuke you for asking. But when you ask him, be sure that your faith is in God alone. Do not waver, for a person with divided loyalty is as unsettled as a wave of the sea that is blown and tossed by the wind. Such people should not expect to receive anything from the Lord. Their loyalty is divided between God and the world, and they are unstable in everything they do."

Dear God, I need Your wisdom in all things. I know You give
it generously. I want to be loyal to You! Please give me more
wisdom each day, and keep me stable in You. Amen.

Day 267

DON'T COMPLAIN

*God is helping you obey Him. God is doing what He wants
done in you. Be glad you can do the things you should be doing.
Do all things without arguing and talking about how you wish you
did not have to do them. In that way, you can prove yourselves
to be without blame. You are God's children and no one can
talk against you, even in a sin-loving and sin-sick world. You
are to shine as lights among the sinful people of this world.*
PHILIPPIANS 2:13–15

Doing all things without ever arguing or complaining, like the Bible
tells us to do, can be super hard. Everyone struggles with this
sometimes. So we sure need God's help and wisdom about why it's
so good to obey this. If we can keep positive with our words and
attitudes as we obey God and follow the plans He has for us, we
shine as bright lights to the sinful world around us. And hopefully
people who do not trust Jesus as their Savior will want to know more
about God's love because they see our lights shining.

---

*Dear God, please help me to be a bright light in the darkness
of sin around me in this world. I want to shine so brightly
that others might know Jesus as Savior too. Amen.*

Day 268

THE RIGHT KIND OF LOVE

God is love.
1 JOHN 4:8 ESV

God is love, and He wants those of us who love and serve Him to share Him with others so they will want a relationship with Him too.

First Corinthians 13:1-8 (CEV) is a popular passage to teach us about love. Read it again, and read it regularly to help you know how important love is and how to share it with the people God has placed in your life: "What if I could speak all languages of humans and of angels? If I did not love others, I would be nothing more than a noisy gong or a clanging cymbal. What if I could prophesy and understand all secrets and all knowledge? And what if I had faith that moved mountains? I would be nothing, unless I loved others. What if I gave away all that I owned and let myself be burned alive? I would gain nothing, unless I loved others. Love is patient and kind, never jealous, boastful, proud, or rude. Love isn't selfish or quick tempered. It doesn't keep a record of wrongs that others do. Love rejoices in the truth, but not in evil. Love is always supportive, loyal, hopeful, and trusting. Love never fails!"

Dear God, help me to read and remember this scripture regularly and try my best to love others like You love. Amen.

Day 269

WISDOM FROM THE BOOK OF EPHESIANS

Let us honor and thank the God and Father of our Lord Jesus Christ.
He has already given us a taste of what heaven is like. Even before
the world was made, God chose us for Himself because of His love.
EPHESIANS 1:3–4

The book of Ephesians is Paul's letter to the church in the city of Ephesus. You can think of it with a big letter *E*, like the first letter in its name, and the letter *e* in the beginning of the word *encouragement*. Because mostly that's what Paul does in this letter. He is not trying to right a specific wrong in the church at Ephesus; he simply wants to encourage the believers there in their faith and identity in Jesus and show them how that faith and identity should play out in their daily lives. You can read Ephesians for encouragement in your life too!

Dear God, thank You for the book of Ephesians.
Help me as I read it and keep coming back to it in the
future. Teach me what You want me to learn from it to
apply to my life and to share with others. Amen.

Day 270

MEMORY WORK

Everything in the Scriptures is God's Word. All of it is useful for teaching and helping people and for correcting them and showing them how to live. The Scriptures train God's servants to do all kinds of good deeds.

2 TIMOTHY 3:16–17 CEV

I hope you like to memorize Bible verses. It's a practice that's so incredibly valuable for your faith and relationship with God—and for sharing your hope in Jesus with others too. I spent several years in middle school and high school on a Bible Quiz team and learned bunches of scripture. I've been amazed through my adult life how those verses pop into my mind just when I need them. I often don't even remember that I had memorized them until all of a sudden there they are in my brain! It's so cool how God works that way to bring truth from His Word to mind exactly at the right moment.

Psalm 119:10–11 (NIV) says, "I seek you with all my heart; do not let me stray from your commands. I have hidden your word in my heart that I might not sin against you." That's another reason to memorize scripture and hide it in your heart—it helps to keep you from sinning against God. Remembering His truth and His commands helps you avoid bad choices.

If you don't already, start now writing down scriptures and posting them in places where you'll be reminded of them and practice them. Hide God's Word in your heart, and then see how He uses it in your life! You will not be disappointed!

Dear God, I want to study and memorize Your Word to help me live my life the best way possible. Amen.

Day 271

BE WISE ABOUT
CONFESSING YOUR SIN

If we say that we have no sin, we lie to ourselves and the truth is not in us. If we tell Him our sins, He is faithful and we can depend on Him to forgive us of our sins. He will make our lives clean from all sin.

1 JOHN 1:8–9

It's not fun to talk about the bad things we've done, but we need to tell them to God. To pretend like we don't sin is silly, because God knows all about our sins anyway. He sees and knows everything about us, even every single thought we have. So we all must take time to pray and confess and ask forgiveness for our sins rather than try to hide them or act like they're no big deal. A soon as we do confess our sins, God cleans us up and takes the sin as far from us as the east is from the west (Psalm 103:12). That's so awesome! He loves us very much and never wants to hold our sins against us.

Dear God, I confess these sins to You today: [name sins]. And I ask for Your forgiveness. Thank You for being such a forgiving and good God who gives me endless grace and love! Amen.

RESURRECTION

"He isn't here! He is risen from the dead!"
Luke 24:6 NLT

At Easter time, I hope you get a basket full of chocolate and treats and maybe even get to hunt around for eggs. It's just so much fun to celebrate, especially when you know the real reason for any springtime holiday celebration is that Jesus died but ROSE AGAIN!

There are plenty of other religions that people follow in this world, but only Christianity is worth believing in because only Christianity worships and spreads the good news of a Savior who died but came back to life, with eyewitnesses to verify His resurrection.

His resurrection is what makes our faith have any purpose and strength. Even Paul said in 1 Corinthians 15, "Unless Christ was raised to life, your faith is useless. . . . If our hope in Christ is good only for this life, we are worse off than anyone else. But Christ has been raised to life! And he makes us certain that others will also be raised to life" (vv. 17, 19–20 CEV).

Your faith in Jesus is not useless because God raised Him from the dead, and your studying and following God's Word and keeping a relationship with God through Jesus is the best thing you can possibly do with your life! You are preparing here in this world for an awesome eternity in heaven!

---

*Dear Jesus, I believe You rose from the dead,
and I praise You! My salvation and faith in You are
the very best things about my life. Amen.*

Day 273

WISDOM FROM THE
BOOK OF PHILIPPIANS

*Be full of joy always because you belong to
the Lord. Again I say, be full of joy!*
PHILIPPIANS 4:4

Another book of the Bible to go to for encouragement is the book of Philippians. Paul wrote this letter to the church in the city of Philippi, and it's known as his letter of joy. The word *joy* is used over and over throughout the letter. The believers there had encouraged Paul and given him great joy, and he wanted to write to show them how much he appreciated them. He also wanted to remind them how real joy always depends on Jesus. As believers in Jesus, we can have joy even during times of suffering because we have faith and hope in Him to make us strong in the middle of it, help us through it, and rescue us from it. Paul said, "I can do all things because Christ gives me the strength" (Philippians 4:13). And we can say that too!

---

*Dear God, thank You for the book of Philippians.
Help me as I read it and keep coming back to it in the
future. Teach me what You want me to learn from it to
apply to my life and to share with others. Amen.*

WEIRD WATERSLIDE STORY

"This is my command—be strong and courageous! Do not be afraid or discouraged. For the LORD your God is with you wherever you go."
JOSHUA 1:9 NLT

I vividly remember a day when I was little and my family went to a water park in Branson, Missouri. I recall it so well because I was miserable. Miserable at a super cool water park. Weird, right?

I was miserable because I let my fear of trying something new control me. I desperately wanted to go down the big waterslides with my dad and three older siblings. But I just couldn't make myself do it. It seemed too scary. So all day, I pouted and cried until finally my mom picked me up and put me on my dad's lap just as he was about to start down the slide. There was no time for me to escape; we were suddenly flying down the slide. I screamed and cried and thought I'd never survive, and then just about the time we were at the bottom, I realized something: THIS WAS SO MUCH FUN!

I got out and wanted to go again and again, but guess what? The park was closing and we had to leave. I'd wasted the whole day in fear over something I finally realized was incredibly fun.

Let the lesson I learned that day be a lesson to you too. If wise grown-ups who love Jesus and whom you know you can trust are encouraging you to try something new, even if it seems scary, go ahead and try. Maybe you won't love it, but at least you'll know for sure. And maybe you will find something you love. To this day, I still love waterslides!

Dear God, help me to get over my fears that are keeping me from amazing things! Amen.

Day 275

WHEN YOU WANT REVENGE

*Never pay back evil with more evil. Do things in such a way
that everyone can see you are honorable. Do all that you can
to live in peace with everyone. Dear friends, never take revenge.
Leave that to the righteous anger of God. For the Scriptures
say, "I will take revenge; I will pay them back," says the LORD.*
ROMANS 12:17–19 NLT

Nothing is worse than having someone do something mean or unfair to you. Sadly, we know what that's like. Our instant reaction is to want to do something mean right back. If someone calls us nasty names, we want to call them nasty names too. If someone lies about us, we want to lie about them too. You know what I mean. But that's not wise because it's not what God's Word tells us to do. God wants us to let Him handle our mistreatment. He will do things with perfect justice in a way that we never could. Our job is never to pay back evil with evil but instead to live in a way that others see we are honorable and that we try to live at peace with everyone.

---

*Dear God, it's so hard not to want to get revenge
on my own, but please help me to let You handle
it when someone treats me badly. Amen.*

Day 276

BE A STAR!

*Do everything without grumbling or arguing, so that you may
become blameless and pure, "children of God without fault in
a warped and crooked generation." Then you will shine among
them like stars in the sky as you hold firmly to the word of life.*
PHILIPPIANS 2:14–16 NIV

In our world, being a star means being famous like a singer or actress
or amazing athlete. But the Bible tells us we can shine like *real* stars
in God's eyes by living a life that follows His Word and strives to be
blameless and pure and without fault in a culture that loves to make
sin look like so much fun. Such a huge part of that is doing what God
asks of us without grumbling and arguing. That's sure easier said than
done sometimes, right?

But if you keep in mind that what God asks of you is always what's
best for you, it will help you to do things without fussing about them.
Philippians 2:13 (NIV) says, "For it is God who works in you to will and
to act in order to fulfill his good purpose." He doesn't expect you to
do hard things without complaining about them alone. He is with you,
in you through His Holy Spirit helping you do them. So remember
that and depend on Him. Then you're a real star!

---

*Dear God, please help me to want to be the kind of star
You want, not what the world says is a star. Amen.*

WISDOM FROM THE
BOOK OF COLOSSIANS

Christ has brought you back to God by His death on the cross. In this way, Christ can bring you to God, holy and pure and without blame. This is for you if you keep the faith. You must not change from what you believe now. You must not leave the hope of the Good News you received.
COLOSSIANS 1:22–23

Paul wrote this letter to the church in the city of Colossae because he had heard that they were listening to false teaching that tried to add ideas from other religions to the Christian faith and the good news of Jesus. Throughout our whole lives, we will hear about false teaching like this too, so it's good for us to come back to read Colossians again and again to stay true to what God's Word wants us to know about Jesus and how to follow Him.

Dear God, thank You for the book of Colossians. Help me as I read it and keep coming back to it in the future. Teach me what You want me to learn from it to apply to my life and to share with others. Amen.

THE BEST KIND OF REST

God gives rest to his loved ones.
PSALM 127:2 NLT

It's so hard for me to sleep at night without some noise. I've become addicted to just the sound of a fan blowing. (On cold nights I just point it against the wall so that it doesn't make me chillier!) The soothing, steady sound of it helps block out the normal creaks of the house or the wind outside—the kinds of noises that make me lie there and imagine creepy things.

Lots of people like what's called "white noise" to sleep, just a simple way to help get a good night's rest. Far more important for helping get good rest, though, is listening to what God's Word says about it. The best kind of rest comes from trusting in Him and living for Him!

* "If you are tired from carrying heavy burdens, come to me and I will give you rest. Take the yoke I give you. Put it on your shoulders and learn from me. I am gentle and humble, and you will find rest. This yoke is easy to bear, and this burden is light" (Matthew 11:28–30 CEV).

* "In peace I will lie down and sleep, for you alone, O LORD, will keep me safe" (Psalm 4:8 NLT).

Dear God, please help me to live a life that honors You and is full of good rest when I need it, the kind of rest that can come only from You! Amen.

Day 279

WISDOM WHILE YOU WAIT

Be gentle and be willing to wait for others.
COLOSSIANS 3:12

Waiting for things to happen or for God to answer prayer can feel like forever and can be so frustrating! Can you think of ways you hate to wait? But with wisdom, you can train yourself to have a good attitude about waiting. God uses those times to teach you to be patient and to depend on Him. Do you think it's fun to listen to someone whine and complain? Probably not. So you want to be careful you don't do that either while you're waiting. Let these scriptures fill your mind and give you wisdom about waiting when you're feeling impatient:

- ✸ "Wait for the Lord. Be strong. Let your heart be strong. Yes, wait for the Lord" (Psalm 27:14).

- ✸ "But they who wait upon the Lord will get new strength. They will rise up with wings like eagles. They will run and not get tired. They will walk and not become weak" (Isaiah 40:31).

- ✸ "The Lord is good to those who wait for Him, to the one who looks for Him" (Lamentations 3:25).

Dear God, it's not always easy, but please help me not to whine and complain but to have wisdom while I wait. Amen.

NO LYING LIPS!

The LORD detests lying lips, but he delights in those who tell the truth.
PROVERBS 12:22 NLT

I have lots of fun babysitting stories, and some crazy ones too—like the time when I was seventeen and I accidentally broke a coffee table with my rear end! I had just sat on the edge to reach down and pick up the baby off the floor to take him upstairs for his nap. But the center glass part of the table broke and I fell right through the middle of it! Yikes! I cut my hand, got a nasty painful scrape on my back, and had to quickly figure out how to vacuum up lots of glass before three very young kiddos got into it and hurt themselves.

After everyone was safe and everything cleaned up, I was so dreading telling the kids' mom! I admit it was tempting to make up a lie. I was embarrassed plus figured she might be mad plus worried that I'd have to use up most of the money I'd earned babysitting to buy them a new table. But I prayed and knew God wanted me to be honest. I admitted my embarrassing mistake and offered to buy the mom a new table. Thankfully, she was so kind and understanding and was just so grateful no one had been hurt worse.

Even if I'd had to pay for the table, I knew the best thing I could do in that situation was be honest. God always blesses honesty in one way or another or sometimes in a zillion ways!

Dear God, please help me to be honest even when it seems like making up a little lie would be so much easier. I know the truth in all things is so important. Amen.

Day 281

WISDOM WHEN YOU'RE REALLY ANNOYED

Most of all, have a true love for each other. Love covers many sins.
1 Peter 4:8

You probably know some kids who are hard to be around because of their annoying behavior. They get on everyone's nerves and just won't stop! In those situations, you need extra wisdom from God about how to be kind without encouraging obnoxious behavior. You shouldn't want to join in with other kids who might be mean to them or gossip behind their backs. Remember that every person, including yourself, can be annoying sometimes, and remember how much God loves each one of us! Ask God to help you interact well with difficult people and find ways to encourage them into better behavior.

Dear God, please give me patience and peace when I'm with difficult kids. Show me how to interact with them with wisdom and grace and love. Amen.

ROAD TRIPS RULE!

Be still before the LORD and wait patiently for him.
PSALM 37:7 ESV

Our family loves to take road trips, especially to Florida! We have all flown before, too, and it's nice to get from one place to another in the speedy way that airplanes provide, but there's something so fun (and usually less expensive!) about a road trip. Enjoying the sights along the way, watching movies and reading books in the car, and stopping when you want to run around at a rest stop or eat a yummy meal at a restaurant we don't have in our home state of Ohio are some of our favorite things. Road trips also make you learn patience to get from one place to another, and that's a really good lesson for life.

God does not always get us from one point in our lives to where He wants us to be next in a quick and easy way. He often lets it take a while, and we learn to patiently keep going, a little at a time, seeing and learning new things along the way, until we reach our next destination. He even lets hard and frustrating things happen too—kind of like car trouble or a traffic jam on a road trip—to teach us more patience and to keep trusting that He will take care of us through hard times.

Dear God, help me to be more patient in life, not always wanting to get from one place to another in the quickest and easiest way. I know You often use waiting times to teach me new things and grow me more in Your grace. Amen.

Day 283

WISDOM FROM THE BOOKS OF 1 AND 2 THESSALONIANS

The Lord is faithful. He will give you strength and keep you safe from the devil. We have faith in the Lord for you. We believe you are doing and will keep on doing the things we told you. May the Lord lead your hearts into the love of God. May He help you as you wait for Christ.
2 THESSALONIANS 3:3–5

Paul wrote to the Christians in the city of Thessalonica to encourage them and teach them more about living for God and growing in their faith. He also encouraged them about hope in Jesus' return to gather all believers to be with Him forever in heaven. Then he wrote a second letter to clear up confusion about Jesus' return and to encourage the believers in Thessalonica to keep working while waiting on Jesus and not to get tired of doing what is right. As we wait for Jesus today, we also must keep doing the good work God has planned for us.

Dear God, thank You for the books of 1 and 2 Thessalonians. Help me as I read them and keep coming back to them in the future. Teach me what You want me to learn from them to apply to my life and to share with others. Amen.

Day 284

LOVELY LIGHTS

*Again Jesus spoke to them, saying, "I am the light
of the world. Whoever follows me will not walk in
darkness, but will have the light of life."*
JOHN 8:12 ESV

Have you ever been to a big, ginormous Christmas light display? So many people in the world just think that the lights are fun and pretty, but those of us who love Jesus know they are fun and pretty *and* they remind us of the fact that Christmastime is when the Light of the World first came into the world—Jesus! He called Himself the Light of the World, and the Bible also talks about how we have His light and can share it with others in our dark world. Read and memorize these scriptures, and work hard to shine your light to everyone around you!

> *For once you were full of darkness, but now you have light from the Lord. So live as people of light! For this light within you produces only what is good and right and true.* EPHESIANS 5:8–9 NLT

> *"You are the light of the world—like a city on a hilltop that cannot be hidden. No one lights a lamp and then puts it under a basket. Instead, a lamp is placed on a stand, where it gives light to everyone in the house. In the same way, let your good deeds shine out for all to see, so that everyone will praise your heavenly Father."* MATTHEW 5:14–16 NLT

---

*Dear Jesus, I want to shine so bright to
share Your truth and love! Amen.*

Day 285

WISDOM FROM THOSE WHO HAVE LIVED A LONG TIME

We. . .gain some wisdom from those who have lived a long time.
JOB 12:11–12 CEV

Who are the oldest relatives in your life—grandparents, great-grandparents, great-aunts and uncles, elderly friends? Do you enjoy talking to them? Maybe you have some great relationships with elderly people, or maybe it sometimes feels too hard to talk to and relate to them because you're young and they're not. But it's so wise to listen and learn from older folks. Think of them as the superstars of wisdom. The longer they have lived, it's likely the more wisdom they have gained from their many life experiences—and they can share that wisdom with you if you let them. Ask God to help you grow in relationship with wise elderly people. If you don't have any elderly relatives nearby, maybe you can start visiting a nursing home and make some new friends. Then let God teach you more wisdom through those new friends.

Dear God, please help me to see how wonderful it is to talk to elderly people and learn from them. Teach me what You want me to know through others who have lived a long time. Amen.

Day 286

YOUR VALUE

"What is the price of two sparrows—one copper coin?
But not a single sparrow can fall to the ground without
your Father knowing it. And the very hairs on your head
are all numbered. So don't be afraid; you are more
valuable to God than a whole flock of sparrows."
MATTHEW 10:29–31 NLT

I read a great little example on Facebook one time that talked about how when you buy a new tablet or smartphone, most people instantly buy both a protective cover for the screen and a case that provides protection too. It seems sad, then, that so many girls these days, each of whom is FAR more valuable (especially in God's eyes) than any electronic device, don't value themselves enough to cover and protect themselves wisely with clothes. I don't mean girls have to only wear things that cover skin from head to toe or always have to be completely out of fashion. It's absolutely possible to both wear cute, fashionable clothes *and* protect and value and respect your body, knowing it's just a fact that sin in the world causes some people to look at girls' bodies with bad thoughts and plans.

While your body is not the most important thing about you (your soul that lives forever is!), it's so incredibly valuable because it carries your beautiful soul! Ask God to help you to be wise in respecting your body and protecting it from harm and from sin in smart ways, including the way you dress!

Dear God, the world gives me such confusing ideas on
what's cool to wear. Please help me know how to value
and respect and protect my body wisely. Amen.

Day 287

WISDOM FROM THE BOOKS
OF 1 AND 2 TIMOTHY

This letter is from Paul, a missionary of Jesus Christ. I am sent by God, the One Who saves, and by our Lord Jesus Christ Who is our hope. I write to you, Timothy. You are my son in the Christian faith. May God the Father and Jesus Christ our Lord give you His loving-favor and loving-kindness and peace.

1 TIMOTHY 1:1–2

In the books of 1 and 2 Timothy, Paul wrote to Timothy, a younger friend and pastor of a church in the city of Ephesus, to encourage him and teach him how to lead his church well, including instructions about how to care for widows (women whose husbands had died) and avoiding the love of money. Paul wrote another letter to Timothy sharing final words of encouragement and motivation that can encourage and motivate us in our faith today too!

Dear God, thank You for the books of 1 and 2 Timothy. Help me as I read them and keep coming back to them in the future. Teach me what You want me to learn from them to apply to my life and to share with others. Amen.

Day 288

DANCING FOR THE LORD

And David danced before the Lord with all his might.
2 Samuel 6:14 NLT

I have very little coordination or artistic physical ability, so I don't really ever dance unless it's just for silly fun, and it's probably ridiculous to watch—LOL! But I do enjoy watching dance, especially watching my girls, Jodi and Lilly! They're part of a church dance group that's not for competition but just for fun and recreation and to be an act of worship to God. Their instructors choose worship music to dance to, and it's such a beautiful sight to watch young people honor God with lovely movement to songs that praise Him with their words.

Our sinful world has turned a lot of dancing into something that does not please God. But when done in good ways, dancing makes God happy, and the Bible talks about it! Read these scriptures and ask God to help you dance with joy—whether it's in a class or on a competition dance team or just for fun wherever you are—in ways that praise Him and make Him smile!

- ✴ "Let them praise his name with dancing, making melody to him" (Psalm 149:3 ESV).

- ✴ "Praise the LORD! Praise God in his sanctuary; praise him in his mighty heaven! Praise him for his mighty works; praise his unequaled greatness! Praise him with a blast of the ram's horn; praise him with the lyre and harp! Praise him with the tambourine and dancing" (Psalm 150:1–4 NLT)

Dear God, when I dance I want it to be in ways that please You! You are awesome, and I praise You! Amen.

Day 289

WISDOM ABOUT HEALING

Jesus came to Peter's house. He saw Peter's wife's mother in bed. . .very sick. He touched her hand and the sickness left her. She got up and cared for Jesus. That evening they brought to Jesus many people who had demons in them. The demons were put out when Jesus spoke to them. All the sick people were healed.
MATTHEW 8:14–16

When Jesus was on earth, He showed that He truly was God with His amazing power to heal people of sickness and demons. Jesus still has the power to heal now, and we can pray and ask God for healing for people who need it. But we also need wisdom about this. Sometimes God chooses not to heal here on earth. We must remember that healing in heaven is far better because it will last forever. So even more important than praying for healing on earth is to pray that the people who need it know Jesus as Savior so that they can be healed in heaven forever with eternal life. As we do pray for healing, we can do it with great faith, knowing that God is absolutely able, but we must ask for it according to His will, knowing He always, always does what is right and good.

Dear God, You have the power to heal and perform any miracle, including healing from any kind of sickness! You are awesome, and I praise You! Please give me wisdom as I pray for Your will to be done. Amen.

Day 290

SING A SONG!

Oh come, let us sing to the Lord; let us make a joyful noise to the rock of our salvation! Let us come into his presence with thanksgiving; let us make a joyful noise to him with songs of praise!
PSALM 95:1–2 ESV

It's amazing how many different styles of music there are and what talent people have for music! God gave people so much creativity when He created us. That makes sense, since we are created in His image and He is obviously so creative! ☺

Even though there are plenty of lyrics in music that are not pleasing to God, I love how many different kinds of songs and lyrics there are now that *do* praise God. If you fill your mind with scripture and praise for God through song, you are so smart! Do you know why? Because when hard times come, your mind will know where to focus and you will find yourself gaining so much strength from God! And even when you're not going through a hard time, you'll just constantly be filled with so much joy in worshipping God!

Read all these scriptures to help you know how important praising God through song is!

- ✦ "I will sing to the Lord because he is good to me" (Psalm 13:6 NLT).

- ✦ "I will sing to the Lord as long as I live; I will sing praise to my God while I have being" (Psalm 104:33 ESV).

- ✦ "Sing to him, sing praises to him; tell of all his wondrous works!" (Psalm 105:2 ESV).

Dear God, I want my mind and my mouth to be constantly full of praise to You! Amen.

Day 291

WISDOM FROM THE BOOK OF TITUS

In all things show them how to live by your life and by
right teaching. You should be wise in what you say.
Then the one who is against you will be ashamed and
will not be able to say anything bad about you.
Titus 2:7–8

Titus was a close friend and travel buddy to Paul, and Paul wrote the letter in the book of Titus to him to instruct him how to organize and lead the church and how to teach others to live for God. We can still learn much wisdom today from the lessons that were originally for Titus. When you act and talk the way God wants you to, others will learn by your good influence.

Dear God, thank You for the book of Titus. Help me as I read it and keep coming back to it in the future. Teach me what You want me to learn from it to apply to my life and to share with others. Amen.

Day 292

THOSE EMBARRASSING MOMENTS

With all humility and gentleness, with patience,
bearing with one another in love.
EPHESIANS 4:2 ESV

Do you like to tell embarrassing-moments stories with your friends? Sometimes it's more fun to hear them from others than tell our own because they're still embarrassing long after they happened! LOL! One time my best friend and roommate in college came back to our dorm room and told me a good one. She had been in biology lab class and all of a sudden got a little sleepy or something and fell off her stool! The worst part? No one else laughed with her. (We sure did laugh together when she told me, though! Hahaha!)

Sometimes it would feel better to have people laugh with us when something embarrassing happens than to just stare at us in shock, right? The Bible says there is "a time to weep, and a time to laugh" (Ecclesiastes 3:4 ESV). As long as others are not being cruel in their laughter and are helping out if the embarrassed person needs it, then finding the humor together in an embarrassing situation actually helps a lot! We all need to not take ourselves too seriously sometimes and remember that everyone makes silly mistakes and has embarrassing moments. Every. Single. One. Of us.

Dear God, please help me to have grace and good
humor in embarrassing situations. Amen.

Day 293

WISDOM ABOUT ANGELS

*"Be sure you do not hate one of these little children.
I tell you, they have angels who are always looking
into the face of My Father in heaven."*
MATTHEW 18:10

Maybe you hear people talk about guardian angels sometimes and wonder if they are real or not. This scripture in the Bible tells you that they are! Jesus said that little children have angels watching over them who are also standing with God, looking right at Him. So anything He tells them to do to help and protect you, they know it in an instant and can come to your rescue! Here are some more scriptures about angels:

* "The angel of the Lord stays close around those who fear Him, and He takes them out of trouble" (Psalm 34:7).

* "I tell you, it is the same way among the angels of God. If one sinner is sorry for his sins and turns from them, the angels are very happy" (Luke 15:10).

* "Keep on loving each other as Christian brothers. Do not forget to be kind to strangers and let them stay in your home. Some people have had angels in their homes without knowing it" (Hebrews 13:1–2).

---

*Dear God, thank You for the angels You have assigned
to protect and care for people! Amen.*

Day 294

HEAVENLY HOME

*For we know that when this earthly tent we live in is taken
down (that is, when we die and leave this earthly body),
we will have a house in heaven, an eternal body made
for us by God himself and not by human hands.*
2 Corinthians 5:1 NLT

Do you like to watch any of those home-improvement or house-hunting shows on television? We do! Especially *Fixer Upper*. It's so fun to see how an old house in need of lots of repair gets an amazing makeover!

Better than any house design or makeover that we can imagine here on earth is the amazing home God is making for us in heaven! John 14:1–3 (NLT) says, "Don't let your hearts be troubled. Trust in God, and trust also in me. There is more than enough room in my Father's home. If this were not so, would I have told you that I am going to prepare a place for you? When everything is ready, I will come and get you, so that you will always be with me where I am."

It's fun to try to dream about all the amazing things God is getting ready for our forever home in heaven! I'm really hoping for some cool waterslides! What do you like to imagine will be there?

---

*Dear God, You are amazing, and I know You must be making
heaven beyond my wildest and coolest dreams! Help me
to keep living according to Your Word and living with
confident hope of my forever home with You. Amen.*

Day 295

WISDOM FROM THE
BOOK OF PHILEMON

*Do not think of him any longer as a servant you own. He is more than
that to you. He is a much-loved Christian brother to you and to me.*
PHILEMON 16

The book of Philemon is all about a slave who robbed and then ran away from his owner Philemon. The runaway slave was named Onesimus, and he met Paul in Rome and became a Christian. So Paul decided to write to Philemon, asking him to please forgive Onesimus and view him not as a slave but as a fellow believer and brother in Jesus Christ. The book of Philemon teaches and reminds us to treat all people as equally loved and respected, especially believers in Jesus, because we are all family.

---

*Dear God, thank You for the book of Philemon.
Help me as I read it and keep coming back to it in the
future. Teach me what You want me to learn from it to
apply to my life and to share with others. Amen.*

Day 296

LIFE'S NOT FAIR

*But if you do what is wrong, you will be paid
back for the wrong you have done.*
COLOSSIANS 3:25 NLT

It's not fair! How many times have you said or thought those words? I can't even begin to count in my own life! So many things in your life are not going to seem fair. It's best just to accept that frustrating fact while you're young. The world became dramatically unfair the moment sin entered in the garden of Eden. I know it's such a bummer, but don't let it discourage you.

God is watching you, helping you, and blessing you along the way—with just enough to keep you trusting in Him and His plans for you day by day. He's watching when you're doing the right thing but keep getting knocked down or overlooked while those who aren't following God's ways seem to keep getting ahead. (*Grrr*, right?) He will make sure those who do wrong get what they deserve, and He will make everything good and right for those who follow Him—if not right now, then for sure forever in heaven someday. Remember that the world is absolutely unfair, but God is absolutely not. Hebrews 6:10 (NLT) says, "For God is not unjust. He will not forget how hard you have worked for him and how you have shown your love to him by caring for other believers, as you still do."

---

*Dear God, please help me to keep up my good work living a life that
honors You. I know You will make all things fair someday. Amen.*

Day 297

WISDOM ABOUT HEAVEN

*Then I saw a new heaven and a new earth. . . . I heard a loud
voice coming from heaven. It said, "See! God's home is with
men. He will live with them. They will be His people. God Himself
will be with them. He will be their God. God will take away all
their tears. There will be no more death or sorrow or crying
or pain. All the old things have passed away." Then the One
sitting on the throne said, "See! I am making all things new."*

REVELATION 21:1–5

It's fun to dream about what heaven might be like, but we also always
need to remember with wisdom that nobody here on earth knows
a whole lot about it yet. The Bible doesn't tell lots of detail about
heaven, probably because our minds couldn't fully understand how
awesome it will be (1 Corinthians 2:9)! But it does tell us everything
will be new and there will be no more death or sorrow or crying or
pain. That fact alone shows us how awesome it will be!

---

*Dear God, how amazing it will be when You make Your
home with us in the new heaven and earth You have
planned. Until then, please keep me close to You as I do
the good things You have for me in this life. Amen.*

OVERCOMERS!

Do not be overcome by evil, but overcome evil with good.
ROMANS 12:21 NIV

Romans 12:21 is a scripture I repeat again and again in my head when I hear bad news of yet another thing gone wrong in our world or when I experience something bad myself. It gives me motivation to keep on loving all the people around me and helping others in the best ways I can. A good habit to get into is to read this verse, memorize it, and apply it specifically when something is going wrong in your life or in the world and you want to do something to help. For example, you could think:

> *I will not be overcome by this classmate who is being mean to me. I can overcome her cruel actions with love and kindness and by praying for her.*

> Or
> *I should not be overcome by this hard family situation I'm in. I can overcome with hope and trust in God for my family and by being loving and helpful to my family.*

> Or
> *I will not be overcome by worry and fear over the bad things going on in our world. I can overcome by asking God how to show His love in my home and in my church and in my community.*

> Or. . .all of the above!

Dear God, You are good, and I know You can help me to DO good toward others until You return and get rid of all evil. Amen.

WISDOM FROM THE BOOK OF HEBREWS

*God made all things. He made all things for Himself. It was right
for God to make Jesus a perfect Leader by having Him suffer
for men's sins. In this way, He is bringing many men to share His
shining-greatness. Jesus makes men holy. He takes away their sins.*
HEBREWS 2:10–11

In the book of Hebrews, the writer (and no one seems to be sure who
that writer is, exactly) wanted to teach the Jewish people who had
become Christians not to go back to the same type of religion that
was practiced in the Old Testament. The book's main point is that
Jesus is above and beyond any kind of religious ritual and sacrifice.
He paid for sin once for all people when He died on the cross—and
then rose again! We can't make ourselves holy through any kind of
religious practice, but we can let Jesus make us holy by accepting
Him as the one true Savior who died for our sins.

---

*Dear God, thank You for the book of Hebrews. Help me
as I read it and keep coming back to it in the future.
Teach me what You want me to learn from it to apply
to my life and to share with others. Amen.*

Day 300

SUPERGIRLS!

*Faith makes us sure of what we hope for and gives
us proof of what we cannot see. It was their faith
that made our ancestors pleasing to God.*
HEBREWS 11:1–2 CEV

Superheroes are kind of a big deal, right?! And they're not just for boys anymore. Maybe you love the movies like *Batman* and *Superman*, and maybe you've seen and even have some of the DC Superhero girl dolls and shows.

There's nothing wrong with enjoying superhero stories, as long as you keep the right perspective. Those are fiction, just for fun, but the Bible talks about the *real-deal* heroes—people strong in their faith in the one true God; people who truly had supernatural power because they believed in God, listened to God, and let God work in their lives!

One of the best places to read about many of them is in Hebrews chapter 11. You'll read snippets there about the great faith of Abel, Enoch, Noah, Abraham, Sarah, Isaac, Joseph, Moses, Rahab, Gideon, Barak, Samson, Jephthah, David, Samuel, and the prophets. Hopefully, that will make you want to look up more details of their stories in the rest of the Bible.

You can believe in God, listen to God, and let God work in your life at all times too! Then you truly will be a superhero—a Supergirl of faith!

---

*Dear God, please inspire me with the stories of real
superheroes—people who believe wholeheartedly in You
and in Your power. I want to be like them! Amen.*

MORE SUPERGIRLS

God is within her, she will not fall.
PSALM 46:5 NIV

Spend some time in the stories of women in the Bible to inspire you as you grow to be a girl of grace. Ruth and Esther have whole books of the Old Testament dedicated to telling their stories of faith and courage and the way God worked through them.

Deborah was one of the judges of Israel who helped show God's loving care of His people. Her story is in Judges chapters 4 and 5.

Hannah's story in 1 Samuel 1 and 2 is of great faith, persistent prayer, and commitment to God.

And of course Mary, the mother of Jesus, whose story is told especially in the Gospel of Luke, is quite the heroic girl who was trusted to carry the hope of the world and be the earthly mother to God in human form!

These are just a few of the courageous women in the Bible. The main thing to remember about their lives is that they were humble girls who loved God and had great faith in His power, not in their own abilities. A true Supergirl knows that the only kind of power that is real is God's power.

Dear God, I'm amazed by the women in the Bible whom You used for great things! Please help me to trust in Your power, and use me for great things too! Amen.

JESUS' WISDOM ABOUT FORGIVENESS

*"Lord, how many times may my brother sin against me
and I forgive him, up to seven times?" Jesus said to [Peter],
"I tell you, not seven times but seventy times seven!"*
MATTHEW 18:21–22

Jesus taught us wisdom in a parable about how important forgiveness is:

> "One of the servants. . .owed [the king] very much money. . . .
> The servant got down on his face. He said, 'Give me time,
> and I will pay you all the money.' Then the king took pity. . . .
> He told him he did not have to pay the money back. But that
> servant went out and found one of the other servants who
> owed him very little money. He. . .said, 'Pay me the money
> you owe me!' The other servant. . .said, 'Give me time, and
> I will pay you all the money.' . . . He had him put in prison
> until he could pay the money. . . . Then the king called for
> the first one. He said, '. . .I forgave you. . . . Should you not
> have had pity on the other servant, even as I had pity on
> you?' The king. . .handed him over to men who would. . .hurt
> him until he paid all the money he owed. So will My Father
> in heaven do to you, if each one of you does not forgive his
> brother from his heart." (Matthew 18:23–35)

---

*Dear Jesus, help me to forgive others because
You love and forgive me. Amen.*

WISDOM FROM THE BOOK OF JAMES

*Obey the Word of God. If you hear only and do not act, you
are only fooling yourself. Anyone who hears the Word of God
and does not obey is like a man looking at his face in a mirror.
After he sees himself and goes away, he forgets what he looks like.
But the one who keeps looking into God's perfect Law and does
not forget it will do what it says and be happy as he does it.*
JAMES 1:22–25

The writer of this letter was the brother of Jesus and a leader of
the church in Jerusalem. If you've heard and understand the saying
"Actions speak louder than words," then you know the main point
James wanted to make. Christians shouldn't just say we have faith.
Our lives and actions should show it by what we do. That never means
our good deeds are what save us from sin. It just means that when
we have committed our lives to Jesus and we have the Holy Spirit
living in us, we shouldn't simply want to listen to the Word of God,
we should want to *do* what it says.

---

*Dear God, thank You for the book of James. Help me as I read it and
keep coming back to it in the future. Teach me what You want me
to learn from it to apply to my life and to share with others. Amen.*

Day 304

HIDE-AND-SEEK

*Anyone who wants to come to him must believe that God
exists and that he rewards those who sincerely seek him.*
HEBREWS 11:6 NLT

I'm guessing you've played a lot of games of hide-and-seek with your family and your friends! It's a classic! My favorite hiding spot is in a bathroom shower. Jodi's is in a closet. Lilly's is under a table. What's yours?

While hide-and-seek is fun, I'm glad that trying to find God is not a game where He's hoping not to be found! It's terribly sad when people today think God doesn't exist because they can't find Him or talk to Him exactly like they do a person here on earth. Or maybe they prayed to Him and didn't get the answers they wanted, so they don't think He's for real. Or maybe they think, sure, God has to exist but He doesn't care one bit what people do or what happens to them.

Those people aren't spending any quality time in God's Word. "For the word of God is alive and powerful," Hebrews 4:12 (NLT) says. And they aren't seeking God sincerely. He promises in Jeremiah 29:13 (NIV), "You will seek me and find me when you seek me with all your heart."

For all those who *do* truly look for God, they will find what a good Father He is, a Father who wants to have a loving, constant relationship with His children and guide them in the awesome plans He created them for (Ephesians 2:20; Jeremiah 29:11)!

---

*Dear God, help me to always remember that You are never hard
to find. Please keep me close to You through Your Spirit and Your
Word, and help me to show others how to find You too. Amen.*

Day 305

BE A PEACEMAKER, PART 1

Do all that you can to live in peace with everyone.
ROMANS 12:18 NLT

Are you always at peace with your family and friends? Probably not. Any relationship is going to have some conflict sometimes, and that's okay if you do it wisely! Kicking-and-screaming kind of conflict is not good, but conflict with wisdom can be really good to work out problems—and we truly need it sometimes. But we shouldn't want to *stay* in conflict; we should work through it until there is peace again. James 4:1 says, "What starts wars and fights among you? Is it not because you want many things and are fighting to have them?" This shows us that so many of our conflicts are caused by selfishness, and when we are willing to work to make peace, we should be willing to admit our own selfishness and mistakes even as we point out selfishness and mistakes in others.

Dear God, please give me wisdom and show me how You want me to do my best to work to live in peace with everyone. Amen.

Day 306

BE A PEACEMAKER, PART 2

*"God blesses those who work for peace, for they
will be called the children of God."*
Matthew 5:9 nlt

Other verses in the Bible, like the following, tell us to work at peace with others.

- ✸ "Work at living in peace with everyone, and work at living a holy life, for those who are not holy will not see the Lord" (Hebrews 12:14 nlt).

- ✸ "Turn away from what is sinful. Do what is good. Look for peace and go after it" (1 Peter 3:11).

When we look at how important it is to God to live in peace with others, it makes us realize how much we need His help with this. We need to keep asking God for His wisdom to know when to have conflict and when to let things go, and on how to show His kind of love and forgiveness to others through it all.

Dear God, please help me to value peace like You do and to have wisdom to work out conflict well with others when I need to. Help me also to love and forgive like You do. Amen.

BE A PEACEMAKER, PART 3

Let the peace of Christ have power over your hearts.
Colossians 3:15

If you want to work toward peace with others, you always need to be working on peace inside yourself first. Philippians 4:4–7 helps you know how. It says, "Be full of joy always because you belong to the Lord. Again I say, be full of joy! Let all people see how gentle you are. The Lord is coming again soon. Do not worry. Learn to pray about everything. Give thanks to God as you ask Him for what you need. The peace of God is much greater than the human mind can understand. This peace will keep your hearts and minds through Christ Jesus." And Psalm 119:165 (NLT) helps you know how to keep God's peace inside too when it says, "Those who love your instructions have great peace and do not stumble."

So, to sum it up—be full of joy because you belong to Jesus; don't worry but instead pray to God about everything; and love God's Word and obey it. That's how you can be full of God's amazing peace and then hopefully let that amazing peace overflow from you and around to others.

Dear God, I love You and trust You and want to know and obey Your Word. Please fill me up with Your amazing peace every day and help me share it with others. Amen.

BiRTHDAY BLESSiNGS

I praise you because of the wonderful way you created me.
PSALM 139:14 CEV

We love to make a big deal about birthdays! It's a time to celebrate the wonderful people God has created, every one a unique individual. I hope you get some great birthday gifts and cards—maybe some of the cards even say "Birthday Blessings." Birthdays are also a great time to remember the blessing prayers that are in the Bible. They're called *benedictions* too, which is a fun word to say! A cool tradition for birthdays is to pray these benedictions over the one who is celebrating a birthday.

Have a loved one pray these for you on your next birthday, and you can pray them for others on their special days too!

* "May the LORD bless you and protect you. May the LORD smile on you and be gracious to you. May the LORD show you his favor and give you his peace" (Numbers 6:24–26 NLT).

* *"May the God of hope fill you with all joy and peace in believing, so that by the power of the Holy Spirit you may abound in hope"* (Romans 15:13 ESV)

* *"I pray that God will make you ready to obey him and that you will always be eager to do right. May Jesus help you do what pleases God. To Jesus Christ be glory forever and ever! Amen"* (Hebrews 13:21 CEV).

Dear God, thank You for the fun of birthdays, and thank You for the prayers of blessing in Your Word that are for each and every one of Your people! Amen.

Day 309

WISDOM FROM THE BOOKS OF 1 AND 2 PETER

You are being kept by the power of God because you put your trust in Him and you will be saved from the punishment of sin at the end of the world.
1 PETER 1:5

Peter wrote 1 Peter to Christians all over the Roman Empire who were suffering in awful ways for believing in Jesus. He wanted to encourage believers and also teach them that suffering could be considered a good thing. That may sound odd, but he said, "Be happy that you are able to share some of the suffering of Christ. When His shining-greatness is shown, you will be filled with much joy. If men speak bad of you because you are a Christian, you will be happy because the Spirit of shining-greatness and of God is in you" (1 Peter 4:13–14). And in 2 Peter, written about three years after 1 Peter, Peter wanted to encourage Christians to keep growing in faith and warn them not to listen to false teachers.

Dear God, thank You for the books of 1 and 2 Peter. Help me as I read them and keep coming back to them in the future. Teach me what You want me to learn from them to apply to my life and to share with others. Amen.

WEIRD IN THE WORLD

Dear friends, you are foreigners and strangers on this earth.
1 PETER 2:11 CEV

Do you ever feel a little embarrassed by your family when you're out in public? Maybe your mom has danced down the aisles of Walmart just to be silly. (I'd never do that to Jodi and Lilly! Haha! Just kidding! Yes, I have!)

Guess what? You need to stop being worried about feeling embarrassed or weird in this world because the Bible tells you that you *should* feel weird in this world! True, it does not say anything specific about whether moms should dance down the aisles in Walmart, but it does talk about living in the world as strangers in a foreign land (1 Peter 1:17; Hebrews 13:14). It also talks about how the world hates those who follow Jesus (Matthew 10:22). And it commands us not to conform to the ways of this world (Romans 12:2).

No one needs to be obnoxious and try to seem crazy and purposefully make others think Christians are to be avoided, and my dancing example is just for fun. The point is, as Christians, we just have to realize that we never will really fit into the culture of this world, and that's a *good* thing. God has better plans and ways and wants you to let Him "change the way you think. Then you will know how to do everything that is good and pleasing to him" (Romans 12:2 CEV).

Dear God, help me to not worry about feeling weird in this world. Please help me to focus on You and how You want me to live. Amen.

Day 311

WISDOM ABOUT JESUS' RETURN

We are to be looking for the great hope and the coming of our great God and the One Who saves, Christ Jesus. He gave Himself for us. He did this by buying us with His blood and making us free from all sin. He gave Himself so His people could be clean and want to do good.

TITUS 2:13–14

We should always be watching for Jesus to return because He promised He would! The idea of Jesus returning might sound a little scary because it will be unlike anything any person has ever experienced, but for those who love and trust Him, His return will be wonderful. Mark 13:24–27 says, "After those days of much trouble and pain and sorrow are over, the sun will get dark. The moon will not give light. The stars will fall from the sky. The powers in the heavens will be shaken. Then they will see the Son of Man coming in the clouds with great power and shining-greatness. He will send His angels. They will gather together God's people from the four winds. They will come from one end of the earth to the other end of heaven."

Dear Jesus, I'm watching and waiting for You to return and gather Your people, including me! I love You and trust You! Amen.

CRAZY BUTTERFLIES

*I love you, L*ORD*, my strength.*
PSALM 18:1 NIV

Do you have something that really makes the butterflies flap around like crazy in your stomach? The thing that does it for me is speaking in front of big groups of people. One-on-one or in a small group, I love to chat, but talking in front of a big crowd? Not so much.

Psalm 18:1 is such an excellent and easy verse to memorize to help you when you're nervous about anything at all—piano or dance recitals, a big gymnastics meet, working on diving in swim class, a big test you have to take or speech you have to give at school. In just a few short words, this scripture focuses your thoughts on God and your love for Him, knowing He loves you too, and reminds you that He is your strength to do anything.

Maybe you've heard this verse too—"I can do everything through Christ, who gives me strength" (Philippians 4:13 NLT). It's another awesome scripture to memorize and repeat, time and time again, when you're faced with any kind of challenge that stirs up those butterflies!

Dear God, there are all kinds of different things that make me nervous. I'm glad to know You always love me, You're always with me, and You're always my strength. Thank You! I love You too! Amen.

Day 313

REAL WISDOM FROM GOD, PART 1

If you have jealousy in your heart and fight to have many things, do not be proud of it. Do not lie against the truth. This is not the kind of wisdom that comes from God. But this wisdom comes from the world and from that which is not Christian and from the devil. . . . The wisdom that comes from heaven is first of all pure. Then it gives peace. It is gentle and willing to obey. It is full of loving-kindness and of doing good. It has no doubts and does not pretend to be something it is not. Those who plant seeds of peace will gather what is right and good.
JAMES 3:14–18

This scripture in James 3 helps us know what real wisdom from God looks like in our lives. It's very different from wisdom from the world. In fact, 1 Corinthians 3:19 says, "The wisdom of this world is foolish to God." So it's important for us always to be praying to know the difference between the world's kind of wisdom and God's real wisdom. And we can only do that by constantly learning from God's Word and asking Him to show us how to use it in our lives through the power of the Holy Spirit who lives in us if we have committed our lives to Jesus as our Lord and Savior.

Dear God, please keep giving me Your real wisdom and help me see the big difference from the world's wisdom. Amen.

Day 314

REAL WISDOM FROM GOD, PART 2

What we preach is God's wisdom. . . . God planned for us to have this honor before the world began. None of the world leaders understood this wisdom. If they had, they would not have put Christ up on a cross to die. . . . The Holy Writings say, "No eye has ever seen or no ear has ever heard or no mind has ever thought of the wonderful things God has made ready for those who love Him." God has shown these things to us through His Holy Spirit. It is the Holy Spirit Who looks into all things, even the secrets of God, and shows them to us. Who can know the things about a man, except a man's own spirit that is in him? It is the same with God. . . . God has given us His Holy Spirit that we may know about the things given to us by Him.
1 CORINTHIANS 2:7–12

This scripture helps us to know more about the difference between the world's wisdom and God's wisdom. The key is the Holy Spirit whom God has given us to show us the secrets of God. How super cool is that to be trusted to know the secrets of God? Keep on asking Him to share them with you!

Dear God, You are awesome Creator of all, King of all kings, and Lord of all lords, and You want to share Your secrets with me. That's incredible! Please keep giving me Your wisdom through Your Holy Spirit. Amen.

HELP FOR BROKEN HEARTS

He heals the brokenhearted and bandages their wounds.
PSALM 147:3 NLT

If you've ever felt like your heart is breaking from disappointment or betrayal or the death of someone you love, I'm so sorry. I hurt for you because I know what that is like. Please don't ever think that God has left you when you're hurting, though. He has promised that He will never leave you (Hebrews 13:5) and that He is near to the brokenhearted (Psalm 34:18) even if you don't always feel like that's true.

Maybe you just can't understand how or why awful things happen to good people. I get it. I've had those same thoughts and questions, and it's okay to tell them to God. He wants you to tell Him every worry and question you have (1 Peter 5:7). In the moments of heartbreak and questioning God, you have a choice to turn away from Him because you're mad, or you can choose to draw closer to Him and trust Him despite your hurt and anger and confusion—and let Him comfort you and help you through the dark, sad days. Little by little they *will* get better. His Word says, "Come close to God, and God will come close to you" (James 4:8 NLT).

When life is at its worst, the worst thing you can do is run from God. If you stick it out and stay close to Him, He will carry you through it.

Dear God, when I'm hurting and confused, please remind me to come closer to You, not get farther away. Only You can truly heal a broken heart. Amen.

Day 316

WISDOM FROM THE BOOKS OF 1, 2, 3 JOHN

I am not writing to you about a new Law but an old one we have had from the beginning. Love means that we should live by obeying His Word. From the beginning He has said in His Word that our hearts should be full of love.

2 JOHN 5–6

Even though these three letters don't mention their writer, most believe it was the apostle John, who was one of the twelve original disciples of Jesus. When writing the first of these letters, John wanted to make sure the Christians then and now would know that Jesus was a real man and that He was also really God and that He loves us very much. Since John knew Jesus so personally, as one of His disciples, we can trust him. The second letter is a very short one to warn against false teachers. And 3 John is another short letter to John's friend Gaius to encourage him always to do what is good and not evil.

Dear God, thank You for the books of 1, 2, 3 John. Help me as I read them and keep coming back to them in the future. Teach me what You want me to learn from them to apply to my life and to share with others. Amen.

Day 317

BEST KIND OF TEST

"When he tests me, I will come out as pure as gold. For I have stayed on God's paths."
JOB 23:10–11 NLT

More important than any test you take for school are the tests you take that show your faith. The Bible is clear that you will go through hard things, but there is a purpose to them. They prove whether you really believe in God and love Him. There are plenty of people in the world who say they love and follow God, but unless their lives show it through hard things, they aren't telling the truth. Read the following scripture and take heart that any hard thing you go through in life is an opportunity to keep proving that your faith is real and sharing it with others who need to know Jesus too.

> *God has something stored up for you in heaven, where it will never decay or be ruined or disappear. You have faith in God, whose power will protect you until the last day. Then he will save you, just as he has always planned to do. On that day you will be glad, even if you have to go through many hard trials for a while. Your faith will be like gold that has been tested in a fire. And these trials will prove that your faith is worth much more than gold that can be destroyed. They will show that you will be given praise and honor and glory when Jesus Christ returns.* 1 PETER 1:4–7 CEV

Dear God, even when I'm going through something so hard, I want to show that my faith in You is for real. Please help me succeed through life's tests. Amen.

Day 318

WISDOM ABOUT FAKE GODS

*Our God is in the heavens. He does whatever He wants to do.
Their gods are silver and gold, the work of human hands. They have
mouths but they cannot speak. They have eyes but they cannot
see. They have ears but they cannot hear. They have noses but they
cannot smell. They have hands but they cannot feel. They have feet
but they cannot walk. They cannot make a sound come out of their
mouths. Those who make them and trust them will be like them.*
PSALM 115:3–8

This scripture compares our one true God with the fake gods of the
world that some people make for themselves. It describes how silly
those fake gods are, with useless mouths, eyes, ears, noses, hands,
and feet. But people often make fake gods because they don't really
want to serve or worship anyone but themselves. And so they will
end up as useless and meaningless as those fake gods. But to trust
and worship and obey the one true God alone is to live the life you
were created for, with love, hope, and peace forever.

---

*Dear God, I'm so thankful I trust in You and not a fake god.
Please keep giving me Your wisdom. Help me to live for You
and do the good things You created me for. Amen.*

Day 319

GOTTA GET YOUR REST

God rested from all his work that he had done in creation.
GENESIS 2:3 ESV

I remember being at summer camp one year in junior high and thinking it was so ridiculous and annoying that we had to take rest times in the middle of the day. Nowadays, I love naps! Whether you do or not, it's important to realize God gave us rest. It's a much-needed gift from Him. He knows we are human (He made us, so *obviously*! ☺) and our bodies have to have rest to function well and to serve Him through the great things He has planned for us to do.

It's hard to get the rest we need sometimes. Life fights us on this like crazy, with so much work to do and so many activities and people demanding our attention! But it's a battle worth fighting to get good rest. Even in one of the Ten Commandments, God commanded us to rest! Exodus 34:21 (ESV) says, "Six days you shall work, but on the seventh day you shall rest."

In the New Testament, Jesus knew He and His disciples needed rest from all the work and ministry they were doing. He says in Mark 6:31 (NLT), "Let's go off by ourselves to a quiet place and rest awhile."

It's important to remember that resting and quietness is how we best come before God to remember who He is and let Him speak to us. Psalm 46:10 (ESV) says, "Be still, and know that I am God."

Dear God, please help me to realize how
important good rest is. Amen.

Day 320

WiSDOM FROM THE BOOK OF JUDE

Dear friends, I have been trying to write to you about what God did for us when He saved us from the punishment of sin. Now I must write to you and tell you to fight hard for the faith which was once and for all given to the holy people of God. Some sinful men have come into your church without anyone knowing it. They are living in sin and they speak of the loving-favor of God to cover up their sins. They have turned against our only Leader and Lord, Jesus Christ. Long ago it was written that these people would die in their sins.

JUDE 3–4

There must have been a lot of false teachers in ancient times, because Jude is another letter written to Jewish Christians mostly to warn them not to listen to false teaching from those who try to cover up their sin. God knew that we would need this warning again in the future—again and again and again—because sadly there are all kinds of people who want to spread false teaching and try to hide their sin. We should always pray for wisdom to choose right from wrong and to recognize false teachers and covered-up sin.

Dear God, thank You for the book of Jude. Help me as I read it and keep coming back to it in the future. Teach me what You want me to learn from it to apply to my life and to share with others. Amen.

MONEY MATTERS

*Honor the LORD by giving him your money and the
first part of all your crops. Then you will have more
grain and grapes than you will ever need.*
PROVERBS 3:9–10 CEV

Are you a saver or a spender? Do you love to shop or think it's boring? Whatever the case, it's super smart to start learning to manage your money well when you're young. Don't blow it all in one place on things that don't last, and don't forget to give generously back to God. The Bible offers the most important money advice you could ever have: Jesus said, "Give, and you will receive. Your gift will return to you in full—pressed down, shaken together to make room for more, running over, and poured into your lap. The amount you give will determine the amount you get back" (Luke 6:38 NLT).

And 2 Corinthians 9:6–8 (NLT) says, "Remember this—a farmer who plants only a few seeds will get a small crop. But the one who plants generously will get a generous crop. You must each decide in your heart how much to give. And don't give reluctantly or in response to pressure. 'For God loves a person who gives cheerfully.' And God will generously provide all you need."

---

*Dear God, please give me wisdom about money,
and help me to be generous. Amen.*

WISDOM ABOUT GOD'S GREAT POWER

[The disciples] took Jesus with them in a boat. . . . A bad wind storm came up. The waves were coming over the side of the boat. It was filling up with water. Jesus was in the back part of the boat sleeping on a pillow. They woke Him up, crying out, "Teacher, do You not care that we are about to die?" He got up and spoke sharp words to the wind. He said to the sea, "Be quiet! Be still." At once the wind stopped blowing. There were no more waves. He said to His followers, "Why are you so full of fear? Do you not have faith?" They were very much afraid and said to each other, "Who is this? Even the wind and waves obey Him!"
MARK 4:36–41

A girl of wisdom always needs to remember how powerful God is. Let this story in the Bible remind you that Jesus was able to command anything in all creation to obey Him. He could simply speak words to a storm to make it stop. He has great power over everything in your life today too, and He loves and cares for you. Remembering that should fill you with courage and peace to face any hard thing.

Dear God, I'm thankful for Your great power over everything! You can do anything at all to protect and help me. I feel so loved and safe because You take care of me. Amen.

Day 323

CONTENTMENT, NOT COMPARING

It's healthy to be content, but envy can eat you up.
PROVERBS 14:30 CEV

Want to know a way to ruin pretty much every single day of your life? Wait, what? Who wants that? Nobody! LOL!

Here's what you *don't* do if you'd rather not ruin your day—don't compare yourself or your life with others. Comparing just leads to envy or jealousy, wishing you had something that someone else does and you don't.

Instead, be content with what you have. First Timothy 6:6–8 (NLT) says, "True godliness with contentment is itself great wealth. After all, we brought nothing with us when we came into the world, and we can't take anything with us when we leave it. So if we have enough food and clothing, let us be content."

It's as simple as that. If you have food and clothing, then be content and trust that God will provide anything else you need.

Dear God, it's so hard not to look around me and see if I have what others have, because I want to fit in. Please help me to focus on You and all the basic needs You provide for me. I'm grateful, and I know You will keep providing. Amen.

STRANGERS AND ALIENS

Dear friends, your real home is not here on earth. You are strangers here. I ask you to keep away from all the sinful desires of the flesh. These things fight to get hold of your soul. When you are around people who do not know God, be careful how you act. Even if they talk against you as wrong-doers, in the end they will give thanks to God for your good works when Christ comes again.
1 PETER 2:11–12

Some versions of this scripture describe Christians as being like aliens here on earth—not ones like you might see in a *Star Wars* or *Star Trek* movie, but aliens in the sense that we are strangers here in this world because it is not our real home. When we believe in Jesus as Savior, we know that He will give us eternal life someday in heaven, which *is* our real home. So we should be careful not to follow what the world says is wise and good and popular but to follow what God says is wise and good—which will often be unpopular in the world. That will help show others the difference of following Jesus, and hopefully they will want to follow Him too. Being a Christian in this world isn't always easy, but it is always totally worth it!

Dear God, help me to follow Your ways and wisdom above all because I know my real home is in heaven with You. Amen.

BOREDOM BUSTER

Take a lesson from the ants, you lazybones.
Learn from their ways and become wise!
PROVERBS 6:6 NLT

As God grows you to be a girl of grace, you'll find it's hard to ever be bored, and that's a good thing! Boredom is often related to laziness, and God's Word tells us very strongly *not* to be lazy.

Check it out:

- ✻ "Lazy people want much but get little, but those who work hard will prosper" (Proverbs 13:4 NLT).

- ✻ "The one who is unwilling to work shall not eat" (2 Thessalonians 3:10 NIV).

- ✻ "Lazy people are soon poor; hard workers get rich" (Proverbs 10:4 NLT).

- ✻ "A lazy person is as bad as someone who destroys things" (Proverbs 18:9 NLT).

- ✻ "If you are lazy and sleep your time away, you will starve" (Proverbs 19:15 CEV).

There's always something to do to serve God and share His love! You can ask yourself the moment you start to sense that bored feeling coming over you: "What could I do right now to be productive, helpful, encouraging, and smart with my time?"

Dear God, I want to use my time wisely. Show me Your
will and the good things You have planned for me to
help others know Your love and grace! Amen.

Day 326

WISDOM FROM THE BOOK OF REVELATION

*John tells that the Word of God is true. He tells of Jesus
Christ and all that he saw and heard of Him. The man who
reads this Book and listens to it being read and obeys what it
says will be happy. For all these things will happen soon.*
REVELATION 1:2–3

God sent an angel to John, one of Jesus' original twelve disciples,
to give him visions to record. These visions were full of prophecy,
imagery, and symbols of what will happen in the last days of this
world. And all of that can often seem very confusing and sometimes
even scary. But the main point of Revelation is that Jesus is coming
soon to bring those of us who love and trust in Him into a new home
to live peacefully and perfectly forever and ever.

---

*Dear God, thank You for the book of Revelation.
Help me as I read it and keep coming back to it in the
future. Teach me what You want me to learn from it to
apply to my life and to share with others. Amen.*

NOT JUST A NICKNAME

See what great love the Father has lavished on us, that we should be called children of God! And that is what we are!
1 JOHN 3:1 NIV

Maybe you have a family member or friend who calls you Princess as a nickname. But if you've asked Jesus to be your Savior, you can totally *own* that name! He is the King of all kings and Lord of all lords (Revelation 17:14; 19:16), and John 1 says about Jesus, "The Word was in the world, but no one knew him, though God had made the world with his Word. He came into his own world, but his own nation did not welcome him. Yet some people accepted him and put their faith in him. So he gave them the right to be the children of God. They were not God's children by nature or because of any human desires. God himself was the one who made them his children" (vv. 10–13 CEV).

So, truly you are royalty, my princess friend! Now, don't let that go to your head and start demanding service from others and a fancy new wardrobe and such! Our King is both sovereign and almighty yet a humble servant of others.

Dear God, I am amazed that You offer anyone who believes in You the right to be Your child! Thank You for letting me be Your princess! Amen.

Day 328

WISDOM FOR THE FUTURE

"I tell you this: Do not worry about your life. Do not worry about what you are going to eat and drink. Do not worry about what you are going to wear. Is not life more important than food? Is not the body more important than clothes? Look at the birds in the sky. They do not plant seeds. They do not gather grain. They do not put grain into a building to keep. Yet your Father in heaven feeds them! Are you not more important than the birds?"
MATTHEW 6:25–26

Maybe sometimes you worry about the future, but Jesus promises that you never need to! He describes in Matthew 6 how the birds don't try to be prepared for the future, and God just feeds them and takes care of them. And you are so much more important to God and loved by Him than little birds are, so you can trust Him even more to take wonderful care of you! Don't ever forget this wisdom, and let it wash your worries right out of your head!

Dear God, please help me to remember how You care for little birds so well and You love and care for me much more than them. Let this truth give me wisdom not to worry. Amen.

Day 329

MORE ABOUT YOUR ROYALTY

"For the LORD your God is the God of gods and Lord of lords.
He is the great God, the mighty and awesome God."
DEUTERONOMY 10:17 NLT

You truly are a princess if you trust Jesus as your Savior, but Jesus set the example of a loving and humble Lord of all lords, and you are called to be like Him (1 John 2:3–6). Philippians 2:3–7 (NLT) says, "Be humble, thinking of others as better than yourselves. Don't look out only for your own interests, but take an interest in others, too. You must have the same attitude that Christ Jesus had. Though he was God, he did not think of equality with God as something to cling to. Instead, he gave up his divine privileges."

It was after Jesus had given up everything in order to save others that God lifted Him to "the place of highest honor and gave him the name above all other names, that at the name of Jesus every knee should bow, in heaven and on earth and under the earth, and every tongue declare that Jesus Christ is Lord, to the glory of God the Father" (Philippians 2:9–11 NLT).

Your life will not be exactly like Jesus', of course, but you are called to copy Him. He did not expect to be honored like royalty here on earth, and neither should you. Instead, you are called to give that honor up and serve people and share the love of the gospel so that others will believe in Jesus too. Then, for eternity someday, you will receive your forever reward of living in a perfect kingdom for all of God's children!

Dear Jesus, I want to have confidence that I am Your princess, but I want to serve others with humility like You did. Please help me. Amen.

Day 330

THE VALUE OF WISDOM

Happy is the man who finds wisdom, and the man who gets understanding. For it is better than getting silver and fine gold. . . . Nothing you can wish for compares with her. Long life is in her right hand. Riches and honor are in her left hand. Her ways are pleasing, and all her paths are peace. . . . The Lord built the earth by wisdom. He built the heavens by understanding. By what He knows, the seas were broken up and water falls from the sky. My son, do not allow them to leave your eyes. Keep perfect wisdom and careful thinking. And they will be life to your soul and a chain of beauty to your neck. Then you will be safe as you walk on your way, and your foot will not trip.
PROVERBS 3:13–17, 19–23

These verses in Proverbs are for all of us—girls and women too!—to realize the great value of having God's wisdom. We should never stop asking for it and appreciating it!

Dear God, I don't want to forget how valuable Your wisdom is. Please keep reminding me and giving it to me. Help me to learn from and use it in everything I do. Amen.

Day 331

GOD'S GREAT FAITHFULNESS

God is faithful, by whom you were called into the
fellowship of his Son, Jesus Christ our Lord.
1 CORINTHIANS 1:9 ESV

If you've ever had a good friendship come to an end for one reason or another, you know how hard it is to lose someone who you thought was a faithful friend. In those hard times, you can be thankful that God is always faithful. All people make mistakes and will disappoint you at one time or another, but God's faithfulness is perfect and endless.

When you feel let down by someone, take heart and focus on these scriptures that describe the great faithfulness of God:

- ✱ "Those who know your name trust in you, for you, LORD, have never forsaken those who seek you" (Psalm 9:10 NIV).

- ✱ "But the Lord is faithful, and he will strengthen you and protect you from the evil one" (2 Thessalonians 3:3 NIV).

- ✱ "If we are unfaithful, he remains faithful, for he cannot deny who he is" (2 Timothy 2:13 NLT).

- ✱ "God is not a man, so he does not lie. He is not human, so he does not change his mind. Has he ever spoken and failed to act? Has he ever promised and not carried it through?" (Numbers 23:19 NLT).

Dear God, Your faithfulness to me amazes me.
I'm so grateful I can count on You no matter what is
going on or who lets me down. I love You! Amen.

Day 332

USE THE WORD OF GOD

Preach the Word of God. Preach it when it is easy and people want to listen and when it is hard and people do not want to listen. Preach it all the time. Use the Word of God to show people they are wrong. Use the Word of God to help them do right.
2 TIMOTHY 4:2

Not too many people like to be told they are wrong. Do you? The Bible will correct us if we read and listen to it, because it holds God's wisdom about what is right and what is wrong. This scripture reminds us that we need to use God's Word to show people when they are wrong and then help them do right according to God's Word. We need to keep sharing God's Word all the time, even when it's hard and people don't seem to want to listen. And we can't share it well unless we are constantly learning from it too. It shows us what we do wrong and need to correct in our own lives too.

Dear God, please give me wisdom and courage to share Your Word and help people stop doing wrong and instead do what is right—and that goes for me too! Amen.

Day 333

LOVE YOUR LEADERS

Remember your leaders, those who spoke to you the word of God.
Consider the outcome of their way of life, and imitate their faith.
HEBREWS 13:7 ESV

When you're young, you have a lot of leaders in your life—pastors and teachers at your church, teachers and leaders at school, coaches and instructors of your sports teams and activities, and especially your older family members like Mom and Dad, grandparents, aunts, uncles, and others.

I know it sometimes feels like they're all just bossing you around or giving you advice you don't need, but next time you're feeling frustrated, take a different approach. Think about how they're trying to help you learn and grow and make good decisions. Thank God for them, even if in the moment you're not feeling very happy with their instructions because you just want to do your own thing. I remember those feelings when I was a girl, and now that I'm a grown-up, I can look back with deep appreciation for all the people who helped teach and guide me—especially my mom who is gone to heaven now. I wish so badly I could still ask her for advice.

Hebrews 13:17 (NLT) says, "Obey your spiritual leaders, and do what they say. Their work is to watch over your souls, and they are accountable to God. Give them reason to do this with joy and not with sorrow."

Dear God, please help me to appreciate and accept
leadership from the good people who love You and who are
in authority over me, especially my parents. Amen.

BUILD YOUR LIVES WITH WISDOM

"For I, the Lord, do not change. So you,
O children of Jacob, are not destroyed."
MALACHI 3:6

Everything in the world around us changes, sometimes quickly and sometimes over longer periods of time. Because of that, we need something that is always steady and stable on which to build our lives with wisdom. And the steadiest and most stable thing we can build on is God's Word. Jesus, who is "the same yesterday and today and forever" (Hebrews 13:8), described building on God's Word like someone building a house on rock rather than on sand: "Whoever hears these words of Mine and does them, will be like a wise man who built his house on rock. The rain came down. The water came up. The wind blew and hit the house. The house did not fall because it was built on rock. Whoever hears these words of Mine and does not do them, will be like a foolish man who built his house on sand. The rain came down. The water came up. The wind blew and hit the house. The house fell and broke apart" (Matthew 7:24–27).

Dear God, thank You for never changing and for being my solid,
stable rock on whom I can build my life with wisdom. Amen.

Day 335

HONOR YOUR PARENTS

"Honor your father and your mother, that your days may be long in the land that the LORD your God is giving you."
EXODUS 20:12 ESV

Not only are you to obey your parents, you are to honor them. That means not just doing what they ask but doing it with a good attitude. You shouldn't grumble and complain as you obey. Appreciate them and respect them and tell them you love them, no matter what's going on in your family. That's a great way to honor them.

As you grow older and eventually become an adult, you will make your own decisions and rules, but you can still honor and bless your parents by maintaining a great relationship with them and spending time with them, even if you don't live close by. With all the forms of communication these days—texting, phone calls, email, and FaceTime, and of course good old-fashioned snail mail—this is not hard. You can keep asking them for advice and to share the wisdom they've gained over the many more years of living they've done than you.

Dear God, please help me to honor and obey my parents now, and when I'm an adult, please help me to continue to have good relationships with them. I thank You for my good parents, God! I love You and I love them! Amen.

Day 336

BE A LEADER

In everything set them an example by doing what is good.
TITUS 2:7 NIV

If you're able to read this book, then you're able to be a leader too. Because if you're at an age when you can read, then you're at an age when you can be a helper to those younger than you, and that makes you a leader and example to others. Jodi and Lilly have been helping me in Sunday school class at church since they were each about four years old. They started helping in the two-and-three-year-olds' class with simple things like passing out cups and napkins at snack time and modeling good behavior like sharing and patiently waiting for their turn. As they've gotten older, they help make up game ideas to keep younger kids occupied, comfort little ones who miss their parents, and read books to little kiddos.

Always remember that you are not too young to be a leader yourself! Live your life according to God's Word, always looking for ways to serve and help others and share your faith. That's the best kind of leader in a world that so desperately needs God's truth and love.

Dear Jesus, please show me how to be the kind of servant-leader You want me to be, to help others know You as their Savior too. Amen.

Day 337

GOD MAKES THINGS NEW

*And the one sitting on the throne said,
"Look, I am making everything new!"*
REVELATION 21:5 NLT

We recently saw the movie *Smurfs: The Lost Village*, and it was so fun! I love when movie producers do a good job of bringing back an old favorite from my childhood in a new way that I can enjoy with Jodi and Lilly. Some remakes are great, and some not so much.

I'm thankful that all of God's remakes are perfect! His grace takes people who were once lost in their sin and turns them into completely new people. Second Corinthians 5:17 (NLT) says, "Anyone who belongs to Christ has become a new person. The old life is gone; a new life has begun!"

Anytime you find yourself headed down a wrong path for a bit, making bad choices or keeping a bad attitude, God's grace can quickly help you turn around and away from sin. Pray this prayer from Psalm 51:10 (NLT): "Create in me a clean heart, O God. Renew a loyal spirit within me."

And remember and trust that God's mercies "begin afresh each morning" (Lamentations 3:23 NLT). Each new day is a day to let God do something new in you!

Dear God, thank You for all You have done and all You are doing to make things new and perfect! Amen.

HAVING GREAT GRATITUDE

*Be thankful in all circumstances, for this is God's
will for you who belong to Christ Jesus.*
1 THESSALONIANS 5:18 NLT

A girl of grace is a girl who is full of gratitude. You can find a reason to give thanks in any and every situation. Yes, even when your siblings are driving you crazy. Even when your homework seems ridiculously hard. Even when a family situation is completely out of control. Even when someone you love dies. Even during the very worst kinds of situations, you can simply thank God that He is with you and hears you. Thank Him for being a good and awesome, loving heavenly Father! Then ask Him to help you focus on the blessings you have right in the moment, even if it's simply the ability to take a big deep breath and pray some more. As you continue to trust in God and thank Him for who He is and what He does, He will show you more and more reasons to have gratitude.

Read and remember these scriptures, and make them your goal:

* "Let all that I am praise the LORD; may I never forget the good things he does for me" (Psalm 103:2 NLT).

* "Give thanks to the LORD and proclaim his greatness. Let the whole world know what he has done" (1 Chronicles 16:8 NLT).

* "And give thanks for everything to God the Father in the name of our Lord Jesus Christ" (Ephesians 5:20 NLT).

---

*Dear God, I thank You for who You are and all
that You do and for all of the blessings in my life.
Please grow me in grace and in gratitude. Amen.*

Day 339

THROUGH EVERY AWFUL THING

"When you pass through the waters, I will be with you; and through the rivers, they shall not overwhelm you; when you walk through fire you shall not be burned, and the flame shall not consume you."

Isaiah 43:2 esv

God has never promised anyone who loves Him a constantly comfortable life. There is no always-easy-peasy path through this world, because sin messed up all the goodness God intended for His creation. But through Jesus Christ, God is working out His plan to defeat sin forever, and in the meantime, He does promise to be with you through every single hard thing you go through, like Isaiah 43:2 describes. This scripture makes me think of the cool Old Testament stories of Shadrach, Meshach, and Abednego, who were literally put into a fiery furnace and did not burn up. Read their story in Daniel 3, especially the awesomeness that after being in the furnace (spoiler alert!), "not a hair on their heads was singed, and their clothing was not scorched. They didn't even smell of smoke!" (v. 27 nlt).

God didn't keep Daniel from being put in the terrifying lions' den, either, but He did protect him through it: "Not a scratch was found on him, for he had trusted in his God" (Daniel 6:23 nlt).

When you're in the middle of something awful or scary or painful or all of the above, remember these Old Testament heroes whom God used to show in miraculous ways how He is right beside us and holding us through every hard thing.

Dear God, please don't ever let me forget how close You are at all times, in every situation. Amen.

TURN PAIN INTO PRAISE

You have turned my mourning into joyful dancing.
PSALM 30:11 NLT

The hardest, most hurtful thing Jodi, Lilly, and I have experienced so far in our lives is the sudden death of my mom and their dear nana. We had such a close relationship with her and shared so much love. We're grateful for all the good memories and all the dear family and friends we still have with us, but it still hurts so bad to have lost her here. We can only focus on God's truth and His promises that everyone who trusts Him as Savior has eternal life with Him in heaven. So we know without a doubt that that's where our mom and nana is now, just waiting till it's our turn to be there too.

God is so close to us in the midst of our pain of missing her. A dear friend reminded us that the best thing to do when the pain hurts the worst is to praise God. It seems impossible at first, but truly, we have found that is the best remedy and comfort for the pain. Focusing our thoughts on who God is and how awesome He is eases the intense pain every single time because it reminds us of His truth and His love and His good plans for a perfect forever for all who love Him!

So, friends, when you are hurting for any reason, remember to let the pain cause you to praise God. Read the psalms and sing praise and worship songs to Him!

---

*Dear God, please help me to praise You in
every painful situation. Amen.*

Day 341

OUR RACE

You know that many runners enter a race, and only one of them wins the prize. So run to win! Athletes work hard to win a crown that cannot last, but we do it for a crown that will last forever.
1 Corinthians 9:24–25 cev

Have you heard that joke that goes something like this: I don't run. And if you ever see me running, you should run too, because something is probably chasing me. Haha! It makes me laugh every time because it's so true for me. I used to jog with friends in college, and that was fun—but I'd much prefer getting some exercise taking a long walk around my neighborhood or preferably on a beach!

What's your favorite kind of exercise? Even though I don't run, I love the inspiring examples of running that scripture gives us for helping us stay strong in our faith in Jesus through our journey of life: "Such a large crowd of witnesses is all around us! So we must get rid of everything that slows us down, especially the sin that just won't let go. And we must be determined to run the race that is ahead of us. We must keep our eyes on Jesus, who leads us and makes our faith complete. He endured the shame of being nailed to a cross, because he knew that later on he would be glad he did. Now he is seated at the right side of God's throne! So keep your mind on Jesus, who put up with many insults from sinners. Then you won't get discouraged and give up" (Hebrews 12:1–3 cev).

Dear God, when my journey through life feels so difficult and I want to give up, please help me keep my eyes on You and keep running with You and toward heaven. Amen.

Day 342

THE LEAST OF THESE

"The righteous will answer him, 'Lord, when did we see you hungry and feed you, or thirsty and give you something to drink? When did we see you a stranger and invite you in, or needing clothes and clothe you? When did we see you sick or in prison and go to visit you?' The King will reply, 'Truly I tell you, whatever you did for one of the least of these brothers and sisters of mine, you did for me.' "
MATTHEW 25:37–40 NIV

Growing up, I spent a lot of time with elderly people in an assisted-living home where my mom worked as a nurse. I also visited people in a nursing home every week when I was in college. Now I'm glad Jodi and Lilly spend lots of time with their grandma and great-grandma at a nursing home. They often play bingo together, and just their presence is an encouragement to the elderly people who need visitors and to see life and the joy of young people in their sometimes dreary days as they struggle with health problems.

Too often, our world doesn't put much value on elderly people because, as their bodies age, they can't seem to do much anymore. But they are so valuable. Every life is priceless to God, and those who are older have much wisdom to share. In caring about them and for them, we are doing what Jesus described in saying, "Whatever you did for one of the least of these brothers and sisters of mine, you did for me."

Dear God, help me to care about and show love to others who seem less important in our world. Amen.

Day 343

NO MORE BLACK-AND-BLUE

For his unfailing love toward those who fear him is as great as the height of the heavens above the earth. He has removed our sins as far from us as the east is from the west.
PSALM 103:11–12 NLT

It's frustrating to struggle with the same kind of mistake again and again. We all have areas like this that vex us! Even the apostle Paul said, "I want to do what is right, but I can't. I want to do what is good, but I don't. I don't want to do what is wrong, but I do it anyway" (Romans 7:18–19 NLT).

Our enemy, Satan, wants us to keep beating ourselves up, figuratively black-and-blue, over everything we struggle with. Because if we keep focusing on what we do *wrong*, we'll never realize all the *right* and awesome things God wants to do through us, all the blessings He wants to give us too! Don't let Satan convince you to turn yourself black-and-blue over your mistakes. Trust God's Word and His grace! First John 1:9 (NIV) says, "If we confess our sins, he is faithful and just and will forgive us our sins and purify us from all unrighteousness."

So when you mess up, admit it to God and make it right with any others who might be involved. Ask for forgiveness and then trust that God takes that sin as far away from you as the east is from the west! Honestly, you're going to have to repeat this process like a zillion times in your life, but that's why we need God so much, and why His endless grace is such an incredible blessing!

Dear God, please help me to confess my wrongs, ask for forgiveness, and then let You shower me with Your grace. Amen.

Day 344

PUTTING ON GOD'S ARMOR

Be strong in the Lord and in his mighty power.
Put on all of God's armor so that you will be able to
stand firm against all strategies of the devil.
EPHESIANS 6:10–11 NLT

When Jodi and Lilly were younger, we enjoyed reading from a fun princes storybook that told a story of a girl who dressed up like a knight so she could joust like her brother. Girls weren't allowed, but no one knew it was her under all that protective armor. In the end, she proved everyone wrong and showed that a girl could joust and win!

In your real-life story, you need armor too, but not for jousting on horses. You need the armor of God to battle the enemies who are constantly fighting against anyone who loves Jesus.

Ephesians 6:12–13 (NLT) says, "For we are not fighting against flesh-and-blood enemies, but against evil rulers and authorities of the unseen world, against mighty powers in this dark world, and against evil spirits in the heavenly places. Therefore, put on every piece of God's armor so you will be able to resist the enemy in the time of evil. Then after the battle you will still be standing firm."

Dear God, please help me to learn more about Your mighty armor
and how to use it to protect against my unseen enemies. Amen.

EACH PIECE OF GOD'S ARMOR, PART 1

Therefore, put on every piece of God's armor so you will be able to resist the enemy in the time of evil. Then after the battle you will still be standing firm. Stand your ground, putting on the belt of truth and the body armor of God's righteousness. For shoes, put on the peace that comes from the Good News so that you will be fully prepared.
EPHESIANS 6:13–15 NLT

Every morning when you're getting dressed and brushing your hair and teeth, you'd be super smart to ask God to help you make sure every piece of His armor fits just right for whatever the day holds. He gives you a belt of truth, which holds everything together by knowing all truth comes from God who is Truth. He gives you the body armor of righteousness that protects your heart and soul from any evil with the righteousness that can only come by the grace of Jesus Christ. He gives you shoes that both protect your feet and equip you to carry the gospel to others.

Almighty God, please help me remember every day to picture my spiritual armor and put it on with Your help. I'm ready to fight my spiritual enemies who want to drag me away from You. Amen.

Day 346

EACH PIECE OF GOD'S ARMOR, PART 2

In addition to all of these, hold up the shield of faith to stop the fiery arrows of the devil. Put on salvation as your helmet, and take the sword of the Spirit, which is the word of God.
EPHESIANS 6:16–17 NLT

God also gives you a shield of faith in Him that protects you from all the weapons and tricky things that Satan and his spiritual armies will throw at you. God gives you a helmet of salvation that protects your head and mind, helping you to trust that no matter what happens here on earth, you are saved for an eternal life forever in heaven. And God gives you an awesome weapon to fight your unseen enemies with—the sword of the Spirit, which is the Word of God.

Don't feel silly every morning, asking God to help you put this armor on. Instead, trust that God's Word is true and that you need this armor. It's not just pretend. Let God empower you like only He can.

Almighty God, I'm so thankful that in a dark world that has so much evil, You have not left me to fight alone. You have given me everything I need to fight against evil with good and to help others know Your truth and love. Amen.

KNOWING YOUR BIBLE WELL

Your word is a lamp to guide my feet and a light for my path.
PSALM 119:105 NLT

I remember doing sword drills at church during vacation Bible school when I was little. A leader would call out a scripture reference, and the first to find it in their Bible would win the race! Being fast is not the important part, though; it's simply so important to know your Bible well as God is growing you to be a girl of grace. God's Word is a living and active book, and it's how He speaks best to us. The more you know about it, the closer you can grow to God, the better able you are to navigate through any situation of life, and the better you can give answers to others for the faith that you have (1 Peter 3:15) and the help that they might need.

If you want a fun way to start learning a whole overview of the Bible, I'd encourage you to watch the What's in the Bible series of movies. There's a whole set that digs in briefly, in fun and interesting ways, through every book of the Bible to teach you more about it!

Dear God, please grow in me a strong desire to know Your Word, the Holy Bible, well. Please guide me through it and draw me closer to You! Amen.

Day 348

CHRISTIANS AROUND THE WORLD

Pray in the Spirit at all times and on every occasion. Stay alert and be persistent in your prayers for all believers everywhere.
EPHESIANS 6:18 NLT

It is no small blessing that we did much of the brainstorming and writing of this book in public places like coffee shops. Did you know that in many countries around the world, there is no way we could have done that? It would not have been safe to openly talk about the one true God and our Savior Jesus Christ, with a Bible open for anyone to see.

I'm extremely grateful for the freedom of religion that we have in the U.S., and I hope you are too. I hope you're also constantly aware of the believers all around the world who do not have freedom like we do but who risk their safety and their lives every day to keep living for Jesus. I'm so amazed and inspired by the way they let God give them incredible courage to spread His truth in dangerous places. Ephesians 6:18 reminds me to pray for them and all others like them at all times. Will you join me?

---

*Dear God, thank You for my freedoms and protections.
I pray that You will also provide freedom and protection
for all the Christians around the world who live in places
where it is dangerous to believe in You. Amen.*

Day 349

SWEET TEETH AND SELF-CONTROL

*For God gave us a spirit not of fear but of
power and love and self-control.*
2 TIMOTHY 1:7 ESV

I don't think I have just one sweet tooth; I think maybe every tooth in my mouth is a sweet tooth! I love chocolate and cookies and dough-nuts and all those yummy things. It's so hard not to eat too much of them! Sweets are an area where I could use a lot more self-control.

Self-control is so important for all areas of life. We can't just say any thought that pops into our head whenever we want to. . . . We can't act on any and every desire we have. . . . We can't always just play or go on vacation. . . . You get the idea! We have to watch our words; we have to act with both the present and the future in mind and knowing our actions affect others too; and we have to do the work and chores and lessons that are required in life. Self-control is incredibly important!

Proverbs 25:28 (NLT) says, "A person without self-control is like a city with broken-down walls." In other words, a person without self-control is in chaos and ruin. Ask God every day to give you more self-control, through His power, so that you live a successful life according to His will!

---

*Dear God, please increase self-control in me, and help me to live
the best kind of life that pleases You and gives You glory! Amen.*

TOTALLY RANDOM

*I urge, then, first of all, that petitions, prayers, intercession
and thanksgiving be made for all people.*
1 TIMOTHY 2:1 NIV

On a shopping trip for Easter dresses one year, Jodi, Lilly, and I were stopped by an older woman who asked if she could walk with us out to the parking lot. She was struggling with anxiety, feeling scared and worried, which she said often happened to her in big busy places. I could tell she was sincere, so we walked her to her car, and then I asked her if she needed anything else or if I could call anyone for her. She assured me she was fine and would be okay to drive home. Then, even though it made me nervous, I asked if I could pray out loud for her. She agreed, and with a simple, short prayer I asked God to bless her and keep her safe.

Jodi and Lilly still talk about that experience sometimes, just how random it was but also good that we could help and pray for a stranger. I was blessed to be able to pray for her and hopefully encourage her and share a bit of God's love.

When you feel the Holy Spirit leading you, don't be afraid to boldly ask if you can pray for someone, especially someone who does not know Jesus. You never can tell how God is going to use those prayers!

---

*Dear God, please help me to be bold in a good
way in praying for others. Amen.*

Day 351

KEEPING SANE WITH SOCIAL MEDIA

*Look carefully then how you walk, not as unwise
but as wise, making the best use of the time,
because the days are evil. Therefore do not be
foolish, but understand what the will of the Lord is.*
EPHESIANS 5:15–17 ESV

I love social media. It's wonderful to stay connected with friends and family all over the country and world, and you've probably seen some of the hilarious things out there that are just for fun like crazy cat videos and babies doing adorably funny stuff.

But in some ways I find social media a frustrating struggle because it's tempting to spend way too much time on my smartphone reading posts and blogs and tweets and such. It's also hard to avoid some of the harmful stuff that's out there everywhere on the Internet, things that do not help us focus on "whatever is true, whatever is noble, whatever is right, whatever is pure, whatever is lovely, whatever is admirable" (Philippians 4:8 NIV).

Whether you're into it much yet or not, as you get older you'll realize our world revolves a lot around social media. There's a lot of good about that but a lot of bad too. Pray for wisdom from God to help you use social media wisely and spend your time on it wisely.

Dear God, I want to start now making good use of my time and being smart about social media. Please give me Your wisdom. Amen.

Day 352

NO MORE IDOLS

Jesus told him. "For the Scriptures say, 'You must worship the LORD your God and serve only him.' "
MATTHEW 4:10 NLT

When you hear the word *idol*, do you think of some big stone or metal statue in ancient times that people bowed down to? Or maybe you think of the golden calf that the Israelites created out of their jewelry and such when they were tired of waiting on God and Moses (Exodus 32).

It may seem ridiculous to those of us who love Jesus to ever think it possible to have an idol. Why would anyone worship some object made of metal or stone or whatever that just sits there and does nothing, right? But did you know that idols can actually be anything that we put above God on our list of priorities?

- ✴ Your family can be an idol if it comes before your relationship with God.

- ✴ Your smartphone and social media accounts can be idols if they take up all your attention.

- ✴ Your sports and activities can be idols if they're your only purpose in life.

God wants us to focus on Him first and foremost in our lives and then let all those other great things fall into place in correct and good order below Him on the list. When He is first, He helps us succeed the best ways possible in everything else.

Dear God, please help me to put You on the very top of my priority list. Amen.

Day 353

BUILDING UP

We should help others do what is right and build them up in the Lord.
ROMANS 15:2 NLT

When you're young, you might not feel like you can do much for God since you still have so much to learn. But the best way to learn about God and how to live life is to serve God now while you also keep reading His Word. And one of the best ways that any young person can serve God now is to encourage others like scripture tells us to. With simply a cheerful attitude and joyful smile, you can spread encouragement. With a phone call or text to let a friend know you are thinking of them, you can build someone else up. You can share hugs, scriptures, and prayer for others who are in need or who simply could use an extra bright spot in their day. Read these scriptures and ask God to help you be encouraging to others every single day.

So encourage each other and build each other up, just as you are already doing. 1 THESSALONIANS 5:11 NLT

Let everything you say be good and helpful, so that your words will be an encouragement to those who hear them. EPHESIANS 4:29 NLT

Dear God, please remind me constantly how easy it is to encourage others and lift their spirits. Show me who You want me to encourage today. Amen.

HOLD ON!

Let us hold tightly without wavering to the hope we affirm, for God can be trusted to keep his promise. Let us think of ways to motivate one another to acts of love and good works. And let us not neglect our meeting together, as some people do, but encourage one another, especially now that the day of his return is drawing near.
HEBREWS 10:23–25 NLT

You've probably seen a movie or television show where the bad guy is trying to push or pry the hands of the good guy off the edge of a cliff or building or something so that he'll fall. You can think of Satan and our enemies in this world like those bad guys—always trying to pry your fingers off your Bible, always trying to get you to let go of your faith and hope and your desire to follow God.

The bad guys will do anything at all to make you fall away from your hope in God. That's why Hebrews 10:23–25 is so important to remember. We must hold tightly to our hope in God, trusting that He keeps His promises, and encourage each other to continue sharing love and good deeds. And we need to go to church regularly with fellow believers so that we can worship God together. God is coming back soon, and we just have to hold on tight until that great day!

Dear God, I don't ever want to let go of my awesome hope in You! Please help me to hold on so tightly! Amen.

Day 355

THE RIGHT WAY TO BRAG

This is what the LORD says: "Let not the wise boast of their wisdom or the strong boast of their strength or the rich boast of their riches, but let the one who boasts boast about this: that they have the understanding to know me, that I am the LORD, who exercises kindness, justice and righteousness on earth, for in these I delight," declares the LORD.
JEREMIAH 9:23–24 NIV

If you know anyone who brags or boasts all the time, you know how annoying that can be. It's wonderful to share exciting, happy news with friends and be excited together. It's just not kind or polite for anyone to constantly try to show off why their blessings and accomplishments and plans are better than yours.

Here's how you can brag and feel good about it:

* *Don't* brag about your plans: When making your plans, you should not brag about them but acknowledge that "what you ought to say is, 'If the Lord wants us to, we will live and do this or that.' Otherwise you are boasting about your own pretentious plans, and all such boasting is evil" (James 4:15–16 NLT).

* *Do* brag about God and His love for us through Jesus Christ! Galatians 6:14 (NLT) says, "As for me, may I never boast about anything except the cross of our Lord Jesus Christ."

Dear God, please help me not to brag about anything but You and Your love and power! Amen.

Day 356

KEEP THE LIGHTS ON

"For all that is secret will eventually be brought into the open, and everything that is concealed will be brought to light and made known to all."

LUKE 8:17 NLT

Secrets are so fun when they're for a good reason—a surprise birthday party, the Christmas gift you can't wait to give, or a big chore you got done around the house like a ninja to help out.

But secrets that you keep because you don't want to tell the truth are usually not okay. And trying to keep a secret from God is never a good idea—not to mention silly. . .since He already knows it anyway. Psalm 44:21 (NLT) says, "God would surely have known it, for he knows the secrets of every heart."

You don't have to always tell every person your every thought; in fact, that's not a good idea at all. But just remember that God hears and knows. Don't ever try to hide anything from Him. Keep an honest, close relationship with God, through the grace of Jesus, and talk to Him about everything. How amazing that the God of all the universe wants you to! If you keep everything in good communication with God, you'll never have to worry about anything hiding in the dark that will be brought out into the light.

Dear God, You are always with me and I can't keep any secrets from You. Please help me never to want to. You are so good and loving, and I'm thankful You want me to live in light, not darkness. Amen.

FLEE!

And give no opportunity to the devil.
EPHESIANS 4:27 ESV

You have quite a challenge ahead of you, growing up in a world that tries to tell girls all kinds of things that are drastically opposite of God's good guidelines in His Word—guidelines that are just meant to protect you and help you live the best life possible. So please, friends, get it in your head now that the Bible talks a lot about FLEEING any situation and experience you're faced with that gives you opportunity to sin (1 Timothy 6:11–12; 2 Timothy 2:22; 1 Corinthians 6:18). Don't mess around with situations you sense the Holy Spirit saying are not good for you, telling yourself, "I just want to do what my friends are doing and this won't hurt me. I've got this under control. I'll just watch and not participate. . .or maybe just a little. . . ." No! The Bible doesn't say you should hang around on the edges of sinful situations. You should run away from them—fast and hard, like the word *flee* expresses.

Yes, you might lose friends this way. And you will be A-OK if you do! I promise you, you do not want those kinds of friends in your life anyway. Any friend who will not respect your beliefs and convictions is not a true friend and never has been. They will only tear you down and away from the best life God wants for you. You can trust that God will bless you time and time again when you obey Him and flee from situations and friendships that tempt you into trouble.

Dear God, please give me courage and wisdom to know when to flee situations that will cause me to sin. I trust that You always want what is best for me, and I want to obey Your Word. Amen.

TRUTH VS. FEELINGS

The sum of your word is truth.
PSALM 119:160 ESV

In general, we girls have pretty strong emotions. All of us show and feel them in different ways, but I think we can all agree how crazy-powerful they seem at times. And they're so fickle (meaning they change a lot), right? That's why it's extremely important to learn that truth is always, always, always more important than your feelings.

For example, you will have times when you don't feel like being a Christian, when it would be easier to just be like the world, but here's truth from God's Word that helps control those feelings: "Do not love this world nor the things it offers you, for when you love the world, you do not have the love of the Father in you. For the world offers only a craving for physical pleasure, a craving for everything we see, and pride in our achievements and possessions. These are not from the Father, but are from this world. And this world is fading away, along with everything that people crave. But anyone who does what pleases God will live forever" (1 John 2:15–17 NLT).

When your feelings might be overtaking you, remind yourself in all situations to slow down, take deep breaths, and think about what is true. No matter how strong your feelings are, they will lie to you sometimes. The truth is what beats feelings. And the truth is always found in God's Word.

Dear God, please help me to keep my feelings in check and focus mostly on Your truth. Amen.

Day 359

UTMOST BLISS

One day as he saw the crowds gathering, Jesus went up on the mountainside and sat down. His disciples gathered around him, and he began to teach them.
MATTHEW 5:1–2 NLT

One of my very favorite passages of scripture is called the Beatitudes of Jesus. *Beatitude* is another word for a blessing, and the Merriam-Webster dictionary describes it as "a state of utmost bliss." I love that! Truly, when we follow these words of Jesus, we will experience utmost bliss both now and ultimately forever in heaven!

> "God blesses those who are poor and realize their need for him, for the Kingdom of Heaven is theirs. God blesses those who mourn, for they will be comforted. God blesses those who are humble, for they will inherit the whole earth. God blesses those who hunger and thirst for justice, for they will be satisfied. God blesses those who are merciful, for they will be shown mercy. God blesses those whose hearts are pure, for they will see God. God blesses those who work for peace, for they will be called the children of God. God blesses those who are persecuted for doing right, for the Kingdom of Heaven is theirs. God blesses you when people mock you and persecute you and lie about you and say all sorts of evil things against you because you are my followers. Be happy about it! Be very glad! For a great reward awaits you in heaven." MATTHEW 5:3–12 NLT

Dear Jesus, please help me to follow Your teaching in the Beatitudes. I want to be blessed for doing what is good and right according to You! Amen.

Day 360

WATCH YOUR WORDS

Watch your talk! No bad words should be coming from your mouth. Say what is good. Your words should help others grow as Christians.
Ephesians 4:29

Our words matter, even if we think they don't. And it's super hard for every single one of us to always say what is good. James 3:2 says, "We all make many mistakes. If anyone does not make a mistake with his tongue by saying the wrong things, he is a perfect man." In other words, it takes a totally perfect person to never, ever make a mistake with words. And there is no perfect person other than Jesus. That's why we need so much help from God through the Holy Spirit to help us with what we say. And when we mess up, which we will, we must ask for forgiveness from God and from the ones our words have hurt. Thankfully, God loves to forgive and help us, and so we should always want to forgive and help others too.

Dear God, please help me to watch my talk and say what is good. Forgive me when I mess this up, help others to forgive me, and help me to forgive others. Thank You for Your love and grace. Please help us all share it. Amen.

Day 361

WHEN YOU'RE ANGRY

If you are angry, do not let it become sin. Get over your anger before the day is finished. Do not let the devil start working in your life.
Ephesians 4:26–27

It's totally okay to be angry sometimes, like when someone is treating you or others in a cruel or unfair way. But let the Holy Spirit help you to not let that anger become sin. Ask God to help you have wisdom to know what to do with your anger in good ways to bring a solution and an end to whatever has gone wrong. If you don't get over your anger in good and quick ways, it can give the devil a chance to start working in your life instead of letting the Holy Spirit work in your life. No way do you want that!

Dear God, please show me clearly when my anger is bad and when it is good. Please show me what to do with anger in ways that please You and help people love You and love others more. Please help me to never let the devil start working in my life. Amen.

Day 362

UNSTOPPABLE

"But before all this happens, men will take hold of you and make it very hard for you. They will give you over to the places of worship and to the prisons. They will bring you in front of kings and the leaders of the people. This will all be done to you because of Me. This will be a time for you to tell about Me. Do not think about what you will say ahead of time. For I will give you wisdom in what to say and I will help you say it. Those who are against you will not be able to stop you or say you are wrong."
Luke 21:12–15

Jesus warned His followers that they would find themselves in dangerous trouble because they loved and obeyed and preached about Him. But He sure didn't tell them to give up. He told them to stay strong and not worry, not even about what they would say. He promised to give them wisdom and words and help so that they would be unstoppable.

Dear Jesus, if I find myself in trouble or danger for following You, I never want to give up my faith or stop telling others about You. Help me to stay strong and trust that You will give me wisdom for exactly what I need to do and say. Amen.

Day 363

LET GOD LEAD YOU IN TRUTH

Show me Your ways, O Lord. Teach me Your paths. Lead me in Your truth and teach me. For You are the God Who saves me.
PSALM 25:4–5

Truth is so important, especially in a world where it seems harder and harder to find. Let God through His Word be your number one source of truth, and let all of these scriptures remind you how important it is:

* "The honor of good people will lead them, but those who hurt others will be destroyed by their own false ways" (Proverbs 11:3).

* "A man who tells lies about someone will be punished. He who tells lies will be lost" (Proverbs 19:9).

* "Do your best to know that God is pleased with you. Be as a workman who has nothing to be ashamed of. Teach the words of truth in the right way. Do not listen to foolish talk about things that mean nothing. It only leads people farther away from God" (2 Timothy 2:15–16).

Dear God, Your Word is the ultimate truth! Help me to grow in truth and love and wisdom and share it all with others. Amen.

BECAUSE OF THE POWER OF GOD

When I came to you, I did not preach the secrets of God with big sounding words or make it sound as if I were so wise. I made up my mind that while I was with you I would speak of nothing except Jesus Christ and of His death on the cross. When I was with you, I was weak. I was afraid and I shook. What I had to say when I preached was not in big sounding words of man's wisdom. But it was given in the power of the Holy Spirit. In this way, you do not have faith in Christ because of the wisdom of men. You have faith in Christ because of the power of God.

1 CORINTHIANS 2:1–5

Do you ever feel afraid and shaking to share your faith like the apostle Paul described in this scripture? Then let Paul encourage you. He didn't feel like he had all the best-sounding words and wisdom that would make everyone want to listen to him either. Paul just knew about Jesus; Paul knew Jesus had transformed his life, and Paul knew that Jesus died on the cross and rose again to save people from their sin and give them eternal life. It is the power of God working in you through His Holy Spirit that helps you share the good news of Jesus. All you have to do is let God work.

Dear God, it's all You! Please just use me as You want, with Your words and wisdom, Your truth and power, to help others know You and trust Jesus as Savior. Amen.

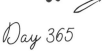

WHEN LIFE IS SO CONFUSING

Oh, how great are God's riches and wisdom and knowledge!
ROMANS 11:33 NLT

Here we are at the end, and I sure hope this book has helped you grow in the awesome grace of Jesus! I know life still feels super confusing sometimes. Living as a Christian in this crazy world seems like you always have to go against the flow. Some people say the Bible is too old and doesn't matter anymore. Sometimes the Bible *does* seem so confusing and disconnected to the present day. But don't get discouraged. Keep following God and trusting Him to show you what you need when you need it and what to do and when to do it. You will never figure out everything about this life and about God here on earth, and that's okay! First Corinthians 13:12 (NLT) says, "Now we see things imperfectly, like puzzling reflections in a mirror, but then we will see everything with perfect clarity. All that I know now is partial and incomplete, but then I will know everything completely, just as God now knows me completely."

Each new day, just keep following God, one step at a time, through His Spirit and His Word, praying to Him constantly. And if you get off track, simply ask for forgiveness and come back to Him! His grace is endless—and remember, He wants to shower you with it! Never forget that the place you're heading and your reward for following Him are beyond anything you can ever dream of, for "no eye has seen, no ear has heard, and no mind has imagined what God has prepared for those who love him" (1 Corinthians 2:9 NLT).

---

*Dear God, I want to keep learning more and growing
in Your amazing grace every single day. Amen.*

SCRIPTURE INDEX

OLD TESTAMENT

NEW TESTAMENT

CHECK OUT THIS FUN FAITH MAP!

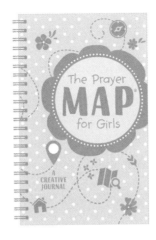

This prayer journal is a fun and creative way to fully experience the power of prayer. Each page guides you to write out thoughts, ideas, and lists. . .creating a specific "map" for you to follow as you talk to God. Each map includes a spot to record the date so that you can look back on your prayers and see how God has worked in your life.

978-1-68322-559-1